Table of Contents

Table of Contents

Into the Heart of Meetings

© Eric de Groot & Mike van der Vijver
a publication of MindMeeting BV
all rights reserved
P.O. Box 936
8901 BS
Leeuwarden
The Netherlands

www.mindmeeting.org
info@mindmeeting.org

Illustrations and cover: Yoko Heiligers
Editorial Polishing: David Cobb
Pre-print and print: WeddingProson, Harderwijk, The Netherlands

ISBN: 9781482553949

first edition, January 2013

Preface

"What the heart thinks, the mouth speaks," is a familiar saying in the Netherlands. If you have a passion for something, you want to tell others about it. You can't wait to transmit some of your enthusiasm to them; share the fervour and the fun. Ultimately, this was our main motivation to write this book. We have a passion for live communication at meetings, and being Meeting Designers is fun; that is what we have experienced in the past one or two decades.

Until recently, nobody knew what we meant when we said that we were Meeting Designers; as a matter of fact, even today relatively few people grasp what we are about. We hope that this book will change that.

To our way of thinking Meeting Designers are professionals who create the programme of a meeting. They base their designs on the connection between meeting content, the established meeting objectives, and the expectations of the meeting organiser and the participants. This profession is still very new, but it is rapidly gaining ground. Up until now, very little has been written about Meeting Design, and that – considering how young the profession is and how few people have any idea what it is about – is hardly surprising. That is the second reason for writing this book: it contains the knowledge and experience of our 40 years' practice in the meeting industry, as a contribution to the understanding and future development of the profession.

Give or take a few, we have calculated that in the course of those years, we must have attended a total of just about 2,500 meetings in various capacities: as participants, interpreters, actors in role plays, or, naturally, as designers. During that time, we never underwent any kind of specific education or gained any official certification – anything that might formally qualify us as Meeting Designers. The reason for that is simple: such education does not exist. So that is a third reason for writing *Into the Heart of Meetings*: we hope that it will prove useful to experienced meeting planners and to young, budding meeting professionals alike, in their quest for better meetings in times of increasing demands for effectiveness and results. Hence our choice of the book's subtitle, Basic Principles of Meeting Design, which characterises what we intend to offer.

You will quickly see that *Into the Heart of Meetings* is a very practical book. Not in the sense that it is a blueprint or step-by-step guide for becoming a Meeting Designer, or something like a compendium of Ten Top Formats for Successful Meetings. It is practical in the sense that all its ideas are based on practical experience. Graphically, you can recognise the examples because they are printed in *italics*. Without exception, these cases derive from our own working practice. On occasions, we have combined several examples into one and/or disguised actual people or organisations involved. Overall, however, everything that is contained in this book is tried-and-tested know-how, developed by the authors thanks to their cooperation with literally hundreds of clients.

At the end of each chapter you will find a short mock conversation between a series of fictitious characters and ourselves. We have called these figures the Sceptics and they are modelled on people we really know. As soon as a chapter is finished, they voice reservations about its contents. In some cases their doubts express prevalent ways of thinking in the meeting industry while in others they point to the need for developing the ideas of the chapter further. And so, that is a fourth reason for this book: the hope that it will stimulate a debate about how Meeting Design can make meetings more effective; and even more generally, how meetings function as a means of communication.

It was no small challenge to write this book "with four hands", as the Italians would say. It took as a couple of attempts and several months before we got the hang of a practice that worked for both of us. Our long-standing friendship was the decisive driving force in getting there, but the unlikely collection of places where we compared notes, hammered out ideas and did the actual writing helped a good deal: Zeist, Wartena, Lunteren, Naples, Amalfi, Montpellier, Zwolle, Rome, Skype. Thanks to Silvana Siciliano for making available her lovely house at Amalfi, Italy!

So as not to weary the reader's eye and patience, we have dealt with the sensitive gender issue by adopting the common short cut of "he" to refer to any human being, rather than the cumbersome "he/she". Perhaps, if this book goes into a second edition, we may reverse that formula, making it "she" to represent "she/he".

This is the place to thank a number of people without whom this book would not have existed, or at least not in the form it now comes to you. Although we had previously both written a number of articles, columns and book chapters, we were always conscious that writing this book was a greenfield operation. We had never really had the need to cultivate what Ernest Hemingway considered the most essential weapon in any writer's armoury, the "crap detector". Early on, therefore, we put together what we called our Anti-Crap Committee. Annemarie van der Meer, Bart Wijnberg and Michiel Rombach read the first version of a good part of the book and during a substantial meal provided encouraging and sobering advice on both form and content. Pier Paolo Mariotti and Germaine Fabrie helped with insightful suggestions for improvement. Naturally, our gratitude goes to Vahid Daemi, Hans Clevers, David Hughes and Martin Sirk for reading the manuscript and giving the book their endorsements. With great patience, David Cobb did an outstanding job of pointing us in the direction of contemporary British idiom for a work of this kind; what he might call 'politely informal register as used between business colleagues.' (Clearly, this last sentence is entirely from him.) Yoko Heiligers devoted her talent and original outlook to the content, producing the lovely illustrations for each of the chapters and the cover design. In that last effort she was helped by Carin Wormsbecher who provided invaluable advice on the graphics and printing. Sosan Hanifi corrected the last imperfections in a final editing round, while Rosa Garriga Mora from Spain helped us to put a marketing plan together.

Finally, special thanks are due to the people who stood by our side gently rocking the cradle of it all: the late Rob Hoelen, Jeroen Busscher, Frank Eijkelkamp, Stephan van der Vlist, Antonello Paliotti and the early clients who believed in us and in this profession even before it really existed: Ton Crepin, Henk Eggens, Sietse Wijnstra, Rieks Perdok, Flip van de Waerdt. Thank you all! In the past 15 years, and especially since the inception of our company MindMeeting, they and our many other clients have rewarded our efforts with the trust and confidence that have allowed us to develop the peculiar mixture of professional insights and practical tools we are now sharing with you. We hope that *Into the Heart of Meetings* will prove a source of inspiration.

Eric de Groot and Mike van der Vijver
Leeuwarden/Naples/Zeist, 2013.

Into the Heart of Meetings

Basic Principles of Meeting Design

Eric de Groot and Mike van der Vijver

Introduction

Men who live together with a pregnant woman gradually begin to show more caring behaviour. This happens because the biology of their body changes: it produces more oxytocin, a hormone which is also known as the 'caring' hormone. So, the fact that a male member of our species meets on a daily basis with a pregnant female member causes a neurobiological modification in his body which in turn, leads to a highly functional behaviour change.[1]

That is fascinating, isn't it?

Why have we written this book? And why would you want to read it? The answer to these two questions is the same: *Into the Heart of Meetings* is a book about the power of meetings as a means of communication. The oxytocin story is an example of the powerful impact of meetings between human beings on their behaviour. Our work as Meeting Designers consists of unleashing that power. So if you have an interest in organising meetings with a heart, meetings that are intense and effective, you should find this book useful.

Of course, everybody is aware that interactions between human beings can be extremely powerful. Think of the shy attraction you felt for a classmate in primary school and how that made you wait every day with infinite patience just to catch a glimpse of him or her. Or think how fascinating you find your colleague in the next office every time he goes to the coffee machine, or of your deep and irrational dislike for everyone in the sales office. Some people inspire you; some turn you off – it is all a matter of dynamics propelled by feelings and perceptions. In today's business meetings, such as conferences, we hardly tap into these human dynamics although more than anything else, they govern our behaviours. Why don't we actually? Why do we apply a set of conventions to meetings, which make it seem they must be performed in a completely rational and predictable way? Meetings involve human beings and the success of meetings depends entirely on how people behave. What we see in practice is that most meetings are flat and boring; they generally fail to bring out the best in participants. The consequence is that the power of meetings remains largely under-utilised.

We feel there are several reasons why meetings suffer from flatness. These reasons essentially boil down to two things: lack of courage or vision, and lack of knowledge. Either of these failings strengthens the other.

This is how we see it: As a means of communication meetings have become bogged down in the quicksand of well-established forms and formats. Just to be on the safe side, their organisers prefer to stick to these solutions,

[1] Delfos, Martine, *De Schoonheid van het Verschil,* Harcourt Book Publishers, Dordrecht, 2008.

even though secretly everybody knows that the outcomes are not going to be optimum. (Actually, what we experience is that in most cases little or no clear and measurable outcomes of meetings are stated or expected, period.) Meeting organisers are afraid to give free rein to the potential of their participants. On the one hand this is because it might make their meeting unpredictable and thus risky and this is something they want to avoid at all costs. Even if they wanted to spare participants marathon monologues and perennial PowerPoints, they wouldn't know where to start.

There is a frankly astonishing lack of knowledge about how meetings actually work. About the dynamics between meeting participants. About what the interaction between them generates in terms of useful or unproductive behaviours. About the impact such behaviours have on meeting outcomes. All of this remains largely a mystery. Admittedly, it is not simple to gain an insight into what happens during meetings. You would need to have an understanding of many disciplines, including but not limited to physiology, endocrinology, sociology, psychology, communication theory, group dynamics, business economics, and art. An unfortunate side effect of this gap in knowledge is that meetings are not even *considered* a specific means of communication, like billboards, television or webpages. Suppose you were the chairman of a company with a staff of 10,000. Would you expect to come up yourself with the graphics design of your corporate brochure or homepage? Chances are that you would be considered a hopeless micromanager if you did (although exceptions are known). Nevertheless, we know of many examples where business executives cheerfully decide how to run the programme for their company's annual management meeting or the launch of the new corporate strategy. This is the more puzzling because often such meetings are *crucially important* for the organisation.

There is a deceptively obvious reason for this mismatch: meetings look a lot like the sort of normal, day-to-day human communications we all engage in. That is a misleading perception. As a result, individuals who know a lot about, say, rocket science, cardiology, corporate strategy or plastic pipes, think they also know about meetings. At least, enough to decide what meeting programmes should look like. Often, this is very unfortunate for the outcomes of meetings and that is an understatement.

Until now the established Meeting Industry has not really gone much out of its way to deal with this basic misunderstanding. It has, no doubt, produced a significant body of knowledge about issues that are related to meetings from the point of view of logistics and hospitality. But it has gleaned little or nothing about what happens with participants' behaviour during meetings and what principles guide those behaviours. The Meeting Industry acts like a car industry that doesn't know what people are doing when they actually sit inside a car.

meetings? In his ground-breaking Manifesto "Meeting Architecture",[3] our Belgian colleague Maarten Vanneste distinguishes three reasons for having meetings: learning, networking and motivation. We would like to add at least three more categories: decision-making, rituals (more particularly, meetings that serve the purpose of satisfying peoples' *need* for having a meeting as a ritual of some kind) and alignment. By alignment we understand bringing meeting participants to a higher level of shared understanding and agreement on something – anything. That encompasses purely 'human' issues, such as emotional engagement and community building. Many scientific and association meetings have this objective. More often than not, meetings combine several of these fundamental reasons.

Why do we continue to have meetings, meetings where people actually, physically *meet*? Today, there seem to be so many alternative ways of communicating which allow us to achieve results for the above six reasons without actually having to get together. Distance learning, virtual teamwork, web-based social media, flat-world interconnectivity, all of these do indeed offer new ways of sharing things with other people. And yet, there is a characteristic of meetings, that gives people and organisations a compelling reason for wanting them. In a way, the difference between these new platforms and live meetings is comparable to that between saying hello to a friend on the phone and hugging him or her. Human beings are essentially social creatures. They *like* to get together with other humans. Moreover, it's not just that they like it, different things happen when they physically meet. The oxytocin release mechanism of the opening example proves this.

The physical presence of other people is the one thing that makes meetings the unique vehicle for human communication they are. When people come together in one place, they are subject to experiences that give them a particular feeling of belonging together, the feeling they are a 'we'. The result is what we have started to call a temporary human ecosystem: a complex interplay between a whole range of factors which interact and thus generate human behaviours that either help to achieve the meeting's objectives or make that more difficult.

As Meeting Designers, we are convinced that it is possible to influence those factors and steer what happens inside the meeting room. On the basis of our shared and ample experience with meetings, our work is to optimise the primary meeting process. On that path and in the many hundreds of meetings we have witnessed, we have sometimes stumbled upon and sometimes consciously developed, tried and tested a number of principles, concepts and notions we are proud and happy to share with you. All of that has experiences have been packed into this book: a guided tour *Into the Heart of Meetings*.

---

18   [3] Vanneste, Maarten, *Meeting Architecture*, a Manifesto, 2009.

Part 1

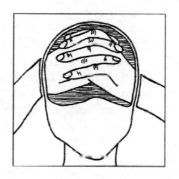

1.1 Mind Meets Matter

Up There, Down Here

 *hat nobody was going to lose their job was just about the only positive message the company had to convey to the employees during the meeting. The rest was all bad news; news about many changes: Changes in positions, changes in salaries, changes in marketing. Many – perhaps too many changes.*

After several years of losses, the company's management team had worked out a radically new strategy, and they wanted to communicate what it meant to the workforce. They were convinced of the urgency and the viability of their plans but at the same time they feared turmoil, negative energy, months of resistance and losing key staff. Instead of confrontation, they wanted the meeting to start off on a positive note, leading to a fruitful discussion of their plans, even though the message was tough.

The first thing the organisers did was to hire a venue, a theatre; then they hired us, to help them design the programme. There were lots of questions to sort out but one seemed to have been answered already: how to present the explanation of the new strategy? That was simple: in the theatre there was a stage with room for the entire Board and a lectern, lighting, and a floor area with seats and a screen for a PowerPoint presentation. The employees would come in, and as soon as everybody had found a seat, the lights would go out for the Managing Director to start his presentation. Wasn't that logical.

Distance and Darkness

Well, was it? As Meeting Designers we often need to think of the question that preceded the answer. On this occasion this was the question we came to: does seating the employees in the theatre in the conventional way, and then switching off the light, deliver the right message at the start of the meeting? From the point of view of logistics, it seemed a 'no-brainer'. Yes, it makes best use of the existing facilities, it is an easy way to assemble the staff, there are no extra costs for technical equipment, high visibility for both speaker and screen is assured, and so on.

But there is another way of looking at it. Having management on the stage in the floodlight and the employees as spectators sitting in the auditorium in darkness carries a powerful message. The message is this: the employees are a passive audience of what the management wants to put across; there is a gap between management and the rest of the company and the employees are kept in the dark. The participants would feel this in an instant. It is not a message that is transmitted through words; it is transmitted through the experience they have when entering the theatre and the lights go out. They undergo a physical experience that tells them: you are mere onlookers, the important people are up there on the stage. In fact, the gap is clearly visible, you can see it because there is an open space between the front row and the stage.

On this particular occasion the gap was very likely to create a perception of 'them and us', those up there deciding about the lives of us, down here. Without saying a single word, seating and lighting would have created an atmosphere of antagonism. Now wasn't that exactly what the management wanted to avoid?

What really happened on the day was quite different. All 450 employees were seated on the stage, in two groups facing each other. This made them actors in their own play. Centre stage stood a small pedestal, with a camera mounted on it. It worked as a whiteboard. Everything that was written on it was projected directly onto big screens, visible for everyone. Those who spoke stood in the middle, between the two stands. Meanwhile, each participant was constantly facing a whole bunch of people, namely their colleagues. This gave an instant feeling of 'us', having a conversation among ourselves.

Physical Presence and Communication

In the original plan for using the theatre, the company management would have ignored the physical experience of participants who were seated on a lower level, at a distance from the place where the action was, and in the dark. The design solution that contributed to this meeting's a success took into consideration the people's physical reactions to specific situations. In our opinion, this example shows the need to understand something that makes meetings different from other ways of communication. An absolutely crucial factor is that participants' bodies are strongly involved in the primary process of communication. If we as Meeting Designers had not taken this into consideration, and not designed an entirely different experience from the one originally planned, the meeting would have been a disaster. Of course, other elements had to be designed as well: the content, the way the audience interacted, the involvement of management team members, and so on. Later in this book we will discuss the use of various design tools to achieve consistent results. In this chapter, however, we shall focus only on the consequences of the fact that the participants are physically present. First of all, when we refer to 'physical presence,' we do not see the body merely as a functional instrument that supplies the mind with the ability to move about, to eat and shake hands. We see it as a complex kind of 'clearing

All of this has major consequences for how meetings work as a form of communication. What happens between participants is not only the outcome of rational and predictable forces and processes, but also of irrational and unpredictable ones. A meeting is a kind of temporary ecosystem, with an enormous number of variables that influence and determine what actually happens there. Some of these variables, and their effect on participants, are relatively obvious: if you give participants a high carbohydrate lunch and a reasonable helping of alcohol, you need an extra effort to keep them focused in the first afternoon session. Others are unknown: How does sexual attraction influence meeting outcomes? It's impossible to establish this using current knowledge. For instance, we have little idea what influence pheromones have on human behaviour[2.] Some processes are highly personal: a certain song may trigger a vivid memory for Person X and result in a mood swing within just a couple of seconds. While Person Y is insensitive to it.

This complex ecosystem is the natural habitat in which meeting participants interact through their differing patterns of behaviour. However, the ecosystem is not immutable – it is something meeting designers can influence in order to improve meeting outcomes. To be able to do this, we need to have a better understanding of how the brain works, having just concluded that the brain is the core of the Mind-Body relationship. So please follow us on a brief excursion into this masterful human organ.

Thinking about Brains

For centuries (probably since René Descartes wrote: "I think and therefore I am"), we have considered mind and body as two separate things. The body was seen as 'inferior', the 'animal' part of the human being, while the mind was 'superior', and therefore the more 'human' part. The body was, and still is, considered primitive and irrational, the mind advanced and rational. Emotions and feelings are usually seen as belonging to the 'primitive' part. Neuroscience provides evidence that processing of emotions and feelings takes place in specific regions of the brain, notably in the limbic system, in areas such as the hypothalamus and the amygdala. These parts, therefore, correspond to the 'primitive' bit of humans. The rational part of the brain, on the other hand, the part used for more complex cognitive tasks, such as reasoning and decision-making, is located in the cortex, especially in the prefrontal cortex. This part of the brain is much bigger in humans than in most other species and that gives us our faculty of abstract thinking – a great source of evolutionary pride.

---

[2] Pheromones are chemical substances that, when perceived, trigger behaviours in members of the same species. They work like external hormones. Especially between insects, pheromones are known to play an important role in communication. The males of certain moths are able to detect only a few molecules of sex pheromones secreted by females, locating them by following the increase in concentration. Little is known about their impact on human behaviour. Some studies suggest that male sweat contains pheromones attracting heterosexual females.

So, that all looks very simple, doesn't it? Reasoning over here, emotions over there in another part of the brain – the location tells you precisely what is done where. Sounds a bit like different departments in a corporation: Sales on the first floor, R&D on the third, the restaurant on the top floor, etc. For many years this picture dominated our thinking about brains. Until recently. Contemporary research in cognitive science is showing us that, in fact, what goes on in our brains is considerably more intricate. It is true that groups of brain cells in certain areas have a primary task. To stick to our analogy of departments in a corporation: of course the sales people are in the company to sell things. And so, the visual cortex primarily processes stimuli from the eyes. But at the same time, all parts of the brain are closely interwoven. Thinking of the office comparison, there are compelling reasons for this. Sales people who only sell, and have no clue about what the people in R&D are doing, could easily turn into a corporate liability. Satisfying every client's wish, they may start selling things that have not been developed yet. Conversely, R&D people working in isolation might come up with the most wonderful products for which there is simply no market. Luckily, our brain is not like that sort of company. In it, there are billions of connections between clusters of brain cells in various functional areas, and clusters in other parts.

Integrated Data Processing

The position held by most neuroscientists today is that the 'higher' brain centres cannot function properly in the absence of processed information from the 'lower' ones. This has become evident by studying the behaviour of people who for some reason suffered brain lesions in the 'lower' centres. People with damage to these 'lower' parts of the brain, while their brain cortex remained intact – allegedly the part of the brain responsible for complex functions such as reasoning, mathematics or speech – continue to have a whole range of 'rational' capabilities. However, often something turns out to be missing. Some patients, for instance, lose the ability to take sound decisions in the real world; in other cases, their capability for meaningful interaction with other humans turns out to be impaired. The literature is full of fascinating cases, the earliest already described in the first half of the 19th century.

What transpires is that in order to properly perform its incredibly complex tasks, the brain does not just separate 'higher' and 'lower' functions. It requires input and processing capacity from all functions and at the same time! The various areas are interdependent and work as an integrated whole. The brain, in other words, is like a company that continuously processes the information generated and collected by many departments working very closely together.

Thanks to sophisticated scan technology, today researchers can actually see which parts of the brain kick into action for certain tasks. And what they see has a bearing on processes that take place during meetings. It reveals unexpected things. In the brains of chess players, for instance. To become a successful grandmaster, chess players need to be able to remember a bewildering number of positions on the chessboard and the optimum strategies that result from these. This is how they do it. They utilise the part of the brain we use to recognise faces, without knowing this! Remembering faces is something humans are particularly good at. As a result, chess players can have a quick glance at a chess board position and immediately say: "Ah, yes. That is Garbashvilli versus Timokhtov, 1928. White plays and wins in twelve moves."

For non-chess players this amounts to a superior display of memory utilisation, until we realise our own ability to recognise faces almost without having to think: "How nice to see you again! Didn't we meet in New York during the first conference on Education and Science in 1999?" Usually we have to make an effort to find the right connection between the face and the circumstances under which we met the person, but the actual *recognition* of the face is almost instantaneous and automatic. We are capable of storing thousands of faces thanks to the complex interaction between visual processing and memory retrieval.

Such findings give us valuable information about meetings and meeting-related behaviour. If the brain uses the constant input of the 'lower' sensors to function properly, shouldn't a Meeting Designer take this input seriously? And shouldn't we learn more about all these strange interactions between mind and body?

Perceptions, the Brain and Behaviour

In this experiment two employees meet in an office elevator. One is an actor who follows a script; the other doesn't know this. The actor says: "Hi, let me introduce myself, I am John, and I am new here. Could you hold my cup for a second? I would like to write your name down, in order to get to know everybody quickly here." Then a short conversation follows, in which the actor asks a few non-committal, scripted questions. When the elevator stops, the actor takes the cup back, and says goodbye. He follows the script so precisely for one reason: to have the same meeting again and again. The only thing that differs between the various encounters in the elevator is one small detail: the temperature of the liquid in the cup.

After an hour, a second member of the experimentation team asks the employee who was in the elevator: "Have you met John? What do you think, does he have the right kind of personality to be the new manager of department X?" The amazing finding is this: the answers the experimenters receive correlate significantly with the temperature of the liquid in the cup which the employees kindly held for a few moments while in the elevator. The correlation was this: the warmer the liquid, the warmer they perceived the personality of John!

All kinds of unwarranted brain processes constantly influence our perceptions, interactions, opinions, judgments, and decisions. Our brain receives an enormous amount of unfiltered information from the outside world that is selected and processed in accordance with existing pathways and connections in our heads. The processing transforms raw information into perceptions. Perceptions depend as much on the objective reality around us, as on the way the brain handles all of this information about the world that streams in. The example shows that the brain does not always deal with the incoming information along rational and conscious pathways. Sometimes you meet somebody and you immediately know that you do not like them, without knowing why really. Or the opposite: love at first sight.

All of the above shows that our brain is not as objective and infallibly single-minded as we think it is. It is not so much a matter of the brain making mistakes, the point is that while we rationally think that our brain is doing one thing, at the same time, somewhere underneath, other 'things' are happening, as well. These other 'things' influence the interactions and relationships we have as a person with the world around us. And often we do not know this.

Now back to 'lower' and 'higher' brain centres and the connection with meetings. Brain processes in the 'lower' brain areas are dealt with several thousand times more quickly than the elaboration of rational thought in the prefrontal cortex. These lower processes especially include physical stimuli coming from the senses but also from our own (and other people's) bodies, such as body posture ('body language') and – very importantly! – feelings and emotions. They include a host of things our brain does in connection with our need for survival and which, for that very reason, it needs to be doing with great urgency. We might call them instinctive. If at a reception the caterers have had a fault in their cold storage system and you end up with a piece of rotten fish in your mouth, your first thought won't be that you're going to have a sleepless night if you swallow it. You'll spit the offending item out. Right away.

In the brains of most human beings, the lower and higher processes are generally well integrated. And, logically, just as the integration between higher and lower brain processes influences people's behaviour in day to day life, it also plays a role during meetings.

Influencing Perceptions through Meeting Design

Let's return to our initial example of the meeting in the theatre. In the original setting, a major difference in perception would have developed between those on the stage and those in the auditorium, because management had overlooked the physical experience employees would have. Management sincerely wanted to create a forum for an open exchange of views. Pity that the employees would have experienced something else on the basis of their perceptions. Inevitably, they would have concluded that the meeting offered them an uneven playing field. If we want to design great meetings we have to work with the fact that the body plays a decisive role in what participants experience.

At the end of the annual corporate meeting the outgoing CEO wanted to introduce his successor. The new man would be given the stage to address just about the entire workforce, but he decided to do something else. He placed himself at the door on the way out and gave all of the 450 employees a firm handshake and a gentle word. In a mind-AND-body way he communicated to his staff the kind of leader he wanted to be in this time of crisis: hands-on, coaching, facilitating and close to his people. No speech could have conveyed that message more clearly than this simple action.

Meeting Design and Outcomes

It is interesting that many meetings are held with the express *intention* of achieving outcomes that require an interaction between rational and non-rational processes. Often, meetings are organised for participants to exchange knowledge and, as a result, develop new ideas and new insights. They also want people to network and extend their connections. However, in practice the participant experience most meetings offer focuses on their rational side. The vast majority of meetings are verbal and cerebral, whereas new ideas and thoughts are spawned by intuition, inspiration and creativity. They have a better chance of emerging during meeting programmes that have been designed to appeal not only to participants' heads but also to their bodies.

One of the easiest examples to illustrate this point is the need for participants to move about. As every experienced conference-goer knows, after a while just sitting and listening becomes unbearable. "The mind can only absorb what the bottom can endure," wrote Mark Twain. In traditional meetings participants crave for their coffee break, and not just because of the caffeine shot. They know that stretching their legs means that their brain will become more active again. A Dutch writer – less famous than Mark Twain[3] – once wrote that our brain is actually located in our legs because we think much

[3] Midas Dekkers.

better when we walk.

It is important, therefore, in meetings that look for productive brain output from participants, to let or even make them move about. The simplest way to do this is to ask participants at some point to go and sit somewhere else. Of course, because most people are already settled in a rut of diehard congress behaviour, they are likely to resist this request. But that resistance usually melts away with some kind insistence and with opinion leaders giving the good example. And especially when people find themselves sitting next to someone who smells a lot nicer.

Mind Meets Matter in Meeting Design

Meeting Design is about creating programmes that influence participant behaviour in such a way that meeting outcomes are achieved and meeting objectives are met. In order to achieve this end, Meeting Designers need to take into account the following principle: people participate in meetings with their minds and their bodies. Good meeting programmes provide participants with a balance of stimuli and activities that appeal to both.

Sceptic

We speak to Klaas, an old friend who works for a Non Governmental Organisation in Zambia.

K: That's a nice idea, putting the participants opposite one another, on a stage. But in the end, what is the impact on the organisation? Surely, you are not suggesting that your meetings change the way organisations work, are you?

E/M: No, of course not. We are Meeting Designers, not agents of organisational change.

K: So what's the point of the example of the people in the theatre? I mean, sitting on that stage didn't change the company in any fundamental way.

E/M: Our point was not to give an example of a successful corporate strategy project; we do feel, though, it is an example of a successful meeting.

K: So results come later, if they come at all.

E/M: In a way, yes – that depends on your time horizon. The day in the theatre was an intense experience and 450 people came out of the meeting

1.2 Meetings Are a Stage

happening in the meeting room will turn out to be useful later, somewhere else.

So participants at meetings essentially have the feeling that they are inhabiting two worlds, or two realities, worlds that coexist in a special relationship: one inside the meeting, and one outside. All who have attended meetings that engaged them deeply will recognise this sensation. When you leave the venue, it feels like returning to the real world. During the meeting, you were somewhere else, somewhere special. In fact, this doubling of reality is one of the attractions of meetings. It also explains why some people are capable of behaving in ways they would rather not talk about after their return to 'normal life'.

Meetings Are a Stage

But there is more to this peculiarity of meetings. We would actually take the line of reasoning one step further: being away from the 'centre of gravity' (as we called it in the previous paragraph), participants at a meeting are somehow involved in fiction, in a story. They are temporarily cast into a different reality. This fictitious reality is not just a random place; it carries a whole series of markers most conference participants immediately recognise as theatre. From our observation that meetings are not the real work or the real world, we derive the following principle:

Meetings are a stage.

Many things that characterise meetings physically prove this point: the actual presence of a stage, the attention focused on the people performing on it, the seating, the need to catch and keep the audience's attention (and the difficulty of doing so), the foyer for food & drinks, the lighting, the sound, etc, etc.

The implications of this principle are huge and they offer tremendous, mostly untapped possibilities to Meeting Designers. Naturally, that is exactly what we are interested in, as we will illustrate in the remainder of this chapter.

Managing the Gap

For meetings to be effective, it is essential to manage the gap between the two worlds we have identified: the world of the meeting and the world outside. Participants are constantly looking for connections, as well as for the divide between them, and trying to make sense of them. This is something that happens to every participant and it is the task of the meeting designer to ensure that they can find that meaning. The impact of the meeting is biggest if the programme allows participants to work within that double reality and figure out the connections, the divide and their meaning. Fiction, and in particular theatre, can help to establish that meaning in two important ways.

For a start, the real world is often hard to grasp. It is complex, elusive and impenetrable. Fiction and imagination can help to make the real world more comprehensible. Meetings can be a place to play with reality, to experiment with thoughts and ideas, to toy with scenarios, to investigate the impossible or the unthinkable. In fact, for some aspects of reality, fiction may be the only acceptable way of addressing them, for instance in the case of taboos, or issues that are politically highly sensitive. The greater the distance between the real world and the reality of the meeting, the greater the chance for participants to develop different perspectives on that outside world and obtain new insights into it. And is that not exactly what many meeting organisers declare they want to achieve?

Secondly, fiction or theatre allows the programme to single out a specific part of the content, or to focus participants' attention in a specific direction. Taking a hard, uncompromising, in-depth look at certain details often helps to clarify the complexities of the real world. A variation of this process is to direct the attention away from particular content, to ensure that negative interactions between participants or participant groups, which is disruptive in the outside world, is kept outside the meeting room. Often, meeting organisers know about these tensions. The opportunities for broaching such sensitive issues are usually extremely limited, while both organiser and participants may be dying for a chance to have them out into the open and do something about them. If a session is not designed properly, a chairperson may cut off any discussion of such issues for fear they will get out of control. Let us take an example and discuss it in-depth to show how all of the above can work out in practice.

Caring for Victims

The National Foundation for the Support to Victims asked us to design a conference about highly needed improvements in the social and financial aftercare for victims of traffic accidents. Participants included actual victims, representatives of the police, of insurance companies and of a broad range of social organisations, both profit and not-for-profit – just about all parties involved in this sensitive societal issue.

What would you do if asked to propose a programme? Most likely you would go in search of the following ingredients: a couple of knowledgeable speakers, one or two exciting testimonials, maybe a panel with people who

Theatre is the art of constructing an experience for a group of people, using actors who pretend to be someone else. The power of theatre to trigger responses from an audience is obvious when children watch a play. Kids just cannot resist the urge to talk to whoever is sitting next to them about what is happening on stage. But it works with adults, as well:

In the 1970s, Brazilian theatre director Augusto Boal used an applied theatre form to generate debate among Argentinians about the political situation in their country. An actor would have a meal in a restaurant and refuse to pay the bill, invoking an old law that guaranteed food for everyone. Other actors would get involved in the debate with the restaurant owner and in no time the whole restaurant would explode in fierce discussions. Even after the instigators declared that they were actors and left, the discussions would not stop.

The function theatre can perform is that of helping meeting participants to bridge the gap that is inevitable in any meeting: the gap between the real world outside the meeting and the artificial, constructed reality of the meeting itself. The very fact that we can construct the reality in the meeting room gives us that opportunity. For our purposes, it is irrelevant that in most meetings this happens only to a very limited extent – the possibility exists, and we have evidence of this in scores and scores of meetings, either thanks to major interventions – such as the car wreck – or to small nudges, for instance by choosing the statements to introduce a provocative debate.

The next question that arises is *how* to use theatre to achieve this goal. Clearly it is not a good idea to turn the entire meeting into a theatrical performance. Although we believe strongly that appealing to participants' emotions may produce much more effective meetings, we do not think that turning meetings into spectacular events is useful per se. As we will argue in Chapter 2.3, every item in the programme needs to be connected with the content and the meeting objectives, as identified by the organisers.

Let us now illustrate three aspects of theatre that can be designed and applied in meetings; these will express the principle that meetings are a stage in concrete terms. The three aspects are: dramatisation, actor performance, and the set.

Dramatisation: Breathe Life into a Story

Suppose your meeting organiser has invited the former CEO of Philips Electronics to inspire a conference on leadership and entrepreneurialism. The audience consists of young academics, alumni of the University that is holding the meeting, all of whom have recently started their own businesses.

What options are there to bridge the gap between this meeting in a lecture hall and the actuality of the participants' day-to-day lives as managers? How can we employ theatre, or drama, to ensure that the powerful personality of the CEO has an impact in the meeting itself, as well as in the world outside? Originally, the University was planning to put the CEO on stage and let him deliver a 40-minute speech from behind a lectern, with a dark blue curtain as the background, and every now and then a chart appearing on a screen. Would that have created a dramatic impact? Hardly, we thought, even though the gentleman in question is a seasoned public speaker.

Thinking of the meeting as a stage, a whole host of alternative opportunities opens up. Firstly, to have any dramatic impact in the meeting, it is necessary to identify a situation we can *dramatise*. The word 'Drama' comes from Greek, and it means 'to act'. The best way to find drama is to look for an action, or a series of actions, that can be performed by a hero. The better the action highlights the strengths of the hero's character – in this case the CEO – the more powerful it is. You want the hero to act, 'to do something', because doing generates much stronger audience involvement than talking. Skiing (actually doing it on a mountain slope) is more intense than talking about skiing. And watching someone skiing is more intense than watching someone who talks about skiing. Therefore, the more the audience acts and the more a hero is experienced at acting out his role, the stronger the impact.

There is a second requirement. Good dramatisation presumes some sort of conflict: a situation that commands the audience's attention and kindles their empathy because they are eager to find out how the hero is going to pull things off.

The reason for inviting the CEO in the first place was to share his business experience with the young entrepreneurs. Instead of preparing a presentation, we asked him if he would be willing to do something else. "Why don't you suggest something?" he replied. We did. The action we asked him to perform was the role of a 'businessmen's priest.' The young entrepreneurs in the audience would get the opportunity to join him on stage and he would listen to their confessions, just as this happens in a Roman Catholic church. We briefed him to anticipate that during the confessions, individuals from the audience would share their deepest worries and business mistakes with him, and he was to give them instant advice and preferably forgiveness. That set up an exciting dramatic situation, for nobody could predict the 'sins' the audience would come up with, nor the way the CEO would respond. We had our action and our conflict. He liked the idea.

Acting out the Script

Now that we had thought of a good dramatic situation, we had to make sure that the action would develop in the desired direction. If you put an actor in the middle of a conflict, he needs to be given a framework and a context to act within. Is he allowed to improvise, to ad lib? How long should the conflict last? How should it end? Is it in fact resolved? In theatre it is the director's task to give the actor the leeway that produces the desired effect. At the same time, the actor needs a script that sets out a number of steps and makes him aware of the beginning, the middle and the end of his act. So, we wrote a small script, in which a facilitator explained the situation on stage and helped individual participants to muster up the courage to talk with this business icon about their essential leadership questions. We also defined the amount of time for each confession and the way it had to end – let us say, the equivalent of an absolution ritual.

Setting the Scene

Finally, the set has to support the actor in his role. At the same time, it needs to provide the audience with the context that makes them understand what it is they are watching. The set adds extra dimensions of involvement: the lighting focuses attention, the choice of colours influences the atmosphere, the way space is used structures the interaction, both implicitly and explicitly. In this case, we gave the CEO a small stage with two chairs and a little table in the middle. His chair was a bit posher than the one on the other side of the table. There were spotlights on both positions. The facilitator, whose status was lower and who had no role in the dramatic action, was at the same level as the audience in the auditorium, next to the small stage. Each time a young manager decided to venture onto the stage for a confession, he was offered the chair next to the CEO. The lights dimmed and there they were: in the intimacy of the CEO's study. The audience listened in utter fascination as each story unfolded and reached its climax when the former Mr Philips gave his advice. The CEO enjoyed his role tremendously, gave of his best, and afterwards told us that, meeting with these young managers, he had actually learned a lot himself (see also Chapter 3.6).

Improving Meetings

As Meeting Designers, we want to offer our clients effective meeting programmes, meetings that actually do what they set out to do. One way or another, this means that participants need to be involved in dialogues: dialogues with the organiser, dialogues with the content experts, dialogues between themselves.

To generate the kind of dialogue participants really want to engage in, it is not enough to merely pinpoint some people who provide content. As we said in the beginning of this chapter, participants are keenly aware that meetings are not real work. In order to catalyse the interaction between all those present at the meeting, you have to think about the gap between the world inside and outside and help participants to bridge it. Good meeting design takes into account the necessity to think through carefully how you want your people in the programme to act. Just an expert, or a series of speakers who convey information about the outside world is insufficient to spark off something unique and powerful. And that is what meeting organisers want, is it not?

There are countless ways in which you can re-present the outside world inside the meeting. You can inject the meeting with a specific view on that reality in order to catalyse the dialogue. You can single out one aspect of the outside reality and set participants the task of diving into it. You can have role-plays in which actors re-present the outside world in a sheltered, safe environment, you can bring events from the outside into the meeting room, as in the car-wreck example. Potentially, the possibilities are unlimited.

The paradox is that in order to re-present reality, you have to enter the realm of imagination. Precisely because the real world is somewhere else, you need imagination to re-present it, to present it again, in the meeting, but slightly differently. Meetings are a stage.

Sceptic

We have a chat with Ben, a retired government official from the Netherlands, who was involved in international policy meetings all his professional life.

B: Sorry, guys, I couldn't disagree with you more. Meetings were definitely real work for me! Everything that was important in my working life happened during the many meetings I went to. That is exactly what the Ministry paid me for!

M/E: Did you ever attend a meeting in which final decisions were taken on policies?

B: Of course not, we live in a democracy. The final decisions are taken by Parliament, not by us. We simply worked out proposals.

M/E: So what did you mostly talk about during your meetings?

B: Oh, about subtle changes in texts, or about the political implications of

1.3 Elementary Meetings

A Dutch Elementary Meeting

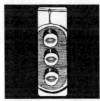 n the front garden of a certain Dutch house there is a strange statue. Everybody who enters knows exactly what rules will apply to the meeting taking place inside and which they will attend. Here are the main ones: do not come uninvited; if you do visit, bring a gift; accept the disc of twice-baked toast sprinkled with sugar-coated aniseed balls and try to eat it without spilling any of it on the floor; treat the specialist nurse who is temporarily in charge of the household with respect; say only kind things about the VIP in the room and do so using a peculiar tone of voice; do not expect answers from the VIP; leave after about 45 minutes, or leave earlier when the total number of people present exceeds 5; avoid speaking about your own personal concerns, unless they have a bearing on the recent experience of the VIP; generally keep your voice down when speaking, avoid loud laughter.

This strange statue is one of a stork, and it stands in the garden of a house where you go to visit a newborn baby and its family.

The Rules of the 'Kraambezoek'

In most of Europe and North America, it was commonly believed that storks brought babies. Only the odd child still believes this, but as a symbol of parenthood, the stork has survived. So that explains the stork.

In the Netherlands about 30% of all babies are born at home.[1] As a result, most people see a newborn baby and its mother for the first time in the family home and not in a hospital. This first encounter is known as the *Kraambezoek*. This meeting kick-starts a round of typical behaviours that illustrate our notion of Elementary Meetings.

Understandably, during the *Kraambezoek* the newborn child is the VIP, but – for obvious reasons – it is its mother who does the talking. Just as obviously, the topics for conversation are restricted: share prices or fly-fishing are taboo. There is one subject that takes up the bulk of the visiting time and on which the mother herself is the main speaker: a detailed description of her labour during the birth of her baby. The pace of the meeting is slow; the visitor asks interested questions, the mother replies, and every now and then, a specialised home care nurse interrupts the meeting for a variety of low-intensity medical checks.

Everybody in the Netherlands knows what a *Kraambezoek* is. The English language, on the other hand, does not even have a word for it. The Dutch

 [1] CBS, Dutch National Statistics Agency, Annual Report, 2009

know all about this meeting and its numerous unwritten rules and make sure not to violate even one of them.

Meeting Markers

How do they know? Well, there are two clear markers that enable them to identify a *Kraambezoek*. The first is a specific invitation. The happy parents announce the birth to the outside world by means of a small card, sent by mail. Family members, friends and relations all receive one. The card is carefully selected at a print shop (or sometimes designed at home, today preferably by older siblings) and it has a specific layout and style. Also, it contains information about the newborn baby: generally the date and exact time of birth, the baby's sex, size and birth weight, and the visiting hours for mother and child. (The father is rarely mentioned – for the time being he is resigned to a back seat) The card counts as an implicit invitation to come over for a *Kraambezoek*.

The statue of the stork in the garden (or sometimes on a balcony) is the second marker. Card and stork are never used in other circumstances. They indicate beyond any possible doubt the kind of meeting people are being invited to and at the same time (and this is important for the Meeting Designer!) what kind of behaviour will be suitable during this first visit to mother and child. Any older children who may accompany visitors are given careful instructions about this, without any room for their own interpretation. In this manner the peculiar characteristics of these meetings are handed down from generation to generation and so meetings of this kind remain part of the fabric of Dutch social life.

Elementary Meetings and Meeting Conventions

We have gone on at some length describing this unique type of meeting. The reason is that we are convinced there are lots of meetings of this kind: specific kinds of encounters that come with specific sets of behavioural rules. What is more, people that have been brought up knowing those rules will not fail to recognise them thanks to a set of unmistakable markers and they will do their utmost to respect them.

We consider this first mother-and-child-visit in the Netherlands, an Elementary Meeting, which we define as follows:

> **An Elementary Meeting has a specific name and consists of an obligatory, tacitly agreed series of actions performed by those taking part in the meeting. It usually originates in a specific national culture.**

This gives a Meeting Designer the exciting possibility of triggering the kinds of behaviour that will help produce the desired meeting outcomes!

Different Elementary Meeting: Different Outcome

Harry is the CEO of a company with 800 employees. In the course of the annual meeting on how the business is doing, he needs to deliver a speech to the entire workforce. He complains that his people are never willing to react to what he says and asks us to design the meeting differently so that this time they will. "A conversation is what I want," Harry sighs, "not talking to a bunch of anonymous faces."

We ask him to explain how his people sit, what he does and where he stands when he does his speech. Nothing particular emerges: Harry's meeting is a conventional classroom-style thing and so we conclude that it is Harry's wish to change an important meeting convention: instead of a passive, listening audience he wants an active, participating audience. As Meeting Designers we are aware that to achieve this we need to change the Elementary Meeting his employees feel they are entering. Instead of picking up the normal markers of a lecture they need to perceive the markers of a conversation. And this has to be done right from the start, when participants are still in the process of figuring out what kind of 'togetherness environment' they are entering.

Design the Markers

We gave the participants three markers to define the situation as a Conversation. The first signal was to break up the audience into 8 batches of just 100. Only 100 participants at a time would listen to Harry's speech; the others would be occupied with other parts of the programme.

The second signal was a little script for Harry. It went something like this: while his colleagues were entering the room, he was to ask one of them a personal question, in a sufficiently loud voice, so that everyone could hear. Something like "Hey, John, is your son back again from Down Under? I guess you and Martha are really pleased if he is?" He had to listen carefully to John's reply and then give him a further response, still on a personal note. This exchange subconsciously induced the idea that he was actually having a conversation, in touch with his people.

The third signal was the scene set.[3] We asked Harry to bring along two comfortable chairs from his office to the meeting room, for which we chose a low status room in the venue: one of the rooms normally used for storage, painted white without any decorations whatsoever. There was no stage, the

[3] *See Chapter 1.2 Meetings are a Stage for an explanation of this notion.*

CEO just sat in one of the chairs at the same level as the participants. The message he conveyed was: "I am just one of you." The second chair was invitingly empty; the distance between Harry's chair and the audience was small.

It worked. To Harry's surprise, when he was about 5 minutes into his speech, the first question came – not generated by a facilitator, but almost by itself, on a subtle cue from Harry that had never worked in the past. We were not surprised. We had changed the meeting conventions by designing clear signals that the participants were in a different Elementary Meeting compared to other years, and they did not fail to respond.

Sceptic

We speak to Mark, a 53-year old entrepreneur who has recently started a new venture producing medical appliances. He is interested in meetings because he has attended so many. In addition, he has vast international experience.

M: So, what you meeting designers do is manipulate people. Cheats!

E/M: If by manipulation you mean influencing people's behaviour: yes, we do that – much as a sports coach manipulates his athletes, a teacher manipulates pupils and parents manipulate their children.

M: OK, I understand you do it for a noble purpose. But if people see through the trick, it does not work anymore. Or does it?

E/M: Framing our work as a trick is not exactly our way of looking at things, but even when people see how it works, its power remains. It just seems so natural to people to go with the flow of a meeting once they are part of it. It is scary to break the rules.

M: As a businessman I sometimes have to break the rules to win a contract. That's international business for you. It's tough out there.

E/M: Do you see business negotiations as an Elementary Meeting, as we have defined it?

M: Certainly, my meetings have a typical set of conventions: the table is never round, there is no booze, we behave like decent, civilized people, and we crack some jokes at the start to break the ice.

E/M: But then you say you break those conventions.

M: Yes, if necessary I drink, get angry and shout at the other party, and I sometimes openly make fun of them. Irritate them.

E/M: And then what happens?

M: Well, of course, then I win! Ha, ha!

E/M: Would you like to change the way your negotiations go?

M: Well, frankly, yes. I hate them. I believe in cooperation more than in aggression, personally. Don't like fighting.

E/M: We use the term 'togetherness environment' in our work. Is that at all relevant to you?

M: Togetherness environment? As in: pub? Or: theatre? Well, I'd prefer an environment like a laboratory setting, or an exciting experiment. Where everybody is invited to see how my invention works. Fun! Or better still: the launches at Cape Canaveral, where all of NASA and their families witness the rocket disappearing in the blue sky!

E/M: Do you think those are Elementary Meetings?

M: Not really, that is the trouble with your idea. Not applicable. Too complicated.

E/M: In the first series of talks between Russian and American presidents in the eighties to end the Cold War, one of them tried to change the Meeting Conventions by inviting the other president for an unusual walk in the garden. On Iceland, wasn't it? Reagan and Gorbachev.

M: That works! Last year I was in Eastern Europe and wanted to conclude a deal. The whole thing was unpleasant and confrontational. Irritating. Then after we broke up this guy who led the negotiations for the other company took me out to the ballet. Seemed just another formality at first. Then after the show he invited me over to his place and we drank a lot of vodka. Good vodka! He showed me his kids who were fast asleep and made a fire. We sat down and after 3 minutes of silence he said: "Mark, I want the deal, I will not break you, but I do not want to be broken either, do you understand?" Then he made me an offer I could not refuse. All problems set aside at a stroke. The next morning, after signing the papers, I asked him what went through his head the night before. He laughed. Then he said: "You know, Mark, my priorities shifted. I want to be rich among friends, instead of just rich." True story.

E/M: He changed the conventions from negotiating with an adversary to having a night out with a friend, didn't he? And that gave a different outcome.

M: Yes, and you know, I'm sure he did it on purpose. Clever. Maybe I can change the next round of negotiations myself. They are in Spain. I have to think about that. Any suggestions?

The Missing Mayor

ver 150 participants from all over Europe are gathered in a Southern European city for an International Conference on Urban Development. The programme should have started 25 minutes ago but the organisers are still waiting for the Mayor to arrive. She was expected to deliver an official opening speech, announced in the programme as "Greetings from the Authorities."

The chair had already announced ten minutes earlier that the Mayor was somewhat delayed due to "reasons of an institutional nature" but she was on her way. Now, the organisers are evidently distressed, but they continue to wait. After ten more minutes of Northern European suffering the meeting starts without the Mayor, who proves to be unable to make it, after all. She sends a message, stating that she would try to be present for the closing session and deliver her speech there.

This scene is not at all rare at meetings taking place in countries around the Mediterranean. National and international conferences there often start with a programme item named "Greetings from the Authorities." It usually boils down to air time for politicians or administrators. Conference diehards from both northern and southern European countries will probably recognise the situation. The southerners (and quite a few easterners, as well) accept the "Greetings" as a somewhat annoying, but inevitable fact of life. In the meantime they are busily networking, while the northerners are slowly stewing with anger, complaining to each other about a lack of professionalism that borders on insult and wondering how on earth the locals can accept this behaviour from their democratically elected representatives.

Diverging Expectations

Clearly, the two groups hold significantly different views about the relationship between the powers that be and ordinary citizens. Generally speaking, national cultures determine to a significant degree what is proper or improper behaviour in a variety of situations, including meetings. To put it differently, behaviour and expectations about behaviour during meetings depend a great deal on the nationalities of the participants and the cultures they represent – just as in society at large. It will probably not have escaped you that we said something similar about behaviours during meetings in the previous chapter on Elementary Meetings. We even indicated that many

Elementary Meetings are connected to specific countries. So what is the difference? In Elementary Meetings it is the recognisable form of the meeting, with its typical markers, that establishes the behavioural conventions. Many of those markers work equally well for people from different countries, as long as they sense them in a similar way. In this chapter we take a much broader look at all kinds of behaviours and especially expectations about the behaviours of others that stem from national cultures. It is the clash between such expectations that the Meeting Designer needs to manage. Here is another example:

The morning session has already eaten well into the lunch break when the last speaker finishes his contribution. No time is left for the planned panel debate, says the chairman, and just as he starts to wind up and invite everybody to their well-deserved pasta, a small, elderly gentleman stands up and grabs a mike. His first two sentences make it clear that he thinks he has an essential point to make and he does not care whether the pasta goes cold. The chairman tries to interrupt him but this only increases his fervour. He starts yelling his question at the panel, ignoring the repeated pleas of the chairman to let them off his hook. Meanwhile, many participants just ignore the speaker and start to leave the room. The session ends amid confused shouts and a furious monologue that only gradually dies out.

Conflict during Meetings

It was fascinating to witness the different ways the audience reacted to this spectacle. Most foreign participants showed their disapproval of the speaker's interruption and were irritated by the incident. They left the meeting in bad spirits. Most local participants, Italians, did not think much of it: just someone who had got carried away a bit and wanted to make his point. So what – they see people doing that in Parliament and on TV every day. Verbal conflict in public is quite acceptable in their country.

For a Meeting Designer, this example shows how culture can impact on programme design and execution. In a country like Italy, if you tell people in your programme that there will be a debate with a panel, then at least some people in the audience will come along determined to say something, whether the organisers like it or not. Trying to shut them up is a futile exercise; they will only feel manipulated and their Latin temperament will get the upper hand. They will not be quiet just because time is up. While such an incident is quite acceptable by Italian standards, it is not by the standards of many other cultures. For different reasons, it is not in Scandinavia or in many countries in Asia. Ultimately, this has a significant impact on the outcomes participants take away from the meeting and should therefore be a concern for the meeting organiser. It is the task of the Meeting Designer to help prevent such disruptions.

Was this incident caused only by poor time-keeping? We do not think so. It was the explosive mixture of poor time-keeping and excitable participants. If you plan a morning programme with several distinguished speakers and a panel debate, in a country such as Italy (and elsewhere – we are not picking on Italy, but the incident just happened to take place there) you know beforehand that it is impossible to make people stick to their allotted time. Not difficult – impossible. At the same time, the fact that the session runs over time will not keep the audience from delivering comments or putting up a verbal fight, especially if the subject matter is controversial. Both of these characteristics are a 'given' of – in this case – Italian culture and society.

You can also predict that people from less flamboyant cultures will be bothered by an incident such as the one depicted above. As a Meeting Designer, you need to take all these ingredients into account and make sure that the programme still satisfies the needs and expectations of all participants.

Meetings and Culture

The theory of cultural differences and communication is a kind of applied anthropology that helps us to understand differences in behaviour between people who come from different countries. Potentially, it has much to say about the relationship between meetings and culture. Clearly, however, this is not the place to present a detailed introduction to intercultural theory; for this, we can refer you to relevant literature on the topic[1]. Most of these writers, however, treat the impact of culture on communication in a generalised way. They don't go beyond offering some insights into the relationship between culture and the type of in-company business meetings we have expressly excluded from our considerations in the introduction to this book. Therefore, in this chapter let us explore the relevance of cultural differences specifically for meetings such as conferences, seminars, etc.

The matter of culture has already briefly surfaced in Chapter 1.3 on Elementary Meetings, where we said that the markers and behaviours of Elementary Meetings often depend on national cultures. We are now going to widen our focus to meeting behaviours and expectations in general, not as they relate to specific types of meetings, but much more broadly how people from different countries hold different views about practically all aspects of meetings, from content to coffee breaks and from interaction to interest. We will also clarify how, in our view, these differences can best be overcome.

[1] See for instance authors such as G. Hofstede, F. Trompenaars, E.T. Hall, G. Ferraro, R. Lewis and others...

What is Culture?

Culture is a set of subjective elements (such as values, norms, customs, self-concepts, stories, myths), shared by groups of people and transmitted across time periods and generations. The degree to which individual members of such groups share these elements may differ, but they know how the 'system' works. One of the most important groups that share a large chunk of such elements are the people who come from the same country. It is true that within national cultures there are enormous differences between individuals and if we apply only limited knowledge about national cultures we run the risk of stereotyping. At the same time, the findings of research – as well as common sense – tell us that differences between national cultures provide useful insights into expectations and behaviours. Everybody with just a bit of international experience will readily acknowledge the impact of cultural, rather than individual, preferences in many situations, including the type of examples described above.

An essential characteristic of cultures, moreover, is that they are transmitted over time from one generation to the next. When you are young, parents, teachers, friends, institutions tell you (mostly indirectly), what is acceptable behaviour and what is not. As a result, "culture is to societies what memory is to individuals."[2]

Culture is part of the identity of people. It influences the way human beings select, interpret, process and use information.[3] In summary, culture is one of the most important systems humans apply to give meaning to their own behaviours and to that of others, to their lives, and to the world in general.

A particular difficulty with cultures is that we don't see them at work overtly or openly. Mostly they influence the choices and decisions of individuals in an implicit way. What we see, is people's behaviours and we tend to attribute meaning to those behaviours, interpret them, on the basis of our own cultural programming. The snag is that we cannot be entirely sure whether our interpretation of this behaviour is the same as the meaning which the person displaying the behaviour gives to it. The culture we know best is our own, even though that knowledge, too, works mostly unconsciously. We apply what is expected under many circumstances without having to think about it and this makes us effective. As Dutchmen, we know with almost surgical precision what kind of behaviour is appropriate in the Netherlands under certain circumstances and what is not. How subtly this ingrained knowledge works can most easily be seen when we want to use humour while addressing an audience. Dealing with a group of fellow-cloggies we know exactly how far we can go. We are less certain about creating the right vibes in front of a group of, say, Icelanders or Japanese. Humour is based on an ambiguity or incongruity about the meaning of situations and behaviours. It requires viewing a situation from two different frames of reference. No

---

[2] Triandis, Harry, *Culture and Social Behaviour*, McGraw-Hill, New York, 1994, p. 1.
[3] Triandis, op. Cit. P. 15.

ambiguity, no fun. Most jokes hinge on that ambiguity. But for a start, people from different cultures may find different things ambiguous. Furthermore they may judge any such ambiguities with a different yardstick (for instance, they may feel embarrassed by things other people find hilarious). And finally, some peoples are simply less comfortable with ambiguity anyway. That is why humour does not travel well.

Impact on Meetings

From the above, it follows that culture has an impact on what people from any country consider acceptable or less acceptable during meetings. Naturally, they themselves will only behave in a manner they consider acceptable. For instance: How do participants go about networking? Are they shy and do they tend to stick with the group of people they already know? Or do they mingle quite freely with others? Naturally, the differences are relative; how people deal with them depends on their individual characters, too. All individuals have to overcome a barrier to socialise with unfamiliar people. But it is clear that Anglo-Saxons are generally much easier-going about networking with people they have never met before than most Finns or Koreans (after all, the invention of the cocktail party is claimed by both a British novelist and an American lady).

Other questions of this sort include: What is the role of the Chair? Must this be a person who has superior content knowledge that gains him the respect of participants? Or does the audience prefer a chair who is more like a facilitator, responsible for the process and with just enough knowledge of the subject to guide the discussion? In the Q/A session will audiences who expect a chairperson with a lot of content knowledge allow themselves to be led or even interrupted by one who knows about the process?

What is the profile and role of speakers and other content experts? Will the audience feel intellectually stimulated by a thought-provoking outsider who tackles their subject matter from a completely different perspective? Or will they dismiss this person's contribution as irrelevant? Do participants expect speakers to start tackling the subject matter in a broad, generalised way? From their own, personal experience? Or from a practical and result-oriented angle?

Of course, some of these preferences depend on the objectives of the meeting, but to a significant extent they depend on automatic, almost instinctive, culture-related choices. Speakers from Latin countries for instance, tend to begin a talk by setting out the legal framework of their topic. This approach is totally alien to most Anglo-Saxons and Scandinavians. They tend to start with a joke.

In international meetings, the stage looks a bit like a chessboard with mahjong stones and backgammon checkers on it at the same time. The task of the Meeting Designer is to come up with a game and rules that will allow everybody to play successfully.

Questions and Answers

"Suppose a speaker or a meeting chairperson at an international conference invites the audience to ask questions in a plenary session. What is the nationality of the first questioner likely to be?" When we ask this question in a workshop with meeting professionals, many agree: "From the US." And we think the same. When we follow up with this question: "And where does the person asking the second question generally come from?" the answer takes some time to pop up. When we suggest "Also from the US?" everybody laughs and agrees.

It is generally known that meeting participants from Asia, especially from East Asia, prefer not to ask questions in plenary. Japanese participants, for instance, usually only ask questions if they have been prepared in advance and they prefer to read them out from a sheet of paper, rather than formulating them off the cuff.

This difference between people from the US and those from East Asia has to do with people's willingness to communicate directly and with how comfortable they feel about speaking up as an individual in public. It is well known that compared to Asians, Westerners (and especially Americans) tend to be much more uninhibited in such situations. It goes without saying that this difference in behaviour has a major impact on the interaction between the key players at meetings: chair, experts and participants. In international meetings, most of your Asian participants are shy to participate in a plenary Q/A session. In private, they say so themselves. You may think that this is just their problem and not adapt your programme to reflect their preference. As a result, however, you may lose a lot of potentially useful input.

Solutions?

How can we solve this problem? The most obvious answer would be for the chair to simply repeat the invitation for questions, perhaps specifically inviting Asian participants to take the floor. Then if they don't, anyone with a Western mind-set might conclude they didn't have any questions, or that they are never disposed to ask questions anyway, or maybe even that they are less knowledgeable on the subject or secretive and unwilling to share their ideas. Perhaps the conclusion is that the wrong people have been invited to the meeting. As we can learn from intercultural knowledge, the truth of the matter is that these conclusions about the observed behaviour are all false. Asking explicitly for participation just raises the bar and makes it harder than ever for the Asians to take part.

A possible solution would be to look for some sort of compromise. Maybe the conference organizers can instruct the Westerners to wait a bit and not take the floor immediately when question time starts. But then, how long exactly? Westerners tend to feel uncomfortable with prolonged silence, while many non-Westerners value silence as a way of showing thoughtful respect for what they have just heard. So how long a silence is long enough? Waiting may cause embarrassment on both sides. And how uncomfortable will the first Asian person feel when they are forced to take the floor this way? How will they know that this is expected of them?

So would it be a good idea then to instruct the chair to invite a random Asian participant to ask the first question? Well, if you come from an Anglo-Saxon country, try to imagine that for thirty or forty odd years you have been shown and taught that speaking in public without prior arrangement is better avoided because it involves a huge risk of somebody – anybody – losing face. That designated 'volunteer' is likely to feel *extremely* uncomfortable.

The Third Way – Not Compromise

The above examples show that some sort of compromise, or asking groups of participants to behave differently from what comes natural to them, generally does not lead to a workable solution. It just creates embarrassment and makes all parties ill at ease.

Solving intercultural differences is not helped by compromises; it requires what we call 'The Third Way.' The Third Way consists of a solution that accords with the 'normal' behaviour and expectations of both (or several) groups of participants at the same time. Finding the Third Way is not always easy because it rarely stares you in the face...

A worldwide association holds its annual conference in Korea. It is their express wish to generate input and feedback on the future of the association not only from their Western participants (who will provide this gladly even without being induced), but also from Asian and in particular Korean participants (who will not).

We design a session in which participants receive pre-printed forms on which they are invited to write down their ideas on an issue that is relevant to the association. They can choose to do this individually or in groups and they can use as many forms as they like. They pin their forms on a wall in the meeting room and they do so anonymously. Next everybody reads the statements and chooses a form that triggers them in some way. In the third stage, we ask *them to **enrich** the ideas that are on it, once again anonymously, individually or in groups, working on as many statements as they like.*

First of all this solution caters for the different preferences between Western and Asian participants whether to work in a group or individually. Secondly, all contributions are anonymous, so that no one risks losing face – a very important consideration for social reasons in Asia. This is reinforced by the fact that during the second stage of the session people can choose from a large number of statements to work on. Nobody will notice if some statements are not selected because their content is not appealing. There are just too many. Finally the assignment to "enrich" the thoughts on the form once again prevents anybody from losing face because no criticism is involved. We deliberately avoided words like "feedback" or "agree/disagree". This kind of expression implies criticism of someone else's work, something that will worry people who are sensitive about 'face' issues.[4] This would have resulted in people giving evasive and politically correct comments only. As this example illustrates, the third way is a reconciliation of different or opposing ways of tackling an issue. As an approach, reconciliation works in any kind of international management and communication situation, including meetings. Finding this kind of solution generally requires some intercultural knowledge, a good deal of common sense and a bit of creativity. Sometimes, but not always, the meeting organiser knows what intercultural issues need to be solved. In the course of the design process (see the Chapters of Parts 2 and 3), it is absolutely essential to enquire into this.

From all of the above, we derive the following principle that applies to meetings as a means of communication:

> International meetings require specific design work to make them culture-proof.

Design Solutions

A useful way of discussing 'Third Way' design solutions is to tackle them according to the six main reasons for holding meetings we gave in our introduction: learning, networking, motivation, decision-making, alignment and rituals.

Learning

A workshop on job-related training has participants from Northern Europe and several Mediterranean and Arab countries. They want to learn about

---

[4] *Face* is a notion Western readers may not be entirely familiar with. It can be considered as a person's social ego, consisting of their and their family's reputation, their position in society, etc. In many non-Western countries considerations about face strongly influence people's choices and behaviours.

What we did was this: we arranged participants in a long line, facing each other two-by-two. We asked them to yell "Goodbye!" as a group and then immediately congratulate the person opposite them on their excellent contribution to the workshop result. Then we told them to move a step to the right, and do the same with the new person they faced.[6] As a result, everybody thanked and said goodbye to everybody else.

This was a simple activity resembling the ritual of sports teams at the beginning or the end of a match, in ice hockey and volleyball for instance. There they do it in a line-up of the two teams, but they don't thank their own team mates.

The ritual was satisfactory to both Asians and Westerners because it acknowledged the contribution of all individuals, while at the same time acknowledging that they were all members of the same group. No individual was singled out.

Decision-making

The Secretary for Public Health in the Netherlands convened an international conference, giving it the following remit: "This Conference should establish a list of priority areas in health care for the elderly, prioritised by the most effective public spending." Or, putting it in language non-politicians can understand: on which specific health problems of elderly people should we spend our limited government money to get the best health outcomes?

To cut a long story short, on day 1, groups of participants used a sophisticated format developed especially for the Conference with the help of subject matter specialists. This produced a provisional list of health priorities. On day 2, a panel of selected experts received further participant input and then had to formulate a final version of the list that would meet with participant consensus. We asked an outspoken elderly British lady to chair this group. When invited, she just looked at us for a couple of seconds and then turned to her fellow panel members and said: "OK, come on my friends. Let's get on with this."

At the end of day 2, the list of priorities was unanimously applauded and forwarded to the Health Secretary.

In this example, the Third Way consisted in capitalizing on the cultural diversity in the audience. The conference took place in the Netherlands and although participants were from all over Europe, the Dutch were in the majority. In the Netherlands, working out compromises has been developed into an art form. On the other hand, the Dutch are not known for quick and decisive action in complex matters because compromising and consensus-

---

[6] To keep the group going, there are several solutions for the persons at the end of the line. We asked them to make a 180 degree turn and continue at the other side in the opposite direction.

building are processes that take a long time. We feel we can safely say so – we both are Dutch. What the conference process needed at this stage was a chair who would appreciate a tough challenge and who would say: "Do you doubt I can pull this off? Well, you just wait and see!"

This is typically the kind of response you get from British people when they are faced with challenges. They will grind their teeth, take it on and make it happen. Which is exactly what this admirable English lady did.

Alignment

Around forty high-level education experts get together in Turin, Italy. They have come from a variety of European and Central Asian countries to start a long-term project on school improvement. The international organisation funding the project have asked us to propose a programme for the first day. They accept our idea for the group to work together on designing a logo for the project.

And so on day 1, we facilitate a session during which we ask participants to draw their Ideal school. With the help of English-Russian interpreters each group describes their drawings and why they have chosen those specific elements. Together they decide which of these elements will prove essential in the course of the project.

Meanwhile a graphic artist listens and sketches. During the tea break, she draws a logo that symbolically incorporates the elements the group have chosen. By the end of the session, the logo is ready.

People have strong feelings about schools, about their shortcomings and how to overcome these. The participants in this meeting needed to become aligned right from the start. In a typical international conference set-up, each of the delegations would have expressed their positive intentions in speeches. But using only words risks confusing issues. It is easy to express beautiful intentions in words and it is equally easy to misunderstand someone else's intentions, especially if people come from very diverse backgrounds. We needed to find a more universal form of communication and take the participants through an actual alignment experience then and there.

At the end of the session all participants recognised that they had offered a contribution toward the creation of the shared logo. At the same time the process had not been about choosing one of the drawings the different groups had produced: an 'outsider,' the graphic artist, came up with the final drawing, encompassing all the elements the group had decided were essential.

Rituals

The conference organisers always gave some time to their major sponsors to present their organisations to participants and explain why they had decided to offer their support. Of course, that public visibility was the main argument for them to put up the money, in the first place. However, in the previous year's evaluation forms, conference attendees had voted this by far the least popular item on the programme: they complained of long and predictably boring talks by inexperienced public speakers. Yet, the sponsors were entitled to their moment in the limelight.

The organisers liked the alternative solution we proposed: to have the Conference anchorman interview them – a different way of performing the unavoidable ritual.

Perhaps the cultural implications of this example are not immediately obvious. Although many participants expressed their frustration about the format for sponsor visibility, their objections to the format were quite different. Participants from the Anglo-Saxon countries found these moments boring, but they were in tune with the needs of the association, so they cheerfully put up with it. In this kind of situation, most South-Europeans, on the other hand, can put themselves in a kind of 'mute' state. They find the thing irritating but unavoidable and hope it will soon come to an end. The Scandinavians and the Dutch are not able to switch off and keep silent. They get irritated – period. And when they are irritated they tend to show it, probably becoming mildly rebellious. More than the others, they also expect organizers to do something with their feedback and if not they become disenchanted.

And so, the association had a problem on at least three fronts. A solution had to be found to deal with different kinds of frustration, while safeguarding the interests of the sponsors.

Participants still recognised the interview for what it was, a ritualised form of communication. But unlike the previous one-dimensional presentation of stale information about the sponsors' activities and organisation, now there was interaction between interviewer and interviewee opening up a more human perspective. Naturally, the meeting's anchor person prepared the interviews so that the essential messages would be covered. But having met the sponsors beforehand, and responding spontaneously to cues in their answers, he was able to arouse a general human interest in the person standing there next to him. "How can your children tell that you are proud of your city?" is a question generally not covered in a sponsor presentation. By transforming the ritual of air time for sponsors into an encounter with a human being of flesh and blood, the audience took a genuine interest. The interaction and reciprocity of the interview format created the right ambience. The human side of things holds a universal value.

Finally

Cultural differences can easily lead to intercultural tensions. In today's world of globalisation, two opposing forces are at work: on the one hand a powerful thrust towards uniformity of products, markets, meetings and views, essentially dominated by Western paradigms, on the other the need for people to reaffirm local identities and feel part of something they can identify with, thus confirming their sense of identity.

It is worth looking at these tensions not only from a narrow angle of meeting efficiency. In a broader view of the world, the notion of the Third Way or reconciliation opens up possibilities for innovative solutions that go beyond populist dichotomies: Those who are not with me, are against me. Many of such dichotomies surface during international meetings. We are convinced that traditional meeting formats and dynamics (the 2009 Copenhagen climate summit is a fine example of this point) are not offering the world satisfactory solutions. Meeting Design that incorporates knowledge about cultural differences AND proposes innovative, tailor-made solutions for live communication processes has a lot to offer to the international community.

Sceptic

We have a talk with Peter, a seasoned international conference goer. He is a well-known specialist in nuclear physics, and comes from Denmark.

P: Wonderful solutions you describe in this chapter! But my idea is that there was no problem to solve in the first place.

E/M: Help us here, Peter, we don't get your point.

P: Maybe the difficulties you talk about apply to national meetings with just a couple of foreigners. But professionally, I attend so many international conferences and the people there know how to behave. They don't need help with inter-cultural problems.

E/M: Are you a culture-sceptic, then?

P: Now the two of you need to do some explaining. What do you mean by that?

E/M: What we mean to ask is, do you side with the people who think

Meetings and Knowledge

articipants do not attend meetings to eat a bunch of bananas; meetings are held to achieve objectives related to the six main reasons we outlined in the introduction: learning, networking, motivation, decision-making, alignment and rituals.

In Chapter 1.1, we referred to meetings as a temporary ecosystem. In ecosystems, organisms interact physically. Meetings, too, create a fuzzy buzz of interactions between the people present there. These interactions permit participants to exchange ideas, express opinions, think out loud on processes, size up other participants and in general respond to each other's verbal and non-verbal cues. While interactions in biological ecosystems principally involve the exchange of matter and energy, the exchange in meeting ecosystems mainly involves *knowledge*. It may be true that some meetings are short on exchange and mostly propose unilateral communication, but that does not really change our point. One of the basic observations about meetings is that somehow knowledge always plays a role. Knowledge is to meetings almost as money is to the economy — the currency that keeps meetings going and feeds their processes.

Of course knowledge is ubiquitous when learning is the reason for having a meeting. When people leave a meeting confident that they have learned something, they and the meeting organiser are happy. The bigger the potential for using that knowledge in their day-to-day working lives, the happier they are. And in the case of companies, the more this learning will contribute to the bottom line at some point, the higher the ROI of the meeting.

In addition to learning, the other main reasons for having meetings are equally linked to knowledge and its exchange. In meetings held for decision-making purposes, knowledge flows back and forth between participants in the form of arguments for or against decisions, or as opinions about them, which is often only a marginal difference. Once the required amount of knowledge has been exchanged, the decision needs to be taken. Continuing the exchange beyond that point will not add anything.

In the case of networking, the knowledge gain is finding out who people are, what they all do, in collaboration with whom else, and in which organisations or contexts. Much, but not all, of that knowledge is available in a compressed form on the business card.

Where motivation is concerned, the discovery may be that you are appreciated by your organisation (or not), for what reasons, and how that appreciation is likely to influence your future. You may also learn what sort of behaviour will make people 'popular' in the organisation and the consequences of such popularity.

In matters of alignment, knowledge helps people to recognise the glue that holds them together (in the case of organisational alignment or community building) or gives them insights into a shared area of interest (in the case of intellectual alignment).

And finally, in the case of rituals, the knowledge is essentially already there before the meeting and it is as if participants chew on it together during the meeting.

Your Knowledge or Your Life

Let us briefly return to the metaphor of knowledge as the 'currency' of meetings. Generally with metaphors the analogy holds together in some respects, but falls down in others. An important similarity between money and knowledge is that, just as cash in society, knowledge needs to flow in order to keep things going. A modern economy is unthinkable without money flowing; when in meetings the flow of knowledge peters out, the life of the meeting drains away. (We shall return to the design implications of knowledge and content flow in chapter 2.2.) Money and knowledge are also similar in that people often have an urge to want more of it; they are avid, insatiable – the more, the better, it seems. And finally, knowledge seems to breed more knowledge – the counterpart of ignorance breeding ignorance. However, there is also a fundamental difference between money and knowledge: If you have knowledge and you give it to someone, your stock of knowledge doesn't decrease. Actually, when donated the right way, it increases. And so, while money obeys the laws of mathematics, knowledge defies them.

In this chapter we discuss the practical consequences for Meeting Design of this last peculiarity of knowledge, as well as another matter of interest suggested by the money metaphor, namely, where is knowledge located? Who has or owns it? In our work as Meeting Designers we have developed a clear view on this and the title of this chapter already partly reveals our answer. It was experiences like the following that led to our convictions:

Just Guessing

Fifteen police experts attended a briefing about an upcoming internal event, called 'Police 2.0.' The brief immediately sparked off some intriguing questions. For example: "Should police patrol in Second Life or on Facebook?", or: "What are the legal implications if under-cover agents visit chat rooms?"

Not surprisingly, our design incorporated the use of as many modern media as possible, with virtual input as well as normal face-to-face conversations. The marketing of the event was also aligned with the theme: viral marketing. We proposed the organizers to attract participants by sending out just five invitations as a start, by e-mail and with a request for confirmation of receipt. It would go to five potential participants, each of whom would be asked to forward the invitation, by e-mail, to five other potentially interested parties. The idea met with enthusiastic police approval: it was in line with the theme and of course they were curious whether the experiment would work.

During the next briefing, four weeks after having infected the first e-mail address, we asked the fifteen experts to guess how many reactions the first month had generated. At first, the policemen hesitated, arguing that they were not experts in marketing, let alone in viral marketing. Nevertheless, we persuaded them to have a try. Most guesses were way off: someone said 2, someone else 300. "Wrong. Way off, all of you, ha, ha...," bellowed the superintendent who was our main contact. But we produced a calculator to check what the average was. We were flabbergasted to find that the mean of their answers was 187, just 3 e-mails away from the actual number of 190 reactions. Their 'mistake' was a mere 1.57%, an extremely accurate guess!

Can You Believe It? Part 1

We defy any expert on viral marketing to come up with an equally precise guess. He or she would have been able to make numerous sensible comments about how viral marketing works and how it has changed the marketing landscape – specialist know-how the group obviously did not have. But predicting the actual number of mails received would have been almost impossible, even for the Philip Kotler of viral marketing. The 15 men and women around the table did a truly remarkable job in coming up with an answer that fell within a very narrow statistical range of error. Of course, that result did not imply that they were now viral marketing experts. The knowledge available for sharing by subject matter experts remains extremely valuable. But the example shows that, in addition to the unilateral transfer of knowledge, at a different level something else may be going on.

All together the group of police officers evidently possessed very precise knowledge about a problem they had never even thought about before. This knowledge was hidden in the group; each on their own had not come even close to the truth, but as a group they missed the target by just a hair's breadth. The essential point is that they were able to produce that precise answer only as a result of their being a group. It is as if the knowledge was *ganglionised*[1] among the 15 people. And to their huge surprise, it emerged by asking them the right question. Jenkins[2] calls this knowledge Collective Intelligence; James Surowiecki uses the term The Wisdom of Crowds.[3] Both authors write about the knowledge groups are capable of 'floating' and how together they can solve problems which no individual would ever be able to. The many examples they give convince readers (us, for instance) that something like collective intelligence not only exists, but that it represents a huge potential for humanity, a potential which so far we have tapped only to a very limited extent.

Can You Believe It? Part 2

Maybe the mathematics of the police experts' session does not surprise you. You see it as a simple matter of statistics, outliers being levelled by other outliers, and common sense materialising somewhere in the middle. Although the police themselves were very surprised, to some extent you are right. Many groups of people, with an average level of common sense, are capable of coming close to the truth in cases such as the viral marketing one. We all know examples of the practical application of this mechanism. Juries in US courtrooms, for instance. They produce a decision about legal issues and these decisions are widely accepted in society as a fair method to establish the truth beyond reasonable doubt. Referenda[4] are examples of this in democratic decision-making.

In the example of the police, we asked them to produce a number. In communication theory, this is called a half-open question: one with a limited number of possible answers. What if you ask a group a fully open question, not a closed or a half-open one? What if the answers cannot be processed in numbers and averages? Will that also enable a group to produce knowledge that the individual group members do not possess? What kind of process does it generate?

Multiplying the Sales Department

A technical company in trouble asked us to design a series of meetings with their complete workforce about cross-selling. Cross-selling was a problem. Despite the fact that the firm had many specialists in different technical fields working for clients – from air conditioning to solar energy, from low

---

[1] We coin this new term here, in analogy with the function of ganglia in the brain. A ganglion is a coordinated group of brain cells that gather and process incoming stimuli, producing outgoing stimuli that have an impact elsewhere in the body.

[2] Henry Jenkins, Convergence *Culture   Where Old and New Media Collide,* New York University Press, New York, 2008 (Paperback Edition).

[3] James M. Surowiecki, *The Wisdom of Crowds – Why the many are smarter than the few and how collective wisdom shapes business, economies, societies and nations,* Anchor Books, New York, 2004

[4] Parliamentary democracy could be an example on a large scale, but in fact is not. In terms of tapping into collective knowledge, voting for a political candidate is not a very productive idea. The reason for this is that the question asked does not have a clear relationship with the outcome of the process (continue reading to find out why that is important).

collective knowledge. People tend to stay in their comfort zones and may be reluctant to face up to a question they did not expect to be asked.

In the example we made the question very concrete. We said to participants that a commercial opportunity meant work that a person present in the room could start doing. Everyone understood that.

3) Supply Motivation

Support the programme's dynamics with clear motivation that resonates with all of the participants. If something important is at stake, people dig deeper, it makes them more willing to think the extra mile. The facilitator can make this happen, without resorting to manipulation. Incidentally, if the group senses even the smallest whiff of manipulation, all credibility is lost in one fell swoop.

In the example we pointed at individual workers and said: "This group is finding work for him, her, and him, so that we can prevent him, her and him from being out of work in a year from now." The participants found that really cool. Of course they wanted to secure a future for the guy or the girl sitting next to them!

The Expert

Nothing said so far means expert knowledge is no longer wanted. A meeting programme should be like a highway along which knowledge moves – expert knowledge, as well as ganglionised, collective knowledge. In effective programmes the two types of knowledge interact and mutually stimulate each other. This requires a careful deployment of the expert. You do not want the expert to shell participants with knowledge projectiles fired at random; you want him to be a sharpshooter, firing at precision targets. You want him to generate the right mix between baffling participants and catalysing their own thoughts. This is tricky and not all experts strike that balance. The best chance of hitting the target is when you create a situation where the expert finds himself in exactly the same position, namely give him an intellectual challenge.

Aristotle When You Least Expect Him

The setting was a meeting of teachers engaged in sharing their know-how about vocational training and education. The professor in didactics was asked to deliver a keynote speech straight after the lunch break. His topic: the difficult behaviour of modern students. You know what we mean. There was no alternative to slotting in the professor; he had to be programmed just before the participants would break up into group sessions. His speech should feed into workshops that same afternoon, but if he gave the usual 45-minute presentation the results would be devastating. The post-prandial dip would feel like a bathe in the Dead Sea.

During the briefing with him, we explained the foreseeable dynamics of the situation and asked him to do the unthinkable. "Could you fit all of your 30 years' experience in pedagogy into a speech of exactly 9 minutes?" For a moment he looked at us as if we were a pair of brainless aliens, then he ignored us for a moment, thought things over and evidently changed gear somewhere in his mind. Finally his face broke into a broad smile. All of this took him about ten seconds. Then he said: "I'd love to".

On the day itself, he started his talk by announcing his brief, produced an egg-timer, set it to go off after exactly 9 minutes and placed it on the lectern in front of him. The audience was now breathlessly agog as he embarked on his seemingly impossible task. In just over eight minutes he managed to deliver a clear story about modern students, their motivations and the way they use modern media. He spent his last 30 seconds reading a piece of text in which someone complained about young students' unruly behaviour. It went something like this: "They eat in an unfashionable way, have no time for studying, behave rudely towards grown-ups and their minds are totally preoccupied with buying things they don't need, thinking about the opposite sex and drinking…" The audience nodded: Yes, that was exactly the student behaviour they knew all too well! Then, seconds before the timer rang, he said: "This text was written by Aristotle, around 340 BC. Thank you." He left the audience in a state that couldn't be more ready for the discussions…

Horizon

The notion that in meetings knowledge is everywhere creates a great many new opportunities. The vast majority of meetings held in ordinary locations are sender-centred. From exhibitions to symposia and from conferences to political gatherings, most meetings have programmes in which speakers speak and audiences shut up and listen.

But just imagine if every big company decided instead to organise sessions in which they tapped into the minds of their workers, drawing on their collective intelligence to identify commercial opportunities. Or if local governments started to tap the wisdom of their citizens to help identify the right measures to solve local problems. To be effective, meetings with these constituents would need to be designed in such a way that their contributions were evoked in an inspiring environment and taken seriously. Not the kind of fluffy citizen participation initiatives we sometimes see taking place in bog-standard local community centres. We envisage quite new dynamics taking with the real content. It took a bit of time at the beginning, but saved us a lot of crap later!

M/E: You are a meeting designer!

A: You must be kidding, is it that simple?

M/E: Well, sometimes it is, yes.

A: Well, that may be, but you're not going to flatter yourselves out of this discussion! Let's go back to my initial point, a normal audience can't know anything useful about science. The Wisdom of Crowds is nonsense!

M/E: Just a second. Did we say that every crowd knows everything about everything?

A: I guess not, because that would be a stupid thing to say. Your ideas may be shaky but I grant you that you're not totally daft.

M/E: Have you ever had the experience that one of your fellow scientists made a useful comment in a discussion about a topic that was not his or her specialty? Something about which he didn't know all the facts.

A: Sure, that happens all the time. Hmm, I can see where you're heading. A conference programme with outsiders who can give feedback becomes more intelligent. It's like turning things around: someone asking a dumb question makes you see something that was below the waterline.

M/E: Isn't it useful from time to time to have an instant peer review during a discussion? Where peers from other disciplines can have their say about an experiment or about research findings? In the process, the group uncovers new insights, maybe even new facts? Serendipity leading the way, although that's a paradox, as well.

A: You mean, finding things you are not looking for, like the three princes from Serendip in the Persian tale? Interesting thought!

M/E: Right. Fleming's discovery of penicillin, just by coincidence, because his laboratory was a mess.

A: Yeah, or like the story of the laboratory assistant who injected viruses into chickens two weeks too late, lazy bum! In the two weeks he had been on holiday the viruses had lost too much of their power to make the chickens sick. But they still sparked off a useful reaction in the avian body. Hence: vaccines!

M/E: That's what we mean!

A: Those discoveries happened in far-away, silent laboratories, though. Don't you think it's a bit utopic to expect a scientific breakthrough to take place in a meeting?

M/E: An experiment is an experiment and a meeting is a meeting. Meetings are always about things that take place elsewhere. You can read about that in chapter 1.2. That doesn't mean that meetings can't be decisive in the evaluation of an experiment. Or lead on to the next useful step.

A: Years ago I was at a conference and one of the sessions was with people who were trying to find water on the moon. Don't look at me like that – this is what astronomy is about! We floated some ideas about methods to investigate the rocks on the surface of the moon. Then someone, an assistant of one of my colleagues, came up with the idea to crash a small rocket into the moon, at the highest possible speed. We actually did that, you know, it was a brilliant plan. Hilarious, of course! This student used to play tennis on gravel courts and he remembered how the gravel dust seemed to explode when a ball hits the court on a hot day.

M/E: You fired the rocket-science equivalent of a tennis ball at the moon?

A: Yes, we did! And we had another rocket fly through the dust to analyse it. That's how we discovered water!

M/E: Did he come up with a fact or an opinion? You said this earlier on. Science is about facts, not about opinions.

A: Who cares, you idiots, it worked! I suppose this student didn't know a lot about the composition of moon dust. Period.

The Laws of the Medium

 eetings are a unique medium for communication; we have called it live communication. The various communication media all 'work' in different ways. By 'work' we mean how a certain medium accomplishes what the people who use it want to achieve, in other words, how the medium carries and transfers messages.

If you want to use a medium successfully, you need to know the specific laws or rules that govern the communicative power of that medium and employ them effectively. These rules result from a mixture of the characteristics of the medium itself and conventions around its use that have developed over time. Paintings are an example of a medium which is totally different from meetings and which have their own communicative potential. Communicating effectively with a painting depends, for instance, on the laws of composition. The laws of composition are partly inherent in the medium itself. For instance, paintings are flat – at least, they are most of the time and before the '60s, they always were. That is why paintings are different from sculptures, which have three dimensions. Composing a flat image is inherent in paintings as a medium. Furthermore, the laws of composition have undergone a long process of development: until the late Middle Ages, little was known about the use of perspective to give depth to images on a flat surface. To us now medieval paintings tend to look somewhat simple and childish. Only later would painters learn how to create three dimensions from two.

To a large extent, this book is an exploration of the characteristic ways in which meetings achieve their communicative potential. We identify aspects of meetings that make them unique as a means of communication compared to other media. Naturally, for Meeting Designers, the next step is to capitalise on those aspects, in order to make any meeting as attractive and effective as possible.

This chapter homes in on another fundamental aspect of meetings, the sixth one so far: their *timeline*. One of the rules of communication for meetings is that they have an unavoidable order and sequence. Meeting organizers should pay attention to a meeting's timeline if they want the best results. Here is a story of a man who did just that.

When, oh When?

Carl is the CEO of a firm with 850 employees and he always has 25 minutes of airtime during the annual corporate convention. This year, he wants to pay a tribute to the people responsible for the huge success of a recently launched product, which we will call product S. Carl hesitates: Which is the better moment to celebrate product S? At the beginning or at the end of the meeting? Intuitively, he knows there is a difference and he wants to get it right. Talking to his communication advisors, two arguments present themselves. The motive for delivering the message at the start is that the good news will get the meeting off to a stimulating start. It gives participants time to talk about S. and celebrate its success together as a corporate milestone. However, the arguments for the other option sound just as reasonable. The audience is more likely to remember this piece of information if they receive it at the end and the impact will last longer.

Isn't Carl overdoing things? Why does he bother, worrying about the difference? Information is information; just give it to the people! They are old and wise enough to decide what they want do with it. But Carl is convinced that, potentially at least, there is a big difference in impact that depends on his choice of the right moment. And impact is what he is after! He understands that meetings are always about things that take place somewhere else (see Chapter 1.2) and that is highly relevant in this situation. As the company leader, he has to make sure that his people do their jobs in the best possible way – not during the meeting, but after it! That is why he picks the brain of his communication advisors, to maximise the motivational effect of his message.

After listening carefully to his consultants, Carl decides to divide his tribute to product S. into two sections. At the beginning he announces that S. is doing much better than forecast, and he congratulates the team on their hard and fantastic work. Then he promises to reveal the exact figures at the end of the meeting, along with a special word for the person who played a decisive role in product S.'s success. People are excited about the good news and throughout the programme, the S. team are the heroes of the day. It lifts the spirits of the whole meeting. Then, at the end, Carl takes the stage again and says: "When we started, I promised I would come back to you about product S. I wanted to give you some numbers and call on the person who gave product S. its biggest boost. Well, the most important number in this story is the number ONE. That is the number of products the person I would like to introduce to you bought from us. Why is this gentleman so important if he bought only one item of S.? Well, he was the very FIRST person to buy it... Ladies and gentlemen: please meet this 32-year old inhabitant of Burgham, Mr Frank du Bon."

It was a stroke of genius for Carl to see how he could play with the meeting's sequence and order and generate the best possible result. In doing so, he made a decision about the timeline.

Meetings, Books and Newspapers

As the example shows, it matters a lot when exactly you deliver a message. We have already made the point that each communication medium has its own set of rules to follow. So now let us explore the rules for timing optimum delivery of messages at meetings and what that implies for the meaning they acquire in the eyes of meeting participants. To get a feeling for this, we will start by exploring some other media and make a comparison.

Have you ever been to a meeting that starts with a lengthy introduction about other conferences, ones that the same organiser has worked on before? Not very likely. However, many books do begin that way: a couple of pages mentioning previous books by the same author, along with short quotes, full of complimentary snippets from reviews. We find this perfectly normal, but giving similar information at the beginning of a meeting sounds rather strange, doesn't it? It would also be strange to have these pages somewhere in the middle of the book. Books have their own specific conventions on what messages to deliver and when to deliver them. We are accustomed to their structure. The first thing you see is the title page. When you open it, you get the endorsements and reviews, followed by a blank page where you will read something like 'for Amy'. Next is the preface. We are all used to this and we know what to do with the information. You can easily skip the reviews; you know they are heavily biased. Also, we do not have to find out who exactly Amy was. The preface may be important, but if it is a very personal preface, we may omit it, as well, unless we are one of the people the author wants to acknowledge. We know that it is essential to read the first sentence of a novel very carefully as it often contains a lot of information about the setting of the story, the storyteller and the basic theme or conflict. The rules governing the order and sequence in newspapers differ greatly from those for books. Suppose our eyes fasten on an article about a missing dog. It is on page 17, in small font. We immediately know that this dog is not particularly relevant. But if that same information is given as the opening message of the evening edition with a headline in large print, that dog must belong to someone special. The place on the imaginary newspaper timeline gives us that information, with the help of the fonts used. It is the first thing you read.

Have you ever been to a meeting where every new topic was introduced by a sentence like "Rooney did it again" or "Argentina cries for more"? The various sessions of a meeting have titles too, but here the objective is generally not to attract your attention by being smart. Newspaper headlines, on the other hand, have become an art form, especially in Britain. Their very purpose is to draw the readers' attention to the article underneath, knowing that they have the choice to ignore pieces that do not interest them. A newspaper editor wages a battle for the reader's attention. Successful headlines define the timeline and the order in which readers will consume the articles.

In meetings such a battle is impossible. The participants are there and undergo the programme in the order established by the organiser, whether they like it or not. You cannot skip the opening page of a conference, as with a newspaper. People may ignore some of the information they receive before the meeting, but as soon as they are invited to enter the meeting room, the time plan of the meeting unfolds inexorably.

Defining Time Experience during Meetings

Let us now zero in on the rules that govern the communicative potential of meetings with respect to time. Leaving aside virtual meetings (see our Epilogue for some thoughts on these), the physical presence of participants in the same place imposes the following combination of rules on meeting communication:

    1) a meeting imposes a shared timeline on participants; and

    2) a meeting offers participants shared experiences.

We have already pointed out a number of consequences of participants' physical presence in Chapter 1.1. Here, we want to underline the fact that participants share their experiences in the same time frame. Next we will discuss the design implications of this particular meeting characteristic.

1) A Shared Timeline

When we design meeting programmes, we have the advantage that we can make decisions about the timing of events the participants will all experience. We can also design the relationships between those experiences and other parts of the programme. A writer cannot do this. He writes for his reader, but he never knows if his reader goes off for a three-week's holiday to his mother-in-law in Cleveland between chapters five and six. Or has a peek at the last page before leaving.

The Meeting Designer has a number of certainties in this respect. He can be relatively sure that participants will arrive within a time slot of roughly 20 minutes, depending on the country where the meeting is held. Once they are there, willy-nilly, they will follow the programme through step by step to its end. Their sole escape route is to leave the meeting, and we have seen in Chapter 1.3 that the threshold between the conference room and the outside

are sometimes hard to grasp, but often understanding them is a matter of common sense. Certain messages *will* create a certain mood and once the mood is there, it is difficult to get rid of. It is a bit like coming over to a friend's place for the first time and tripping over the doormat. The embarrassment will stay with you the rest of the visit. Like a train approaching a railroad switch. If it is diverted in the wrong direction, it may take ages before it is able to get back on the right track again...

In meetings, the opening session determines which shared mental framework is established. Meeting Designers can influence this and make sure the opening session settles participants into the most positive and productive state of mind for the rest of the meeting. Designing it can be real fun.

Opening with a Rock Band

The first programme item during this conference on effective education was a performance by a teenage rock band: four lads with acne, playing far too loud and out of tune. While beaming with enthusiasm, the bass player unwittingly but unmistakably played a different song from their repertoire. The baffled audience couldn't believe their ears. After about one very long minute, a young journalist stepped up onto the stage, motioned the band to stop and started to interview the lead guitarist and singer. His first question was: "Your bass player has a charming smile, but he's a lousy musician. What are you going to do about that?" The audience held their breath, fearing an outburst of Rock and Roll violence aimed at the journalist's nose. But the bandleader laughed a bit sheepishly and admitted they had no plan.

This meeting started with something unusual. People were surprised and curious to understand what a rock band was doing on that stage. They obviously expected the opening to have something to do with the content of the meeting – everything on the meeting timeline must have a meaning. But why a rock band? Initially, the connection was off the chart, yet people wanted to understand! That is why an opening like this tickles people's brains and sharpens their minds. After the first question about the bass player, they quickly got it and the opening fell into place with the conference content and programme. After a few moments of uncertainty, the interview seduced them into the mental framework where they focused on education as a way to improve people's personal performance. It is precisely this sequence – a moment of confusion, subsequent frantic brain activity looking for a connection, and then the relief of recognition – that creates the desired state of mind. During the rest of the conference this 'theme' of improving personal performance came back almost effortlessly. Long talks about bureaucracy in education or school subsidies were not to be heard, much to the organisers' satisfaction.

We call this design approach to an opening *The Push*. It gently pushes participants into the mental framework the organizers are looking for in order to make the meeting fruitful. And with a fine bonus, too: the excitement of the experience gives the meeting instant energy.

Transition from Opening to Middle

The opening finishes when the participants understand the kind of meeting they are in, how they are supposed to behave and how topics are going to be handled. After that we progress to the middle part of the meeting. Normally there is some sort of ritual to underline the transition from opening to middle. This could be the chair saying: "So, now let us get down to business." Or after the plenary introduction at a conference: "Ladies and gentlemen, please now proceed to the break-out rooms, the programme there will start in a few minutes." The transition is most easily recognised if it involves a physical change: in seating, in lighting, and so on.

The Middle and Its Meaning

The middle is the part where 'it' has to happen. Helped by the shared state of mind, participants start to actively explore the content and process it. It is the part where the content starts to 'move', as we will explain from a different angle in Chapter 2.2. Participants dive into things, investigate the content, struggle with it (and maybe with each other). This can be done in many ways, depending on the organiser's objectives: the subject matter can be broken down into small chunks; someone can shed a new light on it; it can be analysed from a broader or narrower perspective; etc.

Compared with the opening, participants process the information they receive much more slowly and thoughtfully. In the opening, they instantly swallow down what is put in front of them; in the middle section they chew it properly for digestion. The Meeting Designer needs to understand the dynamics of this middle part and give shape to it. So let us go into those dynamics.

Two Opposing Forces

When participants get their teeth into the content, two things happen. On the one hand, collaborative work leads to an increase in chaos: some extra chaos in participants' minds and possibly a bit of chaos in their physical mobility, too. It is as if there is an increase in entropy of the subject matter. The processing of the content *should* lead to some added disorder, because if nothing moves, there will not be any noticeable change at the end of the meeting. Meeting organizers want their content to change, to develop. Well, the more people actively participate in exchanges about the content, the more potentially productive chaos there will be and the better the programme of the meeting needs to be designed in order to get the content moving in the right direction.

This diverging force is the unavoidable consequence of the interaction between the people at the meeting. People bring up new viewpoints and arguments about the content; they engage in exciting conversations; they forget about time; and sometimes physical or emotional reactions set in, such as likes and dislikes. If there is a controversy, for instance, adrenalin surges. All of a sudden, the usually meek and thoughtful professor may turn into a dogged street fighter if he feels an opponent in a debate defends utterly wrong opinions. So, on the one hand, the middle brings chaos as a result of interaction related to content.

At the same time, however, there is a second force working against chaos. It is the converging, structuring power of the timeline. Consciously and unconsciously, we attribute meaning to things that happen in connection with their length, beat and rhythm. For instance, if a boy on a bus stares at a pretty girl for a second or two, that is a compliment. But if he does so uninterruptedly for 3 minutes, he scares the living daylight out of her. The duration and sequence of activities in the meeting, yes, the very fact that people know how long a session or the entire meeting is going to last, reduces chaos.

The balance between these forces has an enormous impact on how participants feel and on the outcomes of the meeting. In order to understand this, it is necessary to discuss each of them in somewhat greater detail.

Interaction

As we already saw, the middle part is where participants process the content. To describe what happens at this stage, we introduce the term 'Mental Chemistry'. The content, the ideas in participants' heads, begin to move around, like atoms in a gas. As the temperature rises, these movements increase in intensity. At some point the atoms reach a state where they can react with other atoms, forming new molecules: new insights, new beliefs, new theories. In the middle part, participants are involved in discussions, they do workshop assignments, and contribute to brainstorms. As a result, they not only generate new thoughts about the content, but they also start to develop wishes about their own next steps. The resulting changes in behaviour after the meeting (in line with Chapter 1.2) are the outcomes everybody is hoping for.

The middle part is also the part of the meeting that is 'owned' by the participants, as the following example shows:

During a meeting about international business cooperation, a participant thought it would be a good idea to shoot some video footage and take it home, probably to show to his boss or colleagues. He sat down on a chair in the middle of the meeting room and filmed for about an hour, not at all troubled by the impact his filming had on the other participants and their discussions, exchanges and exercises. Some of them became a bit annoyed with him, but he wasn't doing anybody any harm. Why bother?

This behaviour may be slightly odd, but only slightly. The important point for us is that this gentleman would never have dared to start taping the proceedings this way during the opening or at the end. The middle part, however, belongs to the participants and he was one of them. As owners of the meeting process, participants may start to interfere with it.

The middle is also the time when participants are at the biggest distance from the outside world. Wedged in between the opening and the end (which may be days apart), the meeting programme can put the outside world at any convenient distance. If the programme design makes the distance too big and in due course does not bring participants back to the outside reality, they experience the meeting as woolly and useless. If the programme is too close to reality, it is predictable and produces few new ideas. Whereas, if the design strikes the right balance, participants are totally immersed in the content, guided to a space where the mental chemistry can work without interference and produce extraordinary results.

The Importance of the Timeline

Time is a vital parameter in live communication. It provides structure and gives meaning to experiences. While we are having lunch at a conference, our biological clock is ticking. Suppose this particular lunch takes a bit too long. At some point we will experience a kind of sinking feeling, asking ourselves: "Is something wrong here? Maybe somebody is missing... Or is this an extra pause because the AV for the afternoon plenary does not work properly?" Time defines meaning. Something related to time happens and we look for the meaning.

The sequence of events on the timeline gives a meeting a certain beat or rhythm. No words exist to describe this phenomenon during meetings; we have to borrow them from music. Nevertheless, we immediately recognise their impact on meeting dynamics, both in the spacing of moments in the programme overall, as in the timing of speakers.

which management styles influence the potential for innovation and how to deal with that. The participants had just had the very experience!

The example shows that the crumple zone is able to absorb this kind of incident. Had this episode taken place at the beginning or at the end, it would have been a disaster. Now the chair had the opportunity to straighten things (and himself) out. Even with this somewhat embarrassing exchange between chair and participant, ultimately no harm was done, and the discussion flourished. The crumple zone even offers design opportunities. An incident can be designed into the programme in order to stimulate a healthy debate. A fine example of this are the situations Augusto Boal created in Argentina and which we briefly described in Chapter 1.2.

In the middle, meeting participants are open to detours, unexpected barriers and 'mental snacks'. They accept that as long as it remains clear that it all has a bearing on the meeting objective. This is different in the opening and the end, where the impact of things going wrong is instant and lethal. Speaking about the end...

And in the End

The end is the most vulnerable part of the meeting. Here, the meeting's natural timeline comes to a close, and so messages become irreversible. There is simply no time left to redefine, to correct or to make amends. After the end, there is nothing. Of course, there are endless possibilities for on-line evaluation, digital reports, sending video footage to participants, etc., but whatever effort you make afterwards, the meeting itself is finished. The book is closed.

In our experience, the impressions, the knowledge and the lessons people incorporate at the meeting itself are always infinitely more powerful than anything that is launched at them afterwards. As argued in Chapter 1.1, meetings are inevitably an experience, a physical experience, and so in the meeting participants are subject to the power of experiential learning – a much more potent learning mode than intellectual learning, as any trainer will tell you. The end is the last experience and therefore it will be prominent – dominant even – in the short-term memory. When you ask participants: "How was the meeting?" they tend to refer to the end first, so it had better be good.

There is a funny thing about endings: They are able to colour earlier memories. It is as if they can prime backwards! That may sound complicated but actually the explanation for it is rather simple. Think of this: if the sun was out on the last two days of your holiday, it makes the first ten days of rain seem less wet. Two gorgeous days of sunshine are capable of changing the memory of the first ten miserable days. This is one good reason for preparing the end of a meeting at least as thoroughly as the opening. But there is more to think about...

Harvest Time Lost

Time-wise, the end is closest to the outside world. Towards the final stages, it will gradually start to loom larger and larger over the perception and behaviour of participants and it does so in different ways. On the one hand, people expect the end to generate fuel for action elsewhere. It is the meeting's harvest time; it is when conclusions and summaries re-establish the connection with the real world and tell participants what impact the meeting should have on that world. On the other hand, though, it is also a time when the craving for nicotine or caffeine kicks in, when people's mobile phone starts to burn in their pockets, when they worry about traffic jams, flight schedules or shopping lists. The end is when the voice of day-to-day nitty-gritty starts whispering louder and louder until it becomes a shout. Chairpersons often contribute unwittingly by hurrying through the last bits of the programme, often under the handicap of poor timekeeping. As a result, the meeting loses its momentum. The experience that could leave the deepest imprint gets swept under the carpet by mundane practicalities. What a waste!

What can we do about this? If the end is such a vital moment in the perceived order and sequence, how can we design it so that the hustle and bustle of ordinary life does not spoil it?

Stories Always End

In Chapter 1.2, we introduced the notion of meetings as a stage. Basic mechanisms from theatre and storytelling can help us to improve the power of the programme's finale and increase its resistance against encroachments from outside.

The end of a play or a story needs a final scene that connects the storylines. In an Agatha Christy whodunit, all the main characters get together and the tension of the plot mounts into a final confrontation where the audience's expectations are satisfied as the villain is finally exposed. At the same time, most characters reveal their ultimate and true selves: The evil killer starts crying and becomes the kid who was once so neglected, which explains everything! For the first time the grumpy old uncle proves to have a heart after all, while the timid girl from next door finally proclaims her passionate love for large dangerous dogs...

Apart from the end of the story, there is another thing the audience expects:

the main character must perform the final act or say the final words. He is the bringer of the final message. It looks so obvious: the playwright has to finish what he started, and the main character closes the door. Dead simple. What happens if we apply these two basics laws of a proper ending for a play or a story to the final stage of a meeting?

In meetings, too, things that were started must be finished and all the story lines need to be combined and transformed in a final meaning. The chair – or whoever is in charge of the final moments – has to combine the various 'plots' AND confront them with each other. We often see chairs just summarizing the events of the day, instead of facilitating the clash between storylines that took place during the day. Wrong! Any meeting that is worthwhile presents tensions in content, tensions that represent something dramatic for the participants. The end must be the culmination of that drama. Trivial though it may seem to outsiders, it never is for participants.

Furthermore, the main character has to 'consume' the outcomes of the meeting and show which changes they produce in the real world. This means that everyone needs to know who the main character is, and what he or she is supposed to summarise and subsume. Generally speaking, the main character is not the Chair. Many meeting programmes are unclear about the final player in the meeting's drama! Who owns the meeting's conclusions and outcomes, and who is responsible for the next episode? Who is the 'consumer' of the outcomes? That person needs to have a clearly designed role at the end of the meeting.

In our experience, these relatively simple rules from theatre and storytelling work. The natural timeline of a meeting corresponds to that of the plot of a story. The expectation of participants is for the end to tie the storylines of the plot together into a neat knot. When designed with this in mind, the end has a strength that will easily withstand invasions from the world outside.

The story of this working conference was a sticky one: safety on the oilrigs of a multinational company. Early in the morning, the day had started with the moderator interviewing a worker who had miraculously survived when a 4 ton deadweight had crushed his leg, missing his head by a couple of inches. Participants were moved by his story which combined stupidity and sheer luck.

At the end of the programme, late in the afternoon, the three rapporteurs reported back on the workshops that had addressed safety and subcontracting, attitudes and guilt, responsibilities and money. The company's CEO listened very carefully; the moderator double-checked the rapporteurs' messages with the people from that workshop. Did the debrief truly capture the essential points of the workshop discussion? Then, when all issues were out in the open, the CEO took a deep breath and, to the best of his ability, explained his vision on how to move forward. A real vision that allowed everybody to get a taste of his deepest concerns. The audience was transfixed. Nobody fidgeted, nobody was secretly texting, nobody was thinking of a smoke. When the moderator closed the meeting and invited participants for a drink, the applause was remarkably warm and satisfied.

Meeting Scripts

The simple model of meetings with a beginning, a middle and an end allows us to describe meetings in the form of a script. The script pins down the meaning of everything that happens on the timeline of the meeting. Implicitly, participants of meetings are accustomed to being presented with scripts. And so they anticipate. They know in advance that the opening aims at getting the setting right, that the middle is the part where one can swim around, and that the end generates the fuel for action in the real world outside the meeting. Understanding these dynamics is not rocket science, yet it is astonishing how often people forget their natural feeling for order and sequence when preparing meetings.

The accountancy firm's communication people were close to panic. They were setting up a meeting for all 900 employees to introduce a new style of working. They had hired a basketball stadium, where they would start with break-outs early in the afternoon, then enjoy a shared meal and finally have everybody support the local favourites in a major league match. They had organised excellent catering and the game promised to be spectacular. A high-energy end!
Then the CEO announced that he wanted to deliver a motivational speech, underpinning and explaining the organisational change with facts and figures to create buy-in. He needed about 40 minutes. As his stage, he suggested the basketball pitch, and as the moment: right before the match. He wasn't an awfully good presenter and his audience counted some 800 accountants and clerical staff...
The conference team almost wept when they told us this. "Please, his message will be completely lost, he is setting himself up for disaster." The next day, the first thing on our agenda was an empathic yet stiff talk with the CEO, in the intimacy of his office.

Finally Finale

Order and sequence are an undeniable and unique characteristic of communication during meetings. They produce expectations in participants and the participants will attribute meaning to what happens during the meeting in relation to the meeting timeline.

Naturally we are not the first to recognise the importance of timelines and the related meaning of events. Much research in cognitive psychology provides evidence of this phenomenon. Nobel laureate Daniel Kahnemann writes: "Sequence matters, however, because the halo effect increases the weight of first impressions, sometimes to the point that subsequent information is mostly wasted."[2]

Designing effective meetings with this characteristic in mind means the following: The start conveys many overt and covert messages. What happens in the first ten minutes establishes perceptions in the minds of participants and expectations of what they are all going to have to do and in what manner they will be treated. In the middle part it is essential to strike the right balance between participant interaction and the structuring power of the timeline. And the end should provide for proper harvesting by the main character of the 'story.' We will cover the design implications of creating the right closing more specifically in Chapter 3.7, Finale.

The meeting designer can play with these elements because there are a lot of buttons he can push in order to guide participant behaviour in the desired direction. A proper understanding of the impact of order and sequence is necessary to make the right choices.

Sceptic

We speak to a professional friend, Bibi, a 45-year old meeting professional who runs the marketing department for a large conference centre in the UK.

B: I like this idea of meetings having an inevitable timeline.

M/E: You think it makes sense?

B: Oh yes. I actually recognise it in the different ways participants move around in our venue, depending on where they are in their programme.

M/E: That is fascinating; what do you see?

B: Well, an easy one is that you see most of them hurrying away at the end. There's a huge difference in how they talk to our cloakroom staff in the morning or in the afternoon.

M/E: And during the other stages?

---

[2] Daniel Kahnemann, *Thinking, Fast and Slow*, Penguin Books, London, 2011. The halo effect is described by Kahnemann as: "The tendency to like (or dislike) everything about a person – including things you have not observed – is known as the halo effect." He gives several research cases, as well as examples from his personal life to illustrate the phenomenon and its consequences.

B: I see it there, too, but listen, there is something you mentioned that I would like to hear a bit more about.

M/E: At your service!

B: Thank you, boys! It's about your idea of a beginning, a middle and an end. Sounds almost religious, you know, like the Holy Trinity?...

M/E: As we said, deceptively simple.

B: Yes, I suppose so. In fact, don't you think meetings are far more complex than that?

M/E: Certainly, but what exactly bothers you about that?

B: Well, I'm not really bothered, just wondering. You say that the opening creates certain expectations, and that's fine. Then the middle part is for exploration, and again I can go along with that, as well. Theoretically. But then, what if people attend three workshops, a panel debate and two poster sessions all during the same conference? That commonly happens in the programmes we have in our centre. That means people experience seven openings in two days...

M/E: Why do you think this makes the holy trinity lose its value?

B: Don't you think they get too many of what you call plots? How can you take all of them into account at the end, when you get to the final interaction between plots? Tying up the storylines?

M/E: Ok, we get your point.

B: I'm not saying you're wrong, you know, just wondering how you see it.

M/E: The first thing is to completely forget about logistics and the one-dimensional thinking that traditionally goes into organising a meeting.

B: That's not a very nice thing to say; I earn a living doing that...

M/E: And you're awfully good at it!

B: Thank you! But I know you're just saying that to make me feel better! But do go on!

1.7 The Magic of Meetings

Paradigm Shift for a Party

t was at the end of the 90s, when we received a remarkable request from what could be termed a high net worth individual. He asked us to design and supervise the birthday party for his wife Suzanne, an exceptionally sensitive person. Money was of little consequence, as long as we really hit the mark. He wanted to pay a tribute to her – a gesture in return for all the love she gave him. He had already made up his mind about the venue and the guest list: an up-market hotel smack in the middle of Amsterdam, in the company of fifty of their closest friends. There was one little snag, however: his wife absolutely did not want to be in the limelight...

We quickly reached the conclusion that solving this puzzle required a paradigm shift. How can you pay a tribute to somebody without putting that person in the limelight? How can someone be the centre of attention without everybody constantly focusing on them? It is impossible to find a way out of this dilemma, unless you find a different way of thinking about 'attention.' And so, we invented the principle of the 'recognisable contour.' This freshly coined notion works as follows: the obvious way of representing something – anything, an idea, an entity or an object – is by portraying the thing itself. But it is equally possible to represent it with something that has exactly the same profile, taking the form of a description, or a story, or some other kind of material. We all know the cartoon pictures where a garden fence has a hole in the exact shape of Donald Duck. You look at it and know immediately who made it even though the character is not there. The recognizable contour tells you the story. Rather more sinister examples of this principle are the human shapes recovered from the Roman town of Pompeii centuries after the eruption of Mount Vesuvius. They were found as cavities in the petrified volcanic ashes. Filling these cavities with gypsum produced some of the most moving shapes ever recovered from the past: a mother trying to protect her child from asphyxiation by the hot ashes. A curled-up dog. The recognizable contour, three-dimensional in this case, tells the story.

Throughout Suzanne's birthday party, we applied this principle. Her colleagues told stories about working with her, without mentioning her name even a single time. Family members chronicled special events in which she once took part, but she was never the subject of these anecdotes. As a gift, all guests brought a copy of the book that had been most meaningful in their lives. The whole collection was placed in a delicate little book-case that was put in a visible yet inconspicuous corner of the room. And so, in the course of the evening, a wonderful picture emerged of the world surrounding this lady, while nobody actually talked about her. The Master of Ceremonies, too, never mentioned her name even once; we just focused on her environment – the recognisable contour. Suzanne visibly enjoyed herself. The magic culminated when, towards the end, and to everybody's surprise, she suddenly tapped her glass with her finger. Speaking softly, she just thanked her friends for coming, and the delicacy with which she did this went right to their hearts.

This example illustrates two things: the power of magic and the recognisable contour. The Amsterdam meeting was carefully crafted and thoroughly prepared. With painstaking professionalism, we paid attention to all the things we have broached in previous chapters. We designed the physical experience, the cultural solutions, the right sequence in the programme, the elementary signals and the shared knowledge. But that was not the quintessence of this exceptional evening. There was something else. *There was magic.* Something was in the air that night and everybody in the meeting felt it, recognised it and acknowledged it afterwards. Even the waiters and waitresses were aware of it. At the end of the meeting they said that, while moving around the room, they had a sensation as if they were barefoot, and they served the food with exceptional care. But what exactly was the magic? This brings us to the general question of this chapter: What is it that creates the magic in a meeting? We all know it exists and we can all come up with examples of meetings we attended where we felt it. But where did it come from? What produced it?

The Contours of Magic

The magic of meetings is uncanny. It is as elusive as playing the violin, writing a poem, or conceiving a choreography. As soon as a violinist tries to explain what it is that she does with her fingers, the essence of her fine art is lost. The way in which she caresses the chords, her subtle movements with the bow – it is impossible to catch in words what she does when she plays. It cannot be done because words only *represent* reality, they are not the real world.

To capture the exact sequence and relationship between such delicate movements, language is inadequate. Language seems even more defective when trying to capture the actual sounds a virtuoso produces when playing. This inadequacy applies to a whole range of human experiences, such as beauty, spirituality, tenderness, not just to magic. There must be a meaning behind the fact that so many different art forms try to capture the beauty of the world. Beauty, it often seems, can only be caught indirectly, by a word in a poem, by a perfect high E, by a pirouette in a dance. The beauty manifests itself because the moment is embedded in something that surrounds it: the word is surrounded by silence, the note by pauses, the pirouette by empty space.

We feel that the same applies to the magic of meetings. It is impossible to describe it directly and so the only thing we can do is to depict the contours that surround it, while the thing itself will remain invisible, unsaid; an empty space, which nevertheless has a meaning. The key to grasping that meaning is in the outline, the perimeter of the space.

Kabuki Theatre

Japanese actors who practise traditional Kabuki theatre are following a very different career path from their Western peers. In their lifetime, they learn only one role. Thus, a Kabuki actor may work for thirty years on just one type of movement and voice modulation. Audiences, accustomed to seeing the same play over and over again, delight in the ever greater subtlety and delicacy of the actor's performance. The greatest contribution the actor can give to the performance as a whole is to perfect his own part in it, and this captivates the audience. The result is magic, which – and this is perhaps something you would not associate with Japanese crowds – moves the audience to exuberant expressions of enthusiasm: clapping, shouting, catcalls in outbursts of emotion.

In his book Outliers[1], Malcolm Gladwell asks himself the question how people achieve mastery. One of his conclusions is that roughly 10,000 hours of practice is an absolute must. The consummate skill of the Beatles or Mozart did not materialise out of thin air. The Fab Four's initial songs were not that unique at all – actually, they were relatively commonplace. But after moving from Liverpool to Hamburg and doing two (long!) gigs a day for months on end, their innumerable hours of stage experience sharpened their talent and allowed them to produce all those songs that are now etched in our collective memory. Or maybe not so innumerable, according to Gladwell, because he actually calculated them to be in the order of 10,000. As John Lennon says: "I've got blisters on my fingers."

Mozart's first little compositions were rather mediocre. Of course, they already contained the seed of his genius, but his really masterful work arose after he had pored over paper, pen and keys for many, many hours. There is little doubt that Mozart's and The Beatles' music possesses magic. Not to the same extent for each work or each song, but they are undeniably capable of

 [1] M. Gladwell, *Outliers: The Story of Success,* New York, 2008.

touching people's souls and that is magical.

We believe mastery is one of the contours that delineates the magic of meetings. It probably implies that we, as a team of Meeting Designers, technicians, support staff, speakers, and so on, need to spend 10,000 hours practising and gaining experience! Malcolm Gladwell refers to: 10,000 hours of practising, experimenting, making mistakes, producing *nearlings*,[2] and moving on. And of course, sometimes you may be helped by a streak of beginner's luck, such as in our case with the birthday party.

The Helicopter that Never Was

Eight large sailing barges were moored side by side at a pier alongside a vast lake. At about 10 p.m., two hydrofoils materialised out of the darkness and released the guests, who were welcomed by fireworks and then submerged themselves into an 8-pub corporate party – one in each barge. Each pub had something special. In Pub One, actors played out the final scene of 'The Deer Hunter', in which a round of Russian roulette puts an end to the life of one of the main characters. In one of the others, a jazz band played in semi-darkness. And so on. In the course of the evening, the guests rotated, according to a precise script, from one pub to the other.

At one point when designing this programme we had toyed with the idea of chartering a helicopter to fly the owner/CEO to this staff party and lower him on to the deck of one of the barges, dangling from a rope. That brainchild never matured because of the prohibitive cost and so the idea did not make it to the final script. But the story returned in a magical way ...

A year later, we were asked to design a follow-up party and so we had some talks with staff menbers about their expectations and desires this time. We also asked them about their experience during the previous party with the eight barges and what had been their personal highlight. One of the employees startled us by saying that the absolute climax had been the moment when the director had been lowered from that helicopter... We asked him to explain what he remembered and he told us with no lack of detail how he had experienced this awesome moment. We were flabbergasted; he was not lying, he was not out of his mind, he sincerely thought that this event had taken place and yet it had not!

To achieve a magical meeting there needs to be intensive interplay between the participants, the programme and the broader environment. The word interplay can be taken quite literally here because during a good meeting, the programme and the participants play together. Between them (*inter* in

---

[2] A *Nearling* is something new, undertaken with the right intentions but which has not (yet) led to the desired result. It is an immature idea. This neologism has been coined by Igor Byttebier and Ramon Vullings, to describe useful experiences that should not become lost, even though they have not so far really worked out. I. Byttebier, R. Vullings, Creativity Today, Amsterdam, 2009.

Latin) something new may arise that goes beyond either. The contribution of the participants to the story of the meeting, their imaginative power is an integral part of the quality of their experience. A fairy tale story will only become a fairy tale if we allow ourselves to believe the story at least to some extent.

The man who remembered the illusory helicopter is an example of someone who had an overwhelming willingness to contribute something to the story of the meeting. Even after a time lag of almost a year, the echo of his share in the magic of the party produced the memory of the helicopter. Sure, he crossed the line between fiction and reality, but that does not make his willingness less relevant.

We believe that the willingness of meeting participants to actively engage with their imagination during the meeting is one of the contours denoting the magic that may take place during meetings. Perhaps, when designing meetings that matter, the Meeting Designer has to provide participants with the opportunity to stretch the limits of their imagination and to cross the imaginary border between fantasy and reality.

Authenticity

The symposium on education and social challenges started with a short guided tour through the vocational training college hosting the event. When they reached the boardroom, the group of participants stopped briefly. The teacher conducting the tour was at the same time the symposium facilitator. In a few words, she illustrated the school's mission, its medium-term policy and a couple of details of the building's architecture. Then she stopped, looked the participants straight in the eyes and revealed her biggest personal worries about the school's social environment and student behaviour. Her openness hit home with the participants. She did not approach the day's topic with intellectual distance, instead she sincerely offered the attendees a peek at how it connected with her personal life.

In their evaluations, participants rated the outcomes of the symposium as excellent. Many of them stated that during the day there had been a special atmosphere.

The teacher's courage to share her opinions about the school frankly with the participants gave the meeting right from the start an added layer of depth that could not be overlooked. And nobody *wanted* to overlook it. It is our experience that participants are always susceptible to authenticity. It is true that there is a fine line between genuine personal involvement with the subject matter on the one hand, and sentiments bordering on exhibitionism on the other. Interestingly, what we observe is that meeting participants are perfectly capable of judging which is which and of acting accordingly.

In real life, the spokespersons of organisations sometimes try to stifle any expression of sincerely held views. There are many reasons why they want this, mostly political or related to their own personal agendas. But then, meetings where organisational spokespersons have a great say in the programmes will never be magical.

We are convinced that any disclosures by participants that produce genuine emotions in the audience are likely to contribute to the magic of meetings. Perhaps the Meeting Designer's own personal concerns and beliefs, visions and dreams inspired by the meeting content, also have a significant role to play. This professional approach may increase the likelihood of designing a meeting that has magic.

Shared Destiny

The closing party of an international association meeting took place in a mountain lodge. The decor of the room for the gala dinner was entirely white, making the cocktail dresses of the ladies look like fireworks. The party that followed was fine, but nothing really out of the ordinary: good entertainment, good music, good dancing, good food, good everything.

When the last, big groups of guests stepped out of the lodge, they were forced to stop in their tracks: SNOW! Lots of it! With their marvellous dresses and gorgeous but impractical shoes, the female guests were at a serious risk of breaking an arm or a leg. The men's smart shoes were not particularly practical either. It was necessary to form groups, take each other by the arm and escort the ladies up the doorsteps of their hotels.

The next morning people met again at the small railway station in town. The transfer back to the snowless parts of the world required a 2-hour train ride, which everybody had initially been complaining about. As it turned out, it was perhaps the best part of the entire conference, with all participants still enjoying a magical feeling of togetherness.

This conference had been a good one but not extraordinarily successful. Yet it is etched in our memory as a unique and magical experience. Serendipitously, the snow (in itself a magical thing: Santa Claus, White Christmas, gifts, family unity, light reflected in dark days; and then it suddenly turns into sludge) caused participants to share something they would not during a normal conference: they had to look after each other. Their physical wellbeing, their destiny, became a shared responsibility. Being connected together like this is at the very least pleasant and can become a powerful emotion. It can be especially strong at meetings of associations or clubs, which are characterised by common interests, backgrounds and prospects and less by

are not prodded into vigilance, challenged to manifest themselves, to take positions in discussions that matter, even to defend themselves against the wrong ideas. Thrilling meetings cannot be mainstream. We are convinced that a certain degree of risk and danger contributes to the magic of meetings.

Summarising the Contours

The magic of meetings can be seen in the contours of the space created by the mastery of those who develop and carry out the programme in a professional way: the openness of participants to the meeting's different reality and their willingness to co-create, using their imagination; the way real connections develop between humans and content; the shared destiny of participants; the unique encounters participants hope to have; and the hint of danger they perceive.

There may be other contours. These may include the sincere care for the needs of participants, the impact of topical events on participants' states of mind, yes, perhaps even the effect of certain chemicals on their brains may lead to a magical experience. In the years to come, neuroscience will undoubtedly tell us more about this.

For now, we feel we have drawn six important outlines that give shape to the contours of the magic of meetings. We leave it to the reader to decide about the meaning of these contours. Does the magic of meetings really exist?

Sceptic

Our contributor in this chapter is Hermann, a German IT entrepreneur who studied information engineering at the University of Heidelberg.

H: So far I think you were very clear when writing about the vague things that happen in meetings. But now, yes, I'm sorry, you are going over the top. Pity...!

M/E: Over the top? In what way, Hermann?

H: The top of being reasonable. I mean, I agree it is possible to help people make a shift in their thinking. To achieve that, you need to reason well – that is the top of being reasonable. You have gone over that top. Now you want to work with things that are irrational, not reasonable.

M/E: Magic is unreliable, it is beyond control, it slips through your fingers like water, you cannot grasp it. So, then how can you work with it? Is that your objection?

H: I could not have put it better myself. Thanks! We all know magic does not exist, yes? Some things look like magic, such as conjuring. Remember Tommy Cooper? That funny Englishman with the Turkish hat – what was it called... But those are just tricks, yes, creating an illusion – not magic. You cannot work with magic or illusions!

M/E: Do you ever talk with your colleagues about the magic of IT?

H: Oh, I myself don't believe something like that exists; the Internet is a matter of systems engineering! But I know some colleagues look at the Internet as something magical. It connects millions, actually billions of people, allowing them to communicate about, well, practically anything. It creates new friendships and communities, breeds new products and services – do you know that nowadays there are maths students in India or Singapore who use Skype to give private lessons to school kids in the US? Yes, and they get paid through PayPal! Sometimes the Internet even helps to overthrow regimes. I am proud I can contribute to that with my systems.

M/E: So what is it that makes you feel proud, then?

H: Well, it is the feeling of being connected, yes, of helping to connect people in communities all over the world. Small communities of friends with a shared hobby, or big communities who father around specific issues, such as dealing with climate change, or democratic changes in some countries, facilitated by the Internet.

M/E: To be honest, we don't think that connecting people is a conjuring trick.

H: No, it's not, of course it's a special feeling to be able to create something that has never existed before and which could, potentially, involve all humans on earth.

M/E: How would you describe the moment if or when that really happens?

H: Oh, yes, I think that would be a magical moment!

M/E: Come on Hermann, do you hear what you're saying? Until a minute ago your point was that...

H: Yes, ha, ha! And now I seem to have come around completely to the opposite view! Yes, neat.

M/E: Maybe some things you run into, also in your professional life, simply cannot be completely defined.

H: In *my* professional life?

M/E: No, we mean in general. Some things are fascinating or interesting because of the very fact that they cannot be defined exactly. Don't you think it works like that for many people?

H: That is not an easy thing for me to accept. I am an engineer, you know.

M/E: Sure, but could you really describe what the Internet is today? In words, in language?

H: We can describe it technically, but it is not easy to describe the connectedness. We don't understand the complex factors, yes, that steer the development of the Internet worldwide. If I think about this, your idea of the contours comes to mind. The Internet also has those rims, such as connectedness, new ways of marketing, knowledge as we find it in Wikipedia, but also dating, even adult entertainment, as they call it. The Internet seems to have a life of its own, it grows organically, like an ecosystem. Didn't you use that term for meetings, too, somewhere? Perhaps the Internet is a bit like meetings, yes,...

M/E: Is it ok for you if we leave the magic as it is for the time being? We have touched on it and don't you agree now it is up to the reader?

H: Be my guest, but in the meantime I will continue to search, yes, for the mechanisms that drive developments in my field. I want to see if I can find things that are within the contours. You know what? Let's agree that we meet again in a year's time and compare my results with yours, yes?

M/E: Sounds like fun. We'll have a meeting!

H: Biss dann.

Part 2

2.0 The meeting owner

Until now we have described meetings essentially in terms of their inherent characteristics and as a participant experience. We have identified the consequences of participants' national cultures, their physical presence, the meaning they give to events on the meeting's timeline, the knowledge they bring with them or develop, the impact of meeting conventions and the relationship between the meeting and the participants' work outside the meeting.

It is now time to shift our attention to the people who came up with the idea of having the meeting in the first place: the commissioning party, i.e. the clients of the Meeting Designer. As explained in the introduction to this book, the commissioning role is generally performed by a single person. We prefer to call this person the 'meeting owner', a term first used in Maarten Vanneste's manifesto 'Meeting Architecture' of 2008.[1] We define the meeting owner as the person who has the final decision-making power over the meeting objectives, its budget, its content and its programme features.

There is no doubt that a proper understanding of the meeting owner's requirements (explicit and implicit) is essential to a good design and therefore to a successful meeting. The meeting owner's purpose in holding the meeting at all is to add value to something, generally his organisation, a project, a series of activities, a community, a body of ideas – something for which he has a responsibility and for which he needs the people coming together in a meeting. This guiding principle is not without pitfalls, however. The first one is that often it is not very clear how meetings add value to anything. Secondly, the meeting owner is usually an expert on the meeting's topic but not on how meetings work as a means of communication. Surely, the chairperson of the International Association of Metal Cutlery Producers is fully conversant with knives and forks but offering the participants of his annual world-wide conference an enthusing and effective meeting programme requires a different set of professional skills.

Meeting owners have meetings with goals in mind; such goals tend to be a motley mix, ranging from heavily organisational and strategic to purely personal and even narcissistic. It is the job of the Meeting Designer to translate the meeting owner's objectives into meeting programmes that satisfy both him (the owner) and the participants. Meeting owner and participant are like Yin and Yang. They both influence the meeting, like the two parts of a mould in which some plastic component is formed. If one half of the mould is missing, you do not produce half the component; you make something that is deformed and completely useless. That is how meetings

[1] Maarten Vanneste, op. cit.

take shape: by the combined input from meeting owner and participant, each from their own circle of influence. It is, therefore, also the job of the Meeting Designer to find a balance between their interests.

This consideration begs the following question: who does the Meeting Designer actually work for? Does he work for the meeting owner (who pays his invoice), or for the participants (who experience his work)? There may be differences in interest between the two and in such cases, what choices does the Meeting Designer make? Our position is that the Meeting Designer works for or, more precisely, *together with* the meeting owner, on the assumption that the participant (and not the meeting owner) is the most important person present during the meeting. In our dealings with meeting owners, it is sometimes necessary to make this assumption explicit.

And so let us see what happens in the relationship between the Meeting Designer and the meeting owner. The meeting owner mostly represents an organisation. Meeting programmes depend on the identity of that organisation and at the same time, it can shape that identity (in the case of corporate change processes, for instance). Chapter 2.1 provides insights into the meaning of this for meeting programmes. Chapter 2.2 introduces several new instruments related to meeting objectives: how to establish them and how to measure them – essential exercises for anybody who wants to add value by means of the meeting. Finally, Chapter 2.3 takes up the delicate but vital point of how to deal with the meeting's content.

2.1 Meetings Communicate Identity

Recognition

n the process of developing the programme, the meeting owner and the Meeting Designer function as a left and a right leg. Without either, at best your meeting will hop along but it will never dance. Although we have defined the meeting owner as one specific person, behind that person there will be quite a crowd: he represents an organisation. This has important consequences for the way in which the programme needs to be designed. This chapter will explore the relationship between the meeting owner's organisation, its identity, and the design of the programme.

The first major observation is that the meeting owner wants his organisation to be recognisable in the meeting. This is a peculiar meeting objective that is rarely expressed explicitly. It does not simply mean that the meeting owner wants to be *satisfied* with the meeting and its outcomes – that is a given, but there is more to it. Across a wide range of features, the meeting owner wants the meeting's design and programme to reflect what the organisation is; not what it is like – what it is. If this connection is not recognised, you will hear: "Well, that is not the way we do things here," or "That's a bright idea, but it's not really like us." 'To recognise' means that the meeting and its programme need to match the self-image of the meeting owner's organisation, or in other words, they need to mirror and reveal its identity.

To some extent, this need for recognition also applies to the meeting owner himself as a person, to his profession, role and status within the organisation. In practice, we have found that this part of the recognition works largely through 'common' organisational politics. The dynamics of it are played out in the relationships between the Meeting Designer and the various people in the meeting owner's organisation who cross his path. This may include all kinds of members of the organisation who have a stake in the meeting, its participants or its outcomes. However, these political issues are essentially something that emerges in the work process; it has limited impact on the design as such. For this reason, we will not discuss these relationships here because there is enough reading material in studies of decision-making in organisations. Rather, we will focus on the organisation itself for its identity has a strong impact on the design of the programme. So let us see how meetings and identity are related and what a meeting can tell us about the people who commission it.

Who Are These People?

A friend invites you to come along to a party thrown by some people you have never met before. Of course your friend lures you into coming along by giving you some tempting general and personal details about your future hosts. As you approach their house, you start collecting first impressions of them: OK, so this is their neighbourhood, I see. Hm, this is what their house looks like and this is how they keep their garden.

While you enter these friends of your friend's home and mingle with the other guests, your mind fills up with further impressions, ideas and questions. Those party decorations are really original! Where did they get them? Will there be food later tonight? Do I have to pour my own drinks? But then, what are those waiters doing over there? Dozens of questions are buzzing in the recesses of your brain: what are the other guests like? Does the atmosphere feel formal or informal? Are people drinking lots of alcohol or swigging juices made from organic fruits and vegetables? Are we all expected to join in for a sing-along, with the master of the house behind the piano? Do the hosts get thrown into their swimming pool (without calling the police)?

All these questions are variations on one theme: "Who are these people?" And the party answers an awful lot of them.

Naturally, you don't ask these questions out loud and often not even consciously: you just let the experiences sink in. However, the tacit answers to these unspoken questions give you a lot of information about what kind of people the party organisers are. Swiftly and inexorably, you arrive at an idea or judgment. In the end, the degree of affinity you feel with your hosts and the other invitees makes you decide whether you are at ease and have a pleasant evening, or whether after about an hour you whisper huskily to your friend: "Guess this isn't quite my scene. See you soon, okay?"

Invite Me to Your Meeting and I Will Tell You Who You Are

Meetings transmit many overt and covert messages about the meeting owner and his organisation. In the roughly 2,500 meetings we have witnessed ourselves, we have seen this communication mechanism at work implicitly and yet intensely: Meetings are a powerful vehicle for communicating identity. To glimpse just how powerful, picture the following situation: Suppose you have just got off with a stunning new boy/girlfriend. You have told your parents, and now they are pressurising you to bring her/him over for dinner. The question in your mind is when to do this. You are keenly aware that after that dinner, your new heart throb will know a lot more about the family part of your identity and so you seriously ask yourself when to accept your parents' invitation.

As in our party example, participants in professional meetings draw these conclusions in any case; irrespective of what the organiser does, they will form opinions about what kind of corporate person the meeting organiser is – whether he likes it, or not. Naturally, however, it is possible to influence those conclusions and opinions to a considerable extent.

Event Marketing

Event marketing is a technique to strengthen a brand. It is a particular type of brand communication, different from reading about it or watching a TV commercial. Companies invest lots of money to attract people to these events because their marketing impact is so strong: brands seem to come to life during events; their atmosphere is in the very air the crowd breathes. The rationale for these investments rests on several of the basic principles about meetings we illustrated in Part 1 of this book.

Powerful events – with fashionable artists, glamorous presenters, a strong we-feeling, and so on – capitalise on people's physical presence, offering their senses a roller coaster ride. They centre on a stage and their pursuit is to connect the brand with a positive, yes, a magical experience. The intensity of the experience is immeasurably different from, let us say, a web ad – a communication vehicle way over at the opposite side of the emotional spectrum. Events last a lot longer than commercials. The enforced timeline – the way we described it in Chapter 1.6 – makes it almost impossible for participants to cut themselves off from the experience the event opens up for them.

Event Marketing designers are keen on absolutely all aspects of the experience they offer the crowd because messages about the brand are given by *the entire package* of the event. Therefore, everything is carefully designed to convey exactly the right brand 'feel'; the whole package ensures that it fits minutely with the message the brand wants to put across.[1] Marketing events are meetings designed exclusively to communicate identity. Their basic communication objective is simply to shout: "Hey everybody, this is who and what we are!"

Identity Unveiled

A rock star plugging a particular kind of ice cream or beer in front of 50,000 teenagers flashing their mobile phones is an extreme example of establishing brand identity. Nevertheless, with regard to identity perception, in other types of meetings the process is fundamentally the same: while sitting in a meeting room and listening to a speaker, participants cannot ignore how the

---

[1] A typical example are Redbull's air races which project the kind of image of its product Redbull wants drinkers to remember for ever: energising. You will not see anything around these races that is NOT consistent with this identity.

room has been laid out, how the chair feels, what the quality of the AV is, or what sounds their neighbour is making as he slowly nods off. You cannot switch your perceptions off.

All these stimuli reach your senses and are processed by your brain, rating them as 'WOW', as completely futile impressions or as anything in between. Much of this stays in the unconscious, which does not mean these messages do not have an effect on you; it is just that you are not aware of the impact. All these impulses can create an emotional state, lingering in the back of your head only to surface later, generally as a result of some trigger.

As in the friend-of-your-friends' party example, the whole package of messages and emotions transmits the 'brand' of the family. It answers the 'who-are-these-people' question and it does so by means of a curious mixture of conscious and unconscious perceptions. Equally, the package of a professional meeting unveils the identity of the meeting owner's organisation. That identity is embedded in the organisation's culture.

Identity and Culture of Organisations

The identity of an organisation is closely related to its culture. Organizational culture can be defined as "the pattern of basic assumptions that a given group has invented, discovered or developed in learning to cope with its problems of external adaptation or internal integration, and have worked well enough to be considered valid, and, therefore, to be taught to new members as the correct way to perceive, think and feel in relation to those problems."[2] Sounds convincing but a bit complicated. A definition my auntie understands is simply "the way we do things here."[3] Organisational identity, on the other hand, is what people see when they look at the organisation.

Both culture and identity are dynamic: at any given moment they correspond to a certain state which can be described, even though with difficulty. In the meantime, however, they are gradually evolving into something else, just like the identities of individuals. They are and at the same time they are becoming.

Although there are as many different ideas about the relationship between the culture and the identity of organisations as there are authors, we take the view that culture is the more 'fundamental' notion. The difference is that you can see the identity, while you cannot see the culture; culture is implicit. In meetings, we deal with identity which is visible, overt. However, since it is driven by the invisible culture, it is important to have an idea about the culture of an organisation you design a meeting for.

The organisational culture strongly depends on the culture of the nation

[2] Bjerke, B., *Business Leadership and Cultures, National Management Styles in the Global Economy,* Edward Elger Publishing, Cheltenham, 1999.
[3] Deal, T. E. and Kennedy, A. A. (1982) *Corporate Cultures: The Rites and Rituals of Corporate Life,* Harmondsworth, Penguin Books.

where the organisation originates (see Chapter 1.4 for more details on this). But national culture is only one ingredient in a rich stew; other factors include the size and complexity of the organisation, the type of industry it works in, the kind of tasks the people in the organisation perform, the regulatory framework it needs to accommodate, the expectations of shareholders and stakeholders, etc. There are also less predictable factors: the legacy of a visionary founder, for instance, or the characters of the people at the top; overall levels of trust and respect; particular corporate myths and 'trauma' the organisation has at one time or another suffered.

The stories people tell about their organisations are an important indicator of their organisational culture and identity. For example, a fatal accident in the relatively recent past will have an enormous impact on how people deal with safety. Another example is a hospital where we worked at some point. The financial controller had been caught committing fraud and staff were not very happy with the way the board had dealt with the problem. As a result, trust levels between people in the organisation were dismally low.

These stories determine what the members of an organisation as a group think about how things ought to be done. It is vitally important to find out about any such stories that go the rounds in organisations for whom you are designing a meeting. Therefore, we always ask about such corporate stories during intake interviews. We need to know about them in order to understand our customers, their cultures and their identities. Here is an example of how a particular corporate story played a role in perceptions about an event.

Smoking or Tuxedo?

A manufacturing company in the Netherlands wanted to hold a meeting with all its staff. The communication agency devised what it thought would be an engaging way of announcing the event. The art director designed a series of eye-catching posters, saying Not X but Y! On each poster, X was something boring the workers might have anticipated at such an event (long speeches for instance), while Y was something more appealing, like good food. One of the variations said: "No Smoking but Casual!"

For English readers unfamiliar with the term 'smoking' as the Dutch use it, it means tuxedo or evening dress. Of course that is what the art director was referring to, inviting people to come dressed informally and not in a hired tuxedo. The accompanying drawing of a man in a 'smoking' should have left no room for any misunderstanding. But a couple of weeks into the campaign to advertise the event, the people at the agency began to worry: there had been hardly any feedback and they hadn't a clue why. The explanation came when they received a call from one of the workers who acted as a representative for almost all of the 800 employees. He announced that the workers had collectively decided to boycott the event, because of the ban on tobacco.

What could possibly explain this strong negative reaction? How could the staff suffer from temporary collective blindness to the picture of a man in a tuxedo (who was not smoking!) with a big cross all over him? We found out why.

Smoking had a particular tradition in that company. The late founder and CEO had been so partial to smoking that he had special smoking areas designated in every building. Twice a day people shared the ritual of having a smoke together: mid-morning and again around the afternoon tea break. Smoking was an activity that had roots in the company's culture, an activity that evoked strong feelings of 'belonging' and clear ideas about how it should be handled.

But a fierce conflict a few months earlier between a new manager and his crew in connection with new anti-smoking legislation had left a running sore. The words "No Smoking" triggered an immediate violent reaction, like waving a piece of red cloth in front of a herd of bulls. The poor marketers could not have known this by just looking at the sector of the company or the sort of people that worked there. Inside the organisation there was a time bomb ticking, and its fuse was lighted by this issue of smoking. If only the agency had known about this bomb they could have defused it. We call these types of issues 'social booby-traps.'

Why Bother?

For organisations, culture and identity together form an iceberg: the culture is the unseen part under the surface of the sea; the identity is the tip of the iceberg that sticks out and that you can see.

As in our party example, a meeting confronts participants with the organisational identity of those who commissioned it. However, as we already said, *what kind* of perceptions they have and what kind of conclusions they draw, depends on signals the meeting owner transmits in every single aspect of the meeting – right from the start. Is the venue bristling with security measures when you enter? Are the organisers themselves light hearted about these measures or do they take them very seriously? Is the reception warm and personal or business-like and efficient? Do newcomers receive a special welcome or not? What are the first things you see when you come in: the banners of the sponsors or a bigger-than-life picture of the organisation's founder?

Messages like these are bound to have an impact on the participants' perceptions. The Meeting Designer has to configure the meeting in accordance with the meeting owner's identity, matching physical aspects ('hardware', such as choice of venue, graphics, meals and drinks, etc.) and non-physical aspects ('software', such as modes of communication, conference formats, atmosphere, etc.). It is the task of the Meeting Designer to make the messages about the meeting owner's identity as specific as possible within the margins allowed by the meeting's 'consumers'. After all, this is what other types of design do as well. Product design, for instance, always strikes a balance between identity and functionality and the point of equilibrium tells a story about both. Meetings are just the same.

Design with Identity in Mind

So what choices face the Meeting Designer? Most organisations are relatively well aware of the choices in meeting logistics and hardware. But they are less well versed in choices related to the meeting's software – the primary process as we have defined it in the introduction – or to the connection between hardware and software. Meeting Owners have little insight into the primary process of meetings because their job is usually running a company in accordance with its operational needs. As a result, clients are constantly at risk of making uninformed choices that translate into conflicting messages with regard to their organisation's identity. The Meeting Designer, on the other hand, is supposed to know how meeting communication and organisational identity are connected.

Here are three examples of messages that influence participants' perceptions of the identity of meeting organisers, implicitly communicated through programme features. The first is purely about what we would call hardware:

A world-wide gathering for young people expressly stated in its meeting programme that its purpose was to give a voice to youth from all over the world. At lunchtime on day one, most youngsters had to push and shove in a queue for over an hour to make it to the food counter. By the time the last in the queue actually got there, there were hardly any choices left. Evidently, on food, they could express just one opinion.

This may seem just a matter of poor logistics, but it goes deeper than that. The implicit message of having to spend so long queuing was this: your time does not count. That of the lack of choice: your voice does not count. This, of course, was completely at odds with the organisers' earlier statements, about the importance of listening to the young people gathered there. You can only guess what the impact was on the subsequent commitment of participants in workshops or their willingness to apply any of the resolutions.

The second example is one at the crossroads between hardware and software.

A vocational training institute organises a 2-day conference on good practice in their field: the tourism and hospitality industry. They invite local business representatives and politicians as well as teachers and students. All in all the audience is quite prestigious but the institute has limited funds. For this reason they decide to use their main auditorium to host the plenary and school classrooms for breakout sessions. Their own students act as enthusiastic hostesses, under the guidance of a couple of dedicated teachers. This way, the meeting becomes a playground for the very topic it addresses and all participants are inevitably immersed in the institute's day-to-day environment, teaching hospitality processes and competence building.

In this example, through its choice of venue, the institute managed to give the meeting participants a strong identity message, directly and effectively. That message was: "We are hospitality". Participants could not escape from it! They gained first-hand experience of the identity of the organisers under particular circumstances.

Our third example shows how the software of a meeting, the actual communications in the meeting, can relay a message.

The Association wanted to make the participants at its Annual Assembly feel that the central bureau and paid staff were committed to listening to its members. This identity-related message needed attention because of the way earlier conferences had been shaped: and that was rather traditionally, with keynote speeches and panel discussions. As a result, the attending members were given the impression that the organisers valued the input of the keynote speakers and panellists a lot more than theirs. Since all members had prestigious positions in civic society, that was not very motivating. Not that anybody said so openly, they were too polite for that, but it was apparent in the way they behaved during the conference. Participants would simply start to network and talk loudly when just a few inches outside the meeting room; they would visit the fair in the hall next door; and generally pay little attention to things that were said on stage.

We reshaped that year's programme: All 2500 members were placed at round tables, each seating eight. On stage the chair presented an issue in about three minutes, immediately followed by discussions at the tables about the issue raised and each table casting a vote using an electronic voting system. This cycle, presentation of issue followed by discussion and voting, was repeated three times. At the end of the session, a Government Minister commented on the results of the votes. The conference had great evaluations from all 2500 members.

Let us now consider the specific relationship between organisational identity and Meeting Design. Broadly speaking, we can distinguish five different types of interaction. Below, we will describe these five relationships and comment on the related design features and programme choices.

One: Meetings that Affirm Identity

The first type is when there is a straightforward relationship and the meeting is simply an expression of an organisation's identity. The Meeting Designer develops a programme based on the current identity of the commissioning organisation. The example above of the Association and its Annual Assembly is clearly of this first type. The Designer's solution was to transform the mode of communication and translate the identity into specific features of the programme. This was relatively easy to do because the organisation was so explicit about who they were and what they wanted to convey during the meeting. And there were no corporate myths or trauma that could capsize this approach (although we did escape only by the skin of our teeth from one disaster...[4]).

Two: Meetings that Specifically Communicate Identity

Meetings are a powerful means of communicating the identity of an organisation and are, at the same time, a strong medium for people to identify with an organisation. Apple's famous launches of new products by Steve Jobs himself are a good example of this. They exemplify what Apple is all about not just to the consumer, but also to the corporation's workforce. Jobs' way of doing things was to carefully display a number of values that were easily recognisable and could translate into consumer behaviour, as well as employee behaviour. These included his informal dress (jeans) which said, "be yourself, no frills"; the jokes about Microsoft: "we are a family"; his relaxed attitude to the press: "be confident about your product"; while his air of satisfaction, conveyed the message: "be proud of what you have achieved." New Apple products could have been introduced in hundreds of different ways; but the way Jobs chose was all about identity. And this was felt and welcomed by thousands of Apple workers and millions of Apple buyers. His courage and his skill in these presentations was much admired because they can go horribly wrong — as his main rival once experienced (and just about everyone remembers):

---

[4] On the very morning of the conference, an aircraft overran the runway at the small local airport and crashed into a corn field. The mayor of the host town was supposed to deliver a two-minute welcoming speech after a video snippet announcing him. But in the immediate turmoil after the crash, we lost contact with him. The Conference hall was filled with 2,500 attendees ready to go, and we decided to start the tape, meanwhile praying that he would somehow materialise, which he did just in the nick of time. To everybody's relief, he was able to announce that no one had been hurt in the accident.

Microsoft was launching a new version of Windows, in a huge theatre in Los Angeles. 4,500 journalists from all over the world saw Bill Gates come on stage, for the system's official inauguration, looking as relaxed and confident as could be. The moment his technician booted his laptop, disaster struck: the computer crashed and the hideous blue screen appeared which all Windows users know painfully well. The technician's reactions were as quick as lightning, but not fast enough to trick the 4,500.

The laughter this event produced must have cost billions. The episode, mercilessly broadcast on YouTube, strengthened Microsoft's unfortunate reputation as a suboptimal performer, less than able to present its products effectively.

Three: Meetings that Stretch Identity

The third relationship between meetings and identity is of the stretch type. Sometimes a meeting owner wants to use the meeting to convey a message about a change in the organisation's way of doing things. Instead of affirming the organisation's identity, he wants to stretch it. This can work fine, if the organisation is to a significant degree willing and able to move into the direction of the stretch. In that case, the meeting can become a moment that catalyses the desired shift.

A small accountancy firm wanted to change the way its staff operated internally. The owners asked us to design a programme that challenged the workers to speak out and interact more directly with each other and with management. We offered them a day filled with workshops not related to their daily business, but focusing on human interaction: dance, photography and a philosopher who talked about the meaning of life.

The participants enjoyed the programme tremendously and changed the way they interacted right then and there. Someone said: "I have never seen my colleagues this way." For a meeting of this third type, that is the feedback you want!
Working on meetings in this category is fun. It involves coming up with unexpected features and participants tend to have intense, positive reactions. But you need to be careful. When a meeting owner asks us to design a programme of this sort, there is a severe risk to credibility. It is a bit like people throwing a party who pretend to be different from who they really are; or someone trying to be funnier than he actually is.
Trying to satisfy the organiser's desire to stretch identity can turn into an exhausting expedition. An example is the work we carried out for an

international institution. For several prestigious meetings they expressed the desire to have strongly innovative formats which would allow them to come across as innovative themselves. Unfortunately, there was no internal agreement or clarity on what this kind of innovation really meant. This turned each small decision on programme choices into a Gordian knot. In this institution, political dynamics were rife at many levels. As a consequence, the people working there felt that being innovative where their international conference programmes were concerned was not acceptable. And so in practice they could not avoid lengthy, abstract and vague political presentations and had a problem in handing a measure of autonomy over to participants. The stretch between desired and real identity was too great. It requires careful manoeuvring and high-level Meeting Design to satisfy the programme needs of organisations like this. And sometimes it proves impossible to achieve this at all.

Four: Meetings that Generate Identity

Maybe the closest relationship between meetings and identity is found in meetings that actually help to create identity. Sometimes, for instance during mergers or transition processes within an organisation, meetings aim at creating corporate history. They do so by offering participants experiences that become part of the organisation's identity. In the case of a merger, the first meeting with a large number of members of the two organisations can be crucial in how the shared values will develop.

In the design process for these cases, we have to go the extra mile to achieve an intensity of communication that moves something in people's souls. The emotional engagement in these meetings has to be strong and compelling. Participants need to be drawn into the events of the programme without any means of escape, leaving them with a lasting memory.

To achieve this, we often use the insights that the notion of Elementary Meetings gives us (see Chapter 1.3). People connect strongly to Elementary Meetings; they carry an emotional impact that is unavoidable. As a result, they can produce the power that is necessary to generate identity.

In close cooperation with the general manager who led a merger between two banks, we designed the following, rather unique series of meetings.

"Some years ago I already went through a merger between two banks," the General Manager informed us during our first encounter. "It took me five years to overcome all kinds of hassle between the two groups of staff, because they continued to feel somehow attached to their former organisation. Please help me design a process to avoid that this time." Later he added: "In fact, it is as if these two organisations are about to get married and I

want them to start their marriage on a sound basis, leaving their unmarried status behind them. I want them to head for a new future in a collaborative, entrepreneurial and positive way."

"OK," we replied, "why not take that idea as the concept of the whole series of meetings. Let us lead them through the whole process of what a young couple experiences: start from the first encounter and falling in love, to meeting the parents, getting engaged, having a stag party, and, finally, the actual marriage."

"Well, why not," he said, to our astonishment, "sounds like the kind of approach that could pull this off."

That kick-started five meetings which culminated in an actual fake marriage in a small church. Three couples (each consisting of a husband from one bank and a wife from the other) were married in a role-play with just the right mixture of fun and solemnity. The night before, the two groups of bankers had held two separate farewell parties.

When we met the manager years later he said: "These meetings brought us exactly what we were looking for: a merger of two cultures and identities without all the usual frustration; what a relief!"

Five: Meetings Despite a Lack of Meeting Owner Identity

The impact of organisational culture on meeting programmes – and with that on their effectiveness – is particularly evident in the meetings of some associations. In spite of vigorous efforts, many associations do not have a strongly distinctive identity; they are a lot like other, similar associations. Often, the main thing that distinguishes them is the field they work in, or the personalities of a small number of leading association figures. Medical associations are typical: there is no really significant difference between the organisational identity of, say, the world association of cardiologists or that of orthopaedic surgeons (although as a patient you hope they know the difference). It's a bit like football fans. To outsiders, Arsenal and Tottenham fans are very similar, but don't tell them!

In the absence of a clear identity, it becomes hard to make programme choices that go beyond the largest common denominator. There is no distinctive frame of reference with shared beliefs, experience and values – the stuff that makes up organisational identity – to guide such choices. That makes good Meeting Design difficult.

The consequence is that the meetings held by such organisations tend to be predictable, following a standard pattern and lacking in effectiveness – a polite way of saying that they are boring. They become what Vink[5] calls 'transcultural fields': places such as airport lounges, or today's football teams without any local players, that transmit no clear identity and therefore do

---

[5] Vink, N, *Grenzeloos communiceren, Een nieuwe benadering van interculturele communicatie*, KIT Publishers, Amsterdam, 2001.

not seem to be authentically alive.

To breathe life into association meetings and come up with good conference programmes, a Meeting Designer needs to probe into the direct interests of the association members. Although the people commissioning the meeting are the board or the association's staff, it is actually the members who own it. For a good design, we usually interview at least ten potential participants and use their opinions and expectations so that they have some influence on the programme. That works.

An association for city administrators asked us to design a conference on the subject of green areas in cities and towns. The idea behind the programme was to advance the thinking about how cities should plan and manage their parks and other recreational green areas. Our first interview was with the mayor of one of the biggest cities involved. His opening comment was a candid one: "Good morning, gentlemen. I've heard this year's conference theme is 'Green Areas in towns and cities'. Well, let me confess to you right away, 'Green Areas' is not a topic that will make me jump out of bed enthusiastically and fully charged. I'll probably stay home." That answer clearly meant we had to find a specific slant to the topic and its development. At a later stage, during another interview, someone gave us a clue: "In my city we have to carefully look at the financial consequences of everything we do." And so we designed a programme, focused on the funds that can be generated from green areas and the land they occupy. More about this example in Chapter 2.3.

In associations, there are always many people who have no vested interests but who personify the association's identity. A Meeting Designer is better off speaking to these people, because they give valuable information about participant reactions to the topic and the programme, rather than losing momentum in endless talks with board members and their communication advisers, steering committees and expert groups.

Striking the Balance

The five types of relationships described above stake out the field in which Meeting Designers have to find design solutions. This field lies on the intersection between identity, organisational culture, marketing, practical meeting circumstances and strategic leadership. The day-to-day reality of our profession brings assignments that are always different and call for tailor-made solutions. Nevertheless, our experience is that there is always a demand, but also an opportunity, to design a meeting programme that gives the right answer to the identity needs of the organisation and the meeting owner.

Whether those people always see the implications of these needs for getting an effective meeting programme is a different matter. Sometimes we need to vigorously defend programme proposals because the meeting owner fails to capture the connection with his own identity objectives. While we are generally able to defend such proposals, the meeting owner is not always willing or able to go along. Sometimes this means our ways part...

In any case, what is required of the Meeting Designer is an open eye for and a keen awareness of what meeting owner and meeting participants consider possible and what they do not. It is necessary to challenge the margins up to a point: what is acceptable and normal often risks being poor in communicative power, while on the other hand what is extraordinary and powerful in terms of communication, may be too unconventional. To design meetings that communicate, we need to operate within those margins. A consistent programme, in line with the organisational culture, the objectives of the meeting owner and the particularities of the participants requires a proper understanding of the organisation's identity and its stories.

Sceptic

We speak to Birk, who manages corporate communications in a large International Agency. Birk is from Iceland.

B: Why make things so hopelessly complicated? To me all this talk about values and identity seems unnecessary and irritating. Meetings just have to be effective, that's all there is to it. They have to produce useful outcomes at the lowest possible cost. If you start making things complicated, you always end up paying more.

M/E: Thanks for being so frank, Birk!

B: My pleasure! For heaven's sake, look into things like meeting objectives, measuring meeting outcomes or ROI. That makes sense from a business perspective.

M/E: Money makes the world go 'round – is that a fair summary of your point of view?

B: Right.

M/E: And the more meetings are the same everywhere on the globe the better? Just to avoid confusion? From that angle, the globalisation of meeting formats is the way forward.

B: You're getting my point.

M/E: Well, congratulations, because that is exactly what's happening. All conferences churned out with the same format. And... what do participants say about these meetings if they can afford to be honest?

B: Boring, that's what you're insinuating, aren't you? All these conferences are boring.

M/E: That appears to be the price you pay for global understanding.

B: Maybe, but so what?

M/E: It's not that we don't like this and want to make things interesting for ourselves. The whole reason why Meeting Design is emerging is because of our clients. It's all their fault! They want to do things differently and they are asking us to help them with that.

B: Do they really?

M/E: Meetings that are the same under all circumstances are not necessarily effective meetings. Companies – or organisations in general – want to be recognisable; meetings can express their competitive edge. Money makes the world go 'round...

B: So the very argument I used against you is now used against me. You want to turn the tables on me?

M/E: Well, it's more a matter of looking at facts than of argument. We don't design programmes the way we do because it's more fun to have some outrageous format, cooked up out of the blue. Of course, we think it is more fun but that's not why we produce them. We do it because our clients tell us that they want their identity to become visible. Implicitly, perhaps, but that's what they do. They want their products or services to be distinctive.

B: You guys are actually marketeers.

M/E: A couple of years ago someone wrote that our profession is the meeting point between marketing, sociology and art.

B: So is mine.

M/E: Communication is the focus for both of us; yours in all media, ours specifically in meetings.

B: Still, I haven't heard anything about objectives yet.

M/E: May we suggest you now read the next chapter?

B: If you criticise someone, they always say that you made an excellent point and that they were just going to address it. But all right, I accept the invitation.

What is the Meeting for?

uppose somebody wants to have a meeting; anybody. Well before beginning to think about the meeting programme, the most important question to address is: *what is the meeting for?* As obvious as this question may seem, finding the answer is not always so easy. In our experience most meeting organisers are surprisingly unclear about what it is they want their meeting to achieve. Nevertheless, it is the meeting owner who takes the initiative to hold the meeting and so it is his views, desires and ideas that determine objectives in the first place.

The meeting owner will presumably have good enough reasons in mind to justify investing a significant amount of time and money in the meeting and asking future participants to do the same. He wants to offer these participants the opportunity to learn or exchange something, meet or enthuse someone, develop, change or decide something. The outcomes of these processes are what we call the Business Value of meetings. The Business Value relates to the overall reason why the meeting owner wants to have the meeting. Usually, from that general reason emerge a number of more specific objectives.

Getting to the meeting owner's reason and objectives is the focus of this chapter. We will illustrate the role of the Meeting Designer and provide insights into a number of tools the designer can use in order to excavate from the meeting owners' minds what their objectives really are. We use the word 'excavate' deliberately because – as we will describe in the next couple of pages – it is necessary to shovel away a lot of information we receive from meeting owners so as to lay bare the objectives that lie hidden. We will also make some comments about verifying whether the objectives have actually been met.

Not every meeting is designed. Sometimes this is because the meeting has relatively simple goals, with few participants who have enough facilitation power of their own to achieve good results. Often, meeting owners do not know that such a profession as Meeting Design exists! (Our fault, perhaps.) However, it is our experience that whenever clients engage us, they do so because their meeting is in some respects rather complicated, worrying, even politically sensitive, or because the clients are somehow looking for "something else, something different." As a consequence, the process that ultimately yields a design for the programme is one of close co-operation and co-creation between meeting owner and Meeting Designer. The kick-start for that process is a simple question.

Why Have a Meeting at all?

In the introduction, we defined a meeting as the physical gathering of a group of people in a specific place for a purpose. During meetings people communicate with each other; meetings are a specific means of communication. We have also established that the overall reasons for holding meetings fall into six categories: learning, networking, motivation, decision-making, rituals and alignment.

It is frankly astonishing how often meeting owners find it hard to rationalise that a meeting is the appropriate means of communication for their needs. So one of the first tasks of the Meeting Designer is to sort this out. The first step in cooperation, then, is to check how the views, ideas, expectations and dreams of the meeting owner match up with the definition of what a meeting is. How do we find out? The answer is almost embarrassingly simple: We just ask them. Asking the blunt question why they want to hold a meeting generates a conversation – a conversation that produces an awful lot of insights into the meeting owner's ideas about his meeting. Much more than any written brief would provide. One of the most amazing things in our professional life is that when starting to conceive a meeting, this question is almost always skipped! A conversation with the meeting owner tends to be along these lines:

- Do participants need to be in the same venue with others to learn what you feel they need to learn?
- Do participants need to be under one roof with others to network with them?
- Is there some kind of ritual that participants need to enact together?
- Is it necessary for participants to gather in order to align their views on a subject?
- Will the gathering of the participants increase their motivation?
- Will the gathering produce a step in a decision-making process?

This series of questions yields a good picture of the deeper reasons why the meeting owner wants a meeting. And if he wants it to be a good one, that reason has to be spelled out. Such reasons may take a very concrete form ("We want a signed memorandum of understanding."); sometimes they are subjective or hypothetical ("Wouldn't it be just amazing if..."). In any case, they are the foundation on which to build specific objectives.

A Meeting Designer needs a well-honed array of skills to dig out this information. It is an intensive dialogue directed at finding answers to the list of questions we gave you above. Designers must act at one and the same time as journalists and as talk show hosts; being polite or rude as occasion demands; stubborn and accommodating; massaging the victim's ego one moment and grilling him mercilessly another. It is important to be aware that for every single reason the meeting owner gives, there are probably other, less expensive ways than having a meeting which may satisfy his needs in terms of communication.

Briefings for Meetings

Once the meeting owner has committed himself to a clear stance on the deeper reasons for wanting a meeting, we begin to have a rough idea of what the meeting needs to achieve. However, the initial excavation work has not yet finished. More digging is needed!

When designing the programme, many choices have to be made – about such diverse issues as expressing the identity of the organiser (previous Chapter), or venue and physical circumstances (see Chapter 3.3), or how to treat the content (see Chapter 2.3). The guidelines for making good choices and sound decisions on meeting features such as formats, timing, speakers, pre- and post-meeting communication, as well as many other things, are a function of the objectives or outcomes the meeting owner wants the meeting to generate.

As the starting point for our analysis of objectives, let us take a typical briefing a client might submit. The following is a fabricated request but it is suspiciously similar to many documents we have received from potential clients over the past twenty years.

This document contains the briefing for the event our company wants to commission. The event, hosting 250 of our affiliates, dealers and agencies, upper and middle management levels, is to take place on the 3rd of March, preferably somewhere central in the country. It should leave a lasting impression, contain top-level entertainment and in an appropriate way introduce the product described in attachment 3-b. We expect direct and interactive involvement of our guests. The event should offer opportunities for our sales people to meet clients. The meeting should reflect our corporate Mission: "Electricity for Everyone." The budget for the event amounts to, etc.

Sounds familiar? Probably, because meeting professionals see (or produce) this kind of specification quite a lot. Organise a meeting on the basis of these specs: sounds like a perfectly rational and feasible request, doesn't it?

Well, sorry, we do not agree. A Meeting Designer who needs to come up with a meeting programme based on this kind of input is like a surgeon who operates by candlelight, wearing a pair of sunglasses and with one eye bandaged. The brief falls dramatically short of grasping what a meeting is as a form of communication. Essentially – and this is another possible definition of a meeting – meetings offer participants a physical experience around specific content. As we have argued earlier, the physical and emotional experience for participants is *inevitable*. If you bring people together in a place they *will* have an experience and emotions. Consequently, to design a good programme, it is necessary to understand what the meeting owner wants in terms of experience, emotions and content.

Participant Narratives

What exactly is wrong with the briefing we introduced just now? Well, the objectives for this meeting seem to ignore completely the fact that the meeting involves people – human beings made of flesh and blood. Here is a tiny hint of the sort of information we would be looking for:

A medium-sized municipality organises a meeting for all its staff with the objective of improving the overall level of service it provides to the urban community. The town council wants to achieve this by strengthening the professional pride of staff working at the Town Hall. In order to understand what they mean by that, we start looking for pride among the municipal workers.
One of the testimonies we obtain is from a lady at the municipal cleaning service. She explains what her work means to her and does this by showing us the beauty of her broom. She tells us about the small factory that produces these brooms and how they use natural materials to make them just long and flexible enough to sweep large surfaces without getting too heavy. There is not a trace of cynicism in her voice, only genuine and warm professional involvement. What she conveys is an intense feeling of pride, about the work she does with her most basic tool: a broom. It feels as if the broom is her pet. A testimony like this is incomparably richer than an abstract sentence in a briefing saying, "The meeting has to reflect the pride of our employees."

You get this kind of story only if you talk to the people for whom the meeting is intended and who will undergo the meeting experience. Only if you sit with them during their coffee breaks, smell their lunches, see the view from their work place, hear the siren that ends their shift.

The essential difference is that collecting these narratives – instead of reading a brief – translates the wishes of the meeting owner into something with a broader human perspective. This fact as such produces a better design. Whereas factual descriptive briefings tend to be lifeless and abstract, images and stories depict factual information as well as emotional colour, sharp outlines as well as the depth of real people's lives, even their dreams and visions, marketing language as well as the poetry of workers who talk about day-to-day life and drudgery (or not). This is the raw material from which we can shape the experiences of others.

Paradoxically, in our attempts to establish *objectives* together with the meeting owner, these *subjective* narratives are absolutely essential. They help the meeting owner to embrace the relationship between the meeting experience and the participants. We usually capture these narratives in the form of a series of quotes or pictures. Interestingly, meeting owners practically always agree that the narrative is essential input on which to base the design.

Content Flow

In the course of our work as Meeting Designers, we have developed a view of what meetings are in their essence. That is why, in the previous section, we have defined meetings as a physical and emotional experience around a specific content. Reducing a meeting to its bare essentials, you can strip away many things that seem important, but in fact are not. Of course, they are cinsidered as important by many meeting industry suppliers today, but that is hardly a convincing argument. For instance, people at meetings could do without all the calories they receive – a meeting without eating or drinking is perfectly conceivable. We are not saying that you ought to, simply that you could. Also a meeting room is just an amenity: meetings can be held in the open air; actually, some are – and on occasion that is an excellent idea! Meetings can do without speakers, without a chair, without a time schedule, without a shared agenda. They could even function without certain intangibles: without shared goals, shared positions, a shared motivation.

However, there is one thing that meetings cannot do without. It has to be there. Always. Without it, the meeting cannot be called a meeting; participants will not come; the meeting will die. That one thing is content. All meetings are *about something*. Even more specifically, the meeting causes something to happen with the content: it starts moving. Meetings, therefore, offer participants content in motion, content that changes and develops. It can be anything from the latest developments in nuclear physics to a brainstorm about shaving cream; from skiing opportunities in Austria to *What People Say about Our Company*. To be honest, we are not the first to notice the fundamental role content plays in meetings.[1]

'In motion' means two things. First, the content literally goes from one place to another, for instance from one head into another. One participant learns from someone else that electrons have two ways of spinning. That person heard this from one of the speakers. This byte of content jumps from head to head, it moves. And as it is moves, it multiplies. So now three people know about the spin of electrons, instead of just one. There is something physical

---

[1] Maarten Vanneste, Meeting Architecture, op. cit. Maarten Vanneste is also the founder of the Meeting Support Institute.

in this multiplication of information. That is one way in which content moves. The second meaning is that the content changes in its implications and significance for individual participants. For instance they may conclude that skiing in Austria is less expensive than they thought, or that our company's image among shop owners in Chicago is even worse than we thought. This movement entails a development of the content.

This abstract expectation is in people's heads when they start organising or consider attending a meeting: Something will happen there with content. As a consequence, what we want to know from meeting owners, is this: "What is the movement you want the content to make?" Working on this question with meeting owners has allowed us to develop a specific tool which we decided to call the Content Flow. Our definition is:

> Content Flow is the change in location or in meaning of content during a meeting.

Representing Content Flow

Defined like this, Content Flow sounds like a straightforward and concrete concept, but it is not; it is abstract and finds itself at a different level from the content itself. This makes it difficult to discuss it with meeting owners. They immediately dive into the actual content itself, which is not surprising because content is something meeting owners know a lot about, after all, it is the very reason why they want to hold the meeting! What we want, though, is to make them tell us what they want to happen to the content – what sort of process they envisage, what kind of change as a result of the meeting.

In our talks with the meeting owner, however, it is necessary to give the Content Flow some concrete form and separate the actual content from the flow it can undergo. Every parent knows how hard it is to talk about educating children in general without thinking of your own. Nevertheless, we want meeting owners to talk to us about content without speaking about the content itself. The paradox of this task is obvious and therefore we had to find a technique to allow the meeting owner to do this. We now follow a routine that goes roughly like this:

"OK. Now, we have agreed that the reason for this meeting, is to make the content move in some way or other. So we come to the next step. We would like you to show us that movement. To do this, could you try to visualise the content as some kind of physical substance? Imagine that you could turn the content of your meeting into a material, such as stone, rubber, water, sand, a bunch of plastic pipes, a fireball – anything. If you can visualise the content

in that sort of way, we'll be able to move on."

For most people, asking them to visualise an abstraction as matter, as something you can touch, is not an easy task; their brains need to make something like a minor quantum leap. Luckily, language gives us a helping hand. Matter is exactly the right word because it means substance in the sense of something material as well as substance, in the sense of an object of thought, as information. In English matter is something you can touch, as well as discuss. In the latter case we call it subject matter. We have many expressions that actually qualify informational matter as physical stuff: we speak of thorny issues, a juicy scandal, a burning issue, a delicate topic, etc. We find this in other languages, as well. The French talk of 'matière grave' meaning 'difficult matters' which Germans would translate as 'schwere Sachen' (literally: heavy things).

As soon as the meeting owner, helped with the language examples, begins to see content as physical matter, we give him a large sheet of paper and a fistful of coloured felt pens, and ask him to make a drawing of this content and the way it has to move. Normally, people feel a bit embarrassed, saying they have always been hopeless at drawing since kindergarten, but with some gentle pressure they do get going and get absorbed in drawing the often latent image, the dream of what they want the meeting to do. It is a fascinating process and highly revealing about the meeting owner's agenda. What emerges are rational thoughts, but also motives the meeting owner himself was previously unaware of, as the following example will show.

The HR director of a medium-sized enterprise wanted an in-company symposium about a number of worrying developments in his organisation. He had little difficulty accepting our invitation to do the exercise and draw the Content Flow he had in mind.

After he had put the last stroke on the paper, we examined the result together. "On the left side of the paper, your drawing shows a big empty space. Can you explain what that means to you?" The man peered at the sketch and, with a bemused look on his face, answered: "You're right, I did that without really thinking about it. Hmm. I guess it means we shouldn't start sharing our ideas straight away but have a quiet moment of reflection about where we stand before we do that. I want to start with a kind of emptiness to avoid the discussions we are all familiar with. Yes, that's what I want; actually I did not know that, but my hand drew it, so maybe somewhere deep down I did. That's really odd."

"Well," we answered, "that's something we can definitely incorporate in our programme proposal, so thanks for enlightening us."

Analysis of the Content Flow Drawing

The meeting owner's drawing describes what he wants the meeting to generate in terms of Content Flow but it does not do so in words. Meeting owners often sense that they have drawn a unique document that will help to bring about a unique meeting. When other people are involved, the drawing helps them to make choices about the programme design that will achieve the meeting's Content Flow. It is a transparent tool that serves as a bridge between the wishes of the meeting owner, the ideas of other stakeholders and the process of designing the meeting. The drawing invites a thorough analysis by asking questions about details and peculiarities. The statements obtained that way are again vastly different from written briefs.

The official from the Ministry of Health draws a metal stick that is bent into a particular shape.
"Does that particular form you have drawn have some special meaning for you?" we ask him.
"Yes," he explains, "it's like an Australian boomerang, and come to think of it, that is exactly what I would like to use. I want the symposium to bend the content in such a way that new opportunities surface. And I want those opportunities tested during the meeting, to see if they are relevant for the topic. I want the boomerang to be thrown a couple of times, to test it, to see where it flies, what it hits, and what it brings back to us."
Next we ask him what kind of metal the boomerang was made of.
"Steel," he says without a moment of hesitation. To bend steel you need heat, force, or both. This implies that the symposium has to offer some powerful moments, focussed on changing the overall perception of the content. The drawing produces a remarkably accurate description of a whole series of programme features.

Conclusions like these about what the programme is supposed to do with the content come from meeting owners' drawings and they accept the consequences because they made the drawings themselves. At the same time, for our design purposes we now have a transparent document on which to base our proposals.

Explaining the principle of Content Flow, the way to look at the content as matter, and then making the drawing and reflecting on it, generates a mutual understanding about the meeting between meeting owner and Meeting Designer. Afterwards, the drawing offers guidance in the design process (for this, see Chapter 3.2).

Experience Concept

Though the content of the meeting is the prime thing, it is not the only thing that is on the meeting owner's mind. Another important concern are the circumstances under which that content will be flowing; or at least it should be a major concern, considering that meetings inevitably offer participants an experience with the accompanying set of feelings.

The Content Flow and the circumstances under which it flows are two entirely different things. Every Content Flow can be executed in an infinite number of different ways, with an infinite number of different participant experiences as a result. Suppose we have an extremely unpretentious Content Flow: one idea needs to jump from a single speaker's head into one other participant's head. Even this can be accomplished in an untold number of different ways. The transfer could take place while the two were driving through Ireland in a Landrover, or while cooking and sipping white wine in a French kitchen, or in a classroom in some college building. The idea could be written down for the other person to read, it can be yelled, spoken politely, proclaimed in Shakespearean English; the teacher can wear a bathing suit, a hand-made Italian jacket, or perhaps be stark naked. The room temperature can be anything between minus 40 and plus 50 degrees Celsius, unless participants are in a sauna, where 110 degrees is possible. Before we get carried away even further, the point we are making is clear. In all these situations, the Content Flow may be identical, but the participants' experiences will be utterly different.

As designers, we need to discover if the meeting owner has any thoughts and expectations about the kind of experience he wants the participants to undergo. And in practice, he always has! As discussed in Chapter 2.1, part of these thoughts are related to the messages about organisational identity and the communication processes triggered by the meeting. The meeting owner wants and needs to have a say in this. So what does he want? The sauna, or the Irish countryside?

When we ask meeting owners this question straight out, they are likely to describe the atmosphere they desire to create at their meeting in very broad terms, such as "challenging", or "exciting". These words do not provide a lot of insight into the specific experience they want to offer their participants; they merely suggest a general atmosphere. To get a more precise idea, we have developed the notion of the Experience Concept. Thanks to this concept we can gain an understanding of the kind of experience clients want the participants to have, and we can do so in a more indirect way. Sometimes the indirect route is more effective than the direct one.

Verbs and Experience

To obtain the Experience Concept, we ask the meeting owner to give us a number of verbs. Verbs that express what he wants the participants to do during the meeting. Why verbs? Because people's experiences are closely connected to what they do. The experience – whatever it is – materialises because people perform some kind of act. The experience is the consequence of the activity, even when it involves little real action, so to speak. Sleeping may generate dreams, staring produces daydreams, waiting causes muscles to itch, bungee-jumping terrifies people, and so on. So, the question we ask the meeting owner is:

Could you give us a list of verbs that express the things you want the participants to do? And remember, a verb is a word that expresses an action and starts with 'to'.

Once the meeting owner's supply of verbs dries up, together we whittle the list down to about five or six, eliminating verbs that refer to the same kind of activity, combining meanings and prioritising. All this is done in an open dialogue with the meeting owner, who is in the lead and who also decides when the list is complete.

The final step is to ask the meeting owner to think of some meeting in which all the activities on the list actually take place. This is a trial-and-error process that may take a couple of attempts. It works better if it is done by a group of people who are involved in planning the meeting because their ideas are contagious. And then, magically – and it happens every single time we do this – the meeting owner hits on a type of meeting that will produce the kind of experience he had in mind.

Most often, the meeting envisaged by the meeting owner is an Elementary Meeting. This makes sense, because meetings of this type are the ones that flag up easily in his mind. But even if he picks out some other type of meeting, the reasons for his choice are the distinctive characteristics of just that type of meeting. In the design phase, this is of great help: Elementary Meetings have a characteristic timeline, clear markers of desired behaviour, a specific atmosphere, etc. So if that is the Experience Concept the meeting owner is looking for, these characteristics must be prominent in the design. Chapter 3.2 details the role of the Experience Concept in the actual creation of the programme design but as a prelude we can offer a brief example here. Suppose the Experience Concept is a Christmas dinner. This means that, to the largest possible degree, the design should give the participants a Christmas Dinner experience. The look and feel should resonate with this Elementary Meeting. This does not mean you necessarily cook and eat a turkey, it means the participants will experience markers, feelings, a the meeting owner specifies several desired outcomes which are actually process expectations. We often see this mix-up in documents that initiate meetings, whether written in private industry or in public organisations.

Part of our analysis of objectives is to pinpoint potentially quantifiable outcomes in formulations like the one above. A good candidate is "high-level decision-makers." The questions this noun phrase prompts is: How high is high and what overall level (literally: what height) is a satisfactory outcome? In the above case, we asked the meeting owner to draw up a classification with scores based on the positions participants actually held in their organisations: for instance, a minister was worth ten points, a direct policy advisor to the minister five points, a lower level policy advisor three points, etc. Knowing the number of participants in each catagory, it was possible to arrive at a total number of points the meeting owner considered a satisfactory total 'height' of policy-makers.

This exercise can be done for all sorts of objectives that are initially phrased in vague terms. We recognise such 'hidden' objectives because they often carry a qualifying adjective. Another lead in our example is the formulation "collective analysis." Collective means that *all participants* are to be offered the opportunity to take part actively in the analysis. This is something you can test very easily. You just ask them at the end of the conference to what extent they feel they had the opportunity to contribute to the debate. Ask them to express this on a scale, for instance from 1-10, or 1-6. The meeting owner needs to decide what average level of participation he finds acceptable. Perhaps he thinks that on a scale from 1-10 an outcome of 6.5 is good, because his participants are not accustomed to being actively involved. Or maybe he wants to achieve an average of 8.5 because in his eyes active participation is a vital parameter of a successful conference.

One of the outcome parameters we have developed through this process is what we call Return on Effort (ROE), with a nod to Jack Philips.[2] At the start of the programme, for instance during registration, participants are asked how big an effort they made to attend the meeting and to express this on a scale from 1-10. This is entirely subjective and that is exactly the point. At the end of the meeting, in the exit survey, they are asked this follow-up question: "At the start of the meeting you were asked how much effort you had to make to come here. To what extent was this meeting worth that effort?" Once again, the meeting owner can decide what is a satisfactory level. He certainly gets a more precise outcome than by just asking "Did this meeting correspond to your expectations? Yes/No."

Naturally, drawing up such exit surveys involves all kinds of methodological practicalities, such as asking exactly the right questions and making sure the answers are statistically valid. It goes beyond the scope of this book to go into that level of detail. What is clear, though, is that the process of

[2] Philips, J., op cit.

measuring objectives works as follows:

Together with the client you have to establish:

1. which variable or parameter reflects successful outcomes (and not meeting processes, which describe the way in which those outcomes materialise);
2. when and how to measure this variable and on what scale to express the result; and
3. what is the desired level of satisfaction.

Objectives and the Meeting Programme

The Meeting Designer carries out this analysis together with the meeting owner. Admittedly, the results of this analysis do not specify concrete activities for participants. In other words, they do not yet produce design solutions. What they do provide, however, are essential ingredients in order to make a design that will achieve the Business Value of the meeting. They are part of the specific reconnaissance the Meeting Designer needs to carry out to come up with a good design.

It is our experience that relatively few organizations are capable of expressing clearly what they want to achieve with their meetings. The descriptions of their desired outcomes are generally cloaked in misty language. To a large extent this is because meeting owners know a lot about their own organisations and about the meeting's content, but not very much about meetings as a specific form of communication. Therefore it is the task of the Meeting Designer to guide the meeting owner towards a better understanding of his goals. Difficult? Well, maybe – but is this not typically what clients expect consultants to do?

Sceptic

We speak to Leonardo, a young multi-media professional from Argentina who is a regular speaker at conferences about marketing through social media.

L: Listen, I'm 26, which is about half your age and you wave in front of my eyes this cranky tool you call Content Flow. Man, if you want to use it, you have to be half psychiatrist, and half creative director of an advertising agency. Thanks a million!

M/E: OK, if it doesn't convince you, forget about it.

L: I wasn't saying that; it does get me somehow.

M/E: You know what, just mail us your text…

L: And let me guess, you drop in for the last 5 minutes?

M/E: If we have any questions.

L: I thought arrogance comes with youth, but evidently I was wrong. Are you always that condescending?

M/E: Sorry for that, but we have seen what works in practice. People are not just mouse extensions.

L: Fair enough. There's some arrogance in thinking that as well. I'll send you an invitation anyway. Think about it.

2.3 Attention! Content!

A Warning Sign

he tall, portly man closes the door after us, invites us over to his desk and sinks into the comfortable leather of his tilt-back chair. "Good morning, gentlemen," he booms, "I've heard this year's conference theme is 'Green Areas in towns and cities'. Well, let me confess to you right away, 'Green Areas' is not a topic that will make me jump out of bed enthusiastically and fully charged..."

If you get this input while working on the design of a major conference, as a Meeting Designer you know that you are up against something. The more so, if the person uttering these words is one of the opinion leaders in the organisation that has commissioned the programme. In this case we are talking about the Dutch association of municipalities, whose membership includes all mayors and town clerks – let's say city managers – of the entire country. Incidentally, you may recognise this example from a previous chapter (Chapter 2.1); we are going to use it here for a different purpose.

The interviewee quoted above was the highest public official in one of the largest cities in the country. He gave cast iron reasons for his view on the topic: Green belts are just about normal maintenance and therefore uninteresting. Yet, he was only one of roughly 2,400 intended participants. Should the meeting designer take this offhand reaction as an early warning of a serious problem? Undoubtedly! If a potential participant carries weight and is representative of the organisation for whom the event is being planned, then his doubts are likely to be shared by more members who carry the same organisational DNA. To develop a programme that will truly engage the target population, it is vital to figure out the implications of his doubts about the content.

The mayor expressed himself this way in the first interview of six with typical members of the association. When asked about the proposed content, they all confirmed his judgement. 'Green areas' simply did not catch on with the future audience. Their lack of enthusiasm was about what you might get if you proposed an outing to the National Knot Museum to a group of 17-year-old rockers. Not the sort of starting point that would make it easy to live up to the expectations of the Conference Committee, namely "to design a conference programme that will generate high levels of active participation among the attendees."

Something had to be done with the conference theme, more broadly, with the content. It had to be given a shot in the arm. That is what this chapter is about. We shall explore ways of making content more attractive to meeting owner and participants. We shall also investigate what the Meeting Designer needs to be looking for so that content is approached and dealt with in the most gripping and motivating way. The prime focus will be on the content itself, but we shall also give some examples of design solutions.

What is Exciting?

A topic that irresistibly tickles one person's sensibilities may well leave someone else entirely unmoved. There are few absolute yardsticks for what will arouse a person's interest. Two model airplane constructors may lose themselves in an animated exchange about the strength of balsa wood from country X or Y. Would you get out of bed early for a meeting about the strength of balsa wood? Probably not, but these enthusiasts will! And not just these two – we saw hundreds of them during a gathering of model aircraft builders.

Of course, you may say, these people are hobbyists and hobbyists share loopy interests. We know of a gentleman who owns the world's largest collection of in-flight bags for disposing vomit. It is obvious that some people have interests others do not share. However, when holding a meeting, this issue takes on great relevance. For instance, we can all remember meetings where the chair opened the floor for debate and right away a discussion began that seemed unstoppable. At other meetings trying to get active participation from the floor felt like getting a dead parrot to speak. Why is this?

We are convinced that for a successful meeting, it is not enough to invite a couple of speakers, ask participants: "So, what do you think about what you've just heard?" and simply assume that (hey presto!) you will get a brilliant exchange of views. Interactions during meetings always run the risk of being void or dominated by a couple of self-absorbed individuals. One of the main reasons for this is that the connection between the interests of the participants and the development of the content (the "flow" we would call it, see Chapter 2.2) has not been put in place properly. The meeting and its topic may be intrinsically interesting to participants, but if that interest is not stimulated and developed, the exchanges will be sterile.

The Meaning of Interest

Meeting owners always hope that the meeting will grab the participants' attention; that it will be like a pit-bull terrier: go for the throat and NOT LET GO. As we have already seen, attention depends on the interest the participant has in the content. The English word 'interest' has two aspects. On the one hand it indicates the curiosity a person has about a subject, its attractiveness, perhaps even his fascination with it. On the other, it refers to the person's stake in the issue, the relevance it has for him, the concern he may feel about it. Later in this chapter, we will develop these two aspects of interest into more specific requirements for meeting content. We will work out how content can be made 'hot', since we are convinced that this is an essential part of the Meeting Designer's work. The 'hotness' of content has little or nothing to do with attractive formats or attractive speakers. It comes from the way content is approached, the angle chosen and developed to draw participants in. But let's start at the beginning.

Where Does Content Come from?

Meetings materialise by virtue of an idea conceived by the meeting owner. If it was not for the meeting owner's wish to have a meeting about a certain topic, there would be no meeting. The content, therefore, always starts taking shape in the meeting owner's mind.

In the example at the beginning of this chapter, the association's conference department had come up with a content idea; evidently they thought this was an interesting topic. Our first participant interview indicated the contrary. We find that this is not an exception. Often, participants have a perspective on the content which is essentially different from the meeting owner's.

Typical briefings about content reflect *only* the perspective of the meeting owner. Unlike other people attending the meeting, he has a specific position in the organisation (for instance, he is the CEO, or the communications person – not the manager of operations in location X). He has his own – perfectly relevant – ideas about the content, the facts, their implications for various groups of participants, and so on. However hard he tries to put himself in the shoes of the participants, though, there will be always be a difference between his views on the content and those of the participants. To design meetings that irresistibly draw participants into the action, it is essential to consider the content from a range of angles.

What the Meeting Designer needs is a broader view of the meeting content, bringing in additional angles the meeting owner hasn't thought of. In this way he can establish how 'hot' the original content is and, if necessary, add or twist something to make it 'hotter.' (As indicated earlier, we will define the notion of 'hot' in the next couple of pages). To develop this view with some depth, the Meeting Designer utilises three sources:
- A broad 'journalistic' background with bits and pieces of general knowledge and a sense of issues of current interest to society;
- A sound dose of common sense – a feeling for when things just do not seem to add up. Analysis and a critical stance if you will;

- Participant interviews.

The first two are more or less self-evident in any consultancy-type line of business, so let us focus on the third.

Questions, Questions and More Questions

The pre-design analysis phase needs to bridge the potential gap between the meeting owner's and the participants' vision of the content. If what you need is to discover the participants' angle, there is only one logical option: go and talk to them and listen carefully to what they tell you. And we mean this quite literally: go and look them up in person, and if it is an international meeting, at least speak to them on the phone.

We already introduced the need for participant interviews in the previous chapter. While we take a different angle here – content analysis rather than establishing goals – the two are connected as by an umbilical cord: no clarity about content development without clear goals and no effective goals without an understanding of what should happen to the content. Therefore, participant interviews serve at least two purposes. And hence also the need to do a content flow drawing with the meeting owner, as explained in Chapter 2.2.

A series of participant interviews is not statistically valid market research. What you are looking for in these conversations are shared motives, convictions, statements that help you understand what the meeting means to future participants. It is not about understanding what thousands of breakfast eaters feel when they behold the packaging of a new granola bar wrapper; it is a qualitative investigation in which you look for *other* perspectives on the meeting's content. Usually, an in-depth talk with 6-10 possible participants is sufficient. It is important that these people have ideas about the overall topic and are 'typical' representatives of the organisation. We ask the meeting owner to give us a shortlist, and we refer to them as people who 'carry the DNA' of the meeting's target group.

These conversations need to be in-depth interviews, starting from sincere, human curiosity and pursuing topics as doggedly as a journalist would. The Meeting Designer has to establish confidence, get an overview of the interviewees' general opinions of the content, pursue promising lines of thought, touch on sensitive issues, test ideas on desired outcomes, possible formats, etc.

The insights obtained in this way allow the Meeting Designer to produce an effective perspective of the content. Often, as in our 'Green Areas' example, the outcome of this content analysis brings about a significant shift in what happens to the content during the meeting, as you can read at the end of this chapter.

Making Content 'Hot'

The outcome of this first stage of our content analysis is an approach or an angle that will capture the attention of participants because it has a bearing on their interests. This is the raw material the Meeting Designer starts working with. In many cases, there is a second stage of analysis that leads to optimised design solutions: We make the content 'hot.' For content to be 'hot,' it has to satisfy four criteria:

1. It must be 'sticky';
2. It must have some impact on participants' personal or professional lives;
3. It must present some inner conflict; and
4. It must trigger curiosity, often curiosity of an intellectual kind.

That list looks suspiciously like a post-it memo stuck on the computer screen of someone just starting a career on a tabloid newspaper, doesn't it? Or perhaps of a TV journalist making a human interest programme. Yes, in order to make content hot, they use similar triggers. However, the content of meetings is rarely as mundane as that of tabloid articles or TV reality shows. There is also a further, fundamental difference. Tabloids and reality shows do not take the content anywhere; actually, this is precisely what they try to avoid. Getting the trigger fired is their *raison d'être* after which there is only the emptiness of infinity and beyond. The whole point of the content analysis a Meeting Designer carries out, on the other hand, is to improve the meeting and its outcomes. The purpose is to treat the content during the meeting in such a way that participants can work with it, develop it, take it onto a different plane, reach relevant conclusions about it. That is not really the purpose of the picture on an average tabloid front page. What we do have in common is that we are not after content that is just a bit lukewarm. No, the content has to be really HOT.

Sticky Content

The first criterion for hot content is that it must be sticky. Sticky content is everything that is capable of arousing basic human sentiments. From neuropsychology we know that these reactions come from the most primitive part of our brain, sometimes called the reptile brain because it controls functions we have in common with lizards and snakes. Stimuli entering the reptile brain often stick without us being aware of it; they appeal to such parts of the brain as the limbic system: "Here, in this cerebral underworld, raw emotion is generated: alarm bells are set off in response to threat; false smiles are registered; and lust fires the twitches at the sight of an attractive other."[1] Sticky is about biology, about the drives that come from the four f's: feed, flee, fight and fornicate.

What is it that arouses these basic human feelings? Here is a list of options:

---

 [1] Rita Carter, *Mapping the Mind*, Phoenix, London, 2000-2010.

pain and fear; pleasure, lust and sex; death and decay; a person's loved ones (and in particular threats to them); love of living creatures (baby animals, etc.); but also less obvious things, such as The Best of...!; or a number or series of something (The Five Longest Speeches in Human History, Ten Quick Ways to Overcome Shyness, Fifty Ways to Leave Your Lover, etc.).

Clearly, this is the easiest criterion for making content hotter. It only takes some careful listening during participant interviews and a dash of common sense. Where is the irritation or the pain (for instance during change processes)? What really drives the staff of this organisation? What are people afraid of? The basic sentiments are simple and finite but the number of doors to enter their realm is unlimited.

Content with an Impact on Participants' Lives

Stickiness is largely about unmediated emotions. By an impact on participants' lives we are thinking of content that is hot when it touches people's interests in a broader sense, in relation with the complexity of people's lives in modern society. That contact point may have a literal, physical meaning: what is the place or sphere where the content has an impact. Is it in participants' private lives, in their time at work, or in their leisure time?

It can also relate to a phase participants or their organisations are currently going through. Often, the topicality of issues is a reliable way of making content hot. Reading a couple of newspaper articles or weblogs on the subject matter and asking a couple of probing questions during the participant interviews quickly reveals what is going on in any field. Topicality is like an external gas burner that energises and heats up your content. Which session sounds more attractive to you: a paper on insect life in the suburbs of Dublin? Or one about insect life in your house? Thought so! (Unless you live in Dublin) And if the topic is the sex life of insects in your house, the speaker has added just that cheeky bit of stickiness, as well.

The connection with topical developments is relatively easy to make. Once again, it is a mixture of listening attentively during participant interviews, using one's own knowledge of societal issues and a chunk of common sense. That connection with topical issues need not necessarily come from outside an organisation; it can be internal, too. We distinguish the talk of the day, the talk of the month and the talk of the year. The talk of the day is the sort of thing that attracts people's attention in day-to-day business, for instance a colleague who slipped on a wet floor and ended up doing a somersault. People will laugh about this all day, but not three days in a row. The talk of the month is something like the approval of a major project, or the CEO's marriage. Contracts signed and honeymoon over, and the hotness is gone. The talk of the year could be the impending merger (or... take-over) with this little known former competitor. Such an issue can remain hot for a long time – if the merger talks proceed slowly, easily exceeding a year. And if the merger is managed poorly, several years. Content Analysis should definitely identify what the talk of the year is, and preferably also the talk of the month. The Meeting Designer needs to brief the moderator accordingly. A subtle remark about something topical in his introduction will stoke up the temperature of the content. If the moderator also manages to crack a joke about the talk of the day, that is the icing on the cake. This internal topicality can be obtained most easily from 'archetypical' participants – the sort of people we want the meeting owner to pick out for us.

There is another important way to establish an impact of the content on people's personal circumstances, a very general one, related to human relationships. That is by presenting the content through its meaning for a subgroup with a common interest, a group that is not the participants' default group. For instance, a conference on osteoporosis prevention becomes a lot more interesting if you involve participants in a discussion about what happens when you have to take care of a parent with a broken hip.

Content that Presents an Inner Conflict

The symposium is about the development of medical devices and the soaring costs of health care. The first session is a discussion between a hospital director and a representative of a health insurance company. They exchange arguments about whether to purchase a hugely expensive new MRI-scan machine or a pile of mattresses that prevent decubitus (bed sores caused by lying in the same position for too long). There simply isn't the money for both. The audience can vote for their preferred option. This starting point gives the entire day a very concrete focus.

The choice participants faced was a real one in their world: a potential conflict with two sides that are both realistic but mutually exclusive. Representing the content as a conflict can make it piping hot, as we have concluded from the heated debates that such controlled polarisation generates. Naturally, the two positions must represent a potential and relevant choice for participants or groups of them. Often these conflicts are implicit in what people actually say during participant interviews. Some future participant may comment on a certain development in their organisation: "But of course, in spite of what people on the shop floor say, that is not a viable option," or: "this is broadly felt but unfortunately, the Board will never take it into consideration." Such statements refer to potential conflicts.

Politicians use this technique a lot. They try to find leads in their opponents' speeches so that they can pick a verbal fight and thus gain more attention for their own positions. Some are very skilful at this and get more airtime than others. Drawing attention to their views is exactly what they want.

Of course, we are not talking about a conflict in terms of a quarrel or a fight between individuals, but in a more moral and theatrical sense. Like MacBeth, who is driven by the conflict between his desire for power at any cost and his conscience urging him to take moral responsibility for his acts. The more the conflict presented to the participants is one they really might need to face in their lives, the hotter the content will be for them. Furthermore, the more the conflict involves the two sides of an issue about which people are likely to have strong moral opinions, once again the temperature level of the content will soar.

Naturally, content that is hot because it harbours a conflict will produce emotions. That is exactly the point! However, these emotions are a lot different from the ones spawned by stickiness. They relate on the one hand to participants' concerns (what keeps them awake at night?) and at the same time to higher order human thinking processes on ethics and values, on dilemmas and paradoxes. The ensuing debates tend to centre around value-related positions, such as good and bad, moral or immoral, fair and unfair, healthy or unhealthy, clean and dirty, etc.

Meetings that Arouse...

This header is not finished. As a reader, your mind itches to know what comes after the dots, doesn't it?

The fourth way to make content hot is by arousing people's curiosity. People always want to know how something that has started continues and ends. This implies finding the unfinished story in the content. Storytelling is an age-old human activity and stories come in many forms: a search for something (archetypically: the Odyssey), a whodunit, a love story, a court case, etc. We all know the power of stories and how much easier they are to remember than unconnected facts. Try this one: which number sequence is easier to remember: eight-thirteen, or nine-eleven? Say the numbers out loud. Unfair competition, right? Mnemonics (also aide-mémoires) are based on a similar process. For most of us it is a lot easier to sigh "Now I need a drink, alcoholic of course, after the heavy lectures involving quantum mechanics" than to remember the first fifteen digits of the infinite number Pi (π). The number of letters in each word of the sentence corresponds to one digit.

Stories proper are of course richer than these simple crutches for the memory which we just use to illustrate the point. Stories give access to people's full emotional background. Triggers with arousal value include the sequence of the plot, the attraction of the characters, the connection between their adventures and the day-to-day value of the content for participants. Here we find an easy connection with the previous section on content that harbours a conflict. Clearly, the design options multiply when thinking about the opportunities offered by the idea that meetings are a stage (Chapter 1.2): the theatre is already there, you just need to find the bit of human drama in the meeting content to have content that touches participants.

In rare cases, the storyteller himself can have a 'hotness' value. You just know that some minds will bring a special slant to any bit of content, just because of who they are. A conference about the future of the compression stocking is not very likely to attract large numbers of attendees. But if the next chapter of the story is told by Stephen Hawking (presentation title: "The Future of the Compression Stocking in the Universe"), you suddenly have hot stockings on your hand and an auditorium that cannot hold the crowd! The risk to be managed by the Meeting Designer is that the "hot" storyteller may not bring the sort of angle to the content that fits with the overall programme – much like the contributions of many motivational speakers in our experience.

The Hotness Matrix

In the introduction, we distinguished the six reasons for having meetings. A helpful approach to establish how attractive meeting content is, is to score that content in a matrix made up of these six reasons and the four sources of hotness we have just discussed. This would yield the following table:

	Sticky	Personal Impact	Conflict	Curiosity
Learning				
Networking				
Motivation				
Decision-making				
Alignment				
Rituals				

So how does this matrix work? Each box at the crossroads between a reason and a hotness source can be checked off with symbols, for instance:
- ♪: we have covered this;
- -: we have not analysed our content on this;
- 0: we do not want this in our content;
- blank: this is not relevant.

It is impossible to tick all boxes with a ♪, but in principle: the more boxes ticked, the better. However, one has to be wary as the desirability of ticking certain boxes may depend on the specific objectives of a meeting. In association meetings, for instance, alignment is often an important reason for having the meeting, which excludes the option of having content with an inherent conflict. So that box should have a "0" unless, of course, that conflict is resolved during the meeting, leading to even more alignment! If, on the other hand, decision-making is an important reason for having the meeting, the potential conflict is already there. It then becomes important to establish how to design the decision-making process in such a way that alignment is guaranteed at the same time.

For meetings with an important networking component, it is possible to invite somebody sticky (Bill Clinton, Madonna, a lion) so that there will be a lot to talk about. A strong impulse from the impact on personal circumstances can give rise to very active networking – you get the idea.

Some boxes are obligatory. For a scientific congress the box Learning/Curiosity has to have a ♪ – and generally this is the case. On the other hand, there is a lot to be gained during scientific meetings in the boxes learning/stickiness and learning/personal impact. Also, the ritual part of these meetings tends to be carefully segregated from the content.

Green Areas Revisited

Remember our original example from the start of this chapter? The meeting about 'Green Areas in municipalities?' Clearly, the first of our interviews shouted in our face that the content choice of the meeting owner (in this case the Association's Conference Department) had not done a reliable analysis of the hotness of this content for their members.

We also had a stroke of luck, though: since the very first participant interview produced that insight, we still had the remaining five interviews to figure out what angle on 'Green Areas' would interest municipal administrators.

The other interviews confirmed that, for the average municipality, green areas such as parks are boring. You just need to maintain them: send in the gardeners, the sweepers and every now and then the police and that is all there is to it.

But at one point, one of the interviewees started talking animatedly about a green belt in his town that was subject to building plans. The citizens in the adjoining neighbourhood were worried and had started a NIMBY committee, the project developer was worried by the hostility of the NIMBY committee, and the town council was worried that the contractors might pull out of the deal. There was talk of this but the town needed the funds from the sale of the soil. These funds had been earmarked to pay for a whole range of amenities, including a much needed sports centre. Here we had a green belt everybody was worried about and that caused heated debate. Why?

Because somebody wanted to build on it! So that was the angle we needed to make 'Green Areas' interesting: 'Green Areas' became 'hot' if they met, or – even better – had to fight with 'Red Areas,' i.e. buildings, bricks! Here was the stickiness ("Who is going to disturb the neighbourhood?"), here was the personal impact ("Who is going to spoil my nice view?"), here was the conflict ("powerful project developer pitted against poor city folk"), here was the storyline ("who will win?").

And so, prior to the meeting, all participants could visit an area of 1 m2 somewhere near the conference centre and quote a price for that area if the town council would allow building there. The government minister responsible for land planning and use commented on the figures at the end of his speech. The conference started with two sumo wrestlers, trying to push each other off a tiny plot of land, one wearing a green pair of shorts, the other a red one...

Of course, we are neither land zoning planners, nor municipal administrators, but as Meeting Designers we helped the meeting owner to establish the connection between his participants and the content of the conference. As a consequence, we were able to develop a number of programme features inspired by this angle on the content.

Does the Above Apply Anywhere?

This prompts the question: Can you design a programme for any topic on Earth, say rocket science, even if you are not a rocket scientist yourself? Experience has shown us that our approach to Content Analysis, as described here, can go a long way to achieving that goal. We have applied it to such diverse topics as nanotechnology, education in the tourist industry, pet foods and accessories, and urology. And a myriad of other topics. In every case it proved possible to develop content with a serious edge, holding participants' attention from start to finish. We found that some participants-to-be were always able to tell us in a couple of sentences something that provided us with a hook to which we could fix the four criteria of hotness. From there on, it was possible to develop the content into material that deserved to occupy centre stage and stay there throughout the meeting.

Sceptic:

We have a chat with Michelle, from the UK. Michelle studies political science.

M: This last statement about rocket science, of course, has an inner conflict of itself. I often find that politicians make statements about things they know very little about. I understand they sometimes need to, but as a result people with expert knowledge will not consider them as partners in serious discussion. In science, for instance, but also in business. Does that happen to you?

M/E: That may happen, especially if you haven't explained your position and your counterpart has no clear idea about your professional role in the process of putting together a good meeting programme.

M: Well, explaining is one thing, but another is the need for people on the other side to acknowledge the value of what you say and its relevance.

M/E: Sometimes that requires a bit of manoeuvring.

M: Ooh, that sounds like politics...!

M/E: And often it is! Having our profession officially recognised would help.

M: Do you think that's good enough? Wherever you come from or whatever you're called officially, you'll never be a rocket scientist. One of them.

M/E: But that is exactly the point: acknowledging that and at the same time being able to position ourselves on a different plane. That it is our task as Meeting Designers, to stuff the wonders of rocket science right under the noses of meeting participants. And the very fact that we are outsiders puts us in a better position to do that. We can approach the content and the participants with a fresh look.

M: But all those guys in the auditorium are rocket scientists, as well. So that is not going to help you a great deal. They will probably object: "How can you know what moves us rocket men?"

M/E: Rockets, of course! No – but to some extent you are right, of course. People do not always see the added value of an outsider's perspective on their world. Sometimes we use the argument: "Isn't it worthwhile to make a small investment in a couple of interviews to increase the chances of having conference content that hits the bull's eye?"

M: And that argument, of course, squashes their resistance...

M/E: It often does, but not always. What would you expect? Sometimes they have their own reasons for wanting just that specific content. We often see that in public organisations, for example.

M: Because they have less leeway? What with democratically established plans, and what with approved implementation agendas?

M/E: Exactly.

M: So, as a Meeting Designer, are you a bit into politics?

M/E: Sometimes we have to be. What we prefer, though, is to explain why and especially how we do these interviews. Sometimes a convincing argument is the fact that, being outsiders, we can ask questions no one else thinks of or is allowed to.

M: Such as?

M/E: What makes rocket science sexy? Who is considered the biggest idiot in the field? What keeps rocket scientists awake at night? How do rockets figure in their dreams?

M: And do you get serious answers to those questions?

M/E: We always stress that the interviews are confidential. In our briefings and designs, the outcomes are collated anonymously. You'd be surprised at what people are willing to tell you if you just listen to them with sincere interest. In many cases that is quite a novelty for them…

M: Mmh, I might try that when I need to do the interviews for my thesis in a couple of months' time.

M/E: Have fun!

M: Thanks, and I'm sure I will. But before we move on: who is the greatest idiot in Rocket Science…?

Part 3

3.0 The Design

Part 1 of this book has given you an overview of how meetings work, what makes them unique as a means of communication; Part 2 has established what they are for, what their purpose is. Our discussion of these topics has taken place with our feet in the mud if you will. All our insights are based on our experience as practitioners, which has spawned countless examples of meetings we have attended, designed and conducted.

A major part of the content is still missing, though, and that is the design itself. We hope by now your idea of what constitutes a meeting design is no longer clouded in an impenetrable mist, but still, what is it exactly? How do you make a design? How do you work all the input gained through the techniques described in Part 2 into a programme which will light up a broad smile on the meeting owner's face and a twinkle in his eyes? What, in practical terms, will be the impact of your design on the way you need to manage all those typical meeting amenities such as the venue, technical equipment, facilitation, speakers (although we will take a broader view of their role during meetings) and the outcomes? All of these topics – and a little more – make up Part 3.

To get going, here is our definition of a meeting design:

The design of a meeting is a description of what participant X does with content Y at any point of time Z during the meeting.

In a slightly less condensed form this means that the design of a meeting programme establishes what everybody in the meeting is supposed to be doing at all or any time while it is going on. And since meetings are always about content, participants need to know what they should be doing in relation to that content. On the face of it, that seems a relatively straightforward task. However, meetings are about steering human behaviour. During the meeting you want participants to display the behaviours that will create the value the meeting owner is hoping to obtain, as mentioned in Chapter 2.0.

It is difficult enough to influence the behaviour of one individual, let alone that of whole groups who may have different interests, backgrounds and expectations. This is the very reason why Meeting Design is so useful. All the know-how we have set out in Parts 1 and 2 is needed in order to achieve this. Part 3 introduces you to the method that produces the programme description which will guide the participants through the meeting. We must provide a word of caution: although a programme is generated step-by-step (and in a book the only choice we have is to present it that way), the process

does not necessarily, or even generally, follow a simple linear sequence. The stages are actually much like the steps of a dance – a tango or a salsa for instance. The dancers can choose from a wide range of possible variations that result in a cohesive whole with a logic of its own. Even if you know the basic rhythm, the number of variations is at the same time limited but still unpredictable.

Continuing this metaphor of a dance, who will be the Meeting Designer's dancing partner? There are several options. One is the meeting owner, another could be the participant. But also the content is part of the dance, as are the desired outcomes. All of these need to find themselves incorporated in the final design.

And finally, we like the dance metaphor for another reason. It depicts the design process rightly as it is: a mixture of intellectual analysis, artistic boldness and common sense.

3.1 Meeting Designs: Do We Need Them?

A Good Conversation

he CEO of a multinational company involved in an international project feels the need for a "good conversation" because the venture seems to have run aground. To get it going again, he would like two of his colleagues and an external partner to have an in-depth exchange – no frills, no facilitator, just a fine talk that will take their thinking a significant step forwards.

Suppose this CEO asked for your help in setting up his "meeting". What would you do? What is the first thing that comes to your mind? Would you start with the setting? Place three low, comfortable armchairs in a quiet room? How would you like the lighting to be? A room full of invigorating daylight that conceals nothing? Or a warm top light hanging over the table, encouraging the three men to stick their heads together as if they were arch conspirators? Would you provide coffee, water or some other kind of drink? Ambient music, silence or birdsong?

Or would this not be the direction your thoughts first took you, and would you rather want to know why the CEO wants this conversation to take place anyway? Perhaps know more about the participants – their nationalities for instance? Or get a full understanding of the topic they need to address? Or would you refuse an assignment like this because you felt the whole thing was misconceived from the very start? Misconceived because it was based on the assumption that it is possible to steer such a personal process as a conversation between three people.

A Fundamental Question

Part 3 of this book treats the process of designing meeting programmes. This could be programmes with three people, such as in the example above, or with hundreds or even thousands of participants. However, before discussing the design process, we need to stop and address the doubt raised in the last part of the previous section. We need to ask ourselves the fundamental question: is it possible to influence the core of human interactions during meetings by means of a designed programme? In other words: does meeting design make sense, or is it a mission impossible?

The question here is not whether it is possible to come up with some neat fun activities for meeting participants. That question is a no-brainer. Of course anybody can figure out that is advisable to put important topics at the beginning of in the agenda, as books on effective business meetings recommend. And of course anyone can think of a good ice-breaker at the start of the meeting to energise participants. Chairpersons, secretaries with clout and professional communication advisors provide these suggestions routinely. The question we are raising goes beyond these more or less cosmetic interventions: "Is it possible to influence the dynamics and outcomes of meetings through Meeting Design?"

If the answer to this question is no, then that is the end of this book. Then the only thing that people can do with meetings is organise them, look after the logistics and the budget, collect a good set of speakers and that is all there is to it.

It will not surprise you that we are of a different opinion. The reason why we nevertheless feel we need to address this question is that for many people, our answer is not that obvious at all. And so we need to substantiate our position. In fact we can see a couple of weighty arguments against our proposition. In the example of the three men, is it not simply their personal responsibility to turn their meeting into a "good conversation?" Is it not true that their characters, emotional intelligence, mood of the day and a number of coincidences determine how "good" their conversation will turn out to be? And above all, isn't the conversation the result of the immediate interaction between the thoughts and words of the three men, something which by definition cannot be anticipated or influenced? Nobody can know beforehand what any one of them will say exactly and what response that will prompt from the others. As long as you cannot predict these reactions, the argument runs, the idea of designing the meeting programme does not make sense. We can compare the dynamics with chemical engineering: applied chemistry exists by virtue of the fact that you can predict how chemical substances will behave when mixed with others. No predictable chemical reactions, no chemical industry.

This would apply to meetings if thoughts and words were their sole ingredients. The truth is they are not. The examples in the chapters of Part 1 of this book demonstrate that in meetings more is going on than words and ideas coming together. There is a wealth of human interaction which is independent of content; there are the involuntary physical reactions of participants; there is the regulating impact of culture; there are the reactions to meeting conventions; there is the meaning derived implicitly from order and sequence; there are the changed perceptions of people who experience magic.

All of these factors are part of the chemistry of a meeting. They can radically alter the meaning of content, as we have seen in chapters 1.6 and 2.3. The characteristics of meetings as a means of communication (analysed in Part 1) supply an impressive choice of instruments that may determine the course of any meeting. These instruments do allow the Meeting Designer to influence the essential content-related quality and outcomes of meetings.

At the same time, it is fair to say that the exact conduct of the conversation remains elusive – which is one of the attractions of meetings: they have this shifting balance between predictability and unpredictability. It is a bit like ocean sailing: the skipper cannot do anything about the direction and force of the wind, currents and waves, but what he can control is the ship's course and waypoints, the position and the trimming of the sails and the team spirit of his crew. The choices he makes there allow him to steer the boat more or less successfully to its destination. The same applies to the work of the Meeting Designer. The moods and characters of his participants and content providers, accidental circumstances (a snowstorm, a public transport strike) and such factors are not in his hands. Nevertheless, as we will show in the next chapters, the Meeting Designer does have control over an exciting range of methods to steer the meeting's dynamics. Applying those methods is the work of the Meeting Designer.

Proof?

In parts 1 and 2 we have given many examples of design solutions. Do these examples provide clues about the effectiveness of Meeting Design methods and instruments? In other words, can we prove that a well-designed programme does actually influence the content-related dynamics of any meeting? Or is it just chance and wishful thinking?

We are afraid that strictly speaking we cannot. With isolated examples it is almost impossible to show with scientific, statistical validity that a meeting would have produced different dynamics and different results had there not been a carefully designed programme. But every now and then, a streak of luck produces a glimpse of proof of the influence of designs on meeting outcomes.

We designed and moderated four meetings commissioned by an association of directors in a certain industry about its new policy. These meetings between the association's board and small groups of members were extremely short – one hour each – so there was a detailed script, with precise indications for the moderator's introduction, followed by a format to find out whether participants saw any merit in the proposed policy outline. Three out of the four meetings were downhill skiing for the board: participants were positive and cooperative and the atmosphere was light and conducive to good results. The fourth seemed to drag along with the handbrake on. The people there were more distant, behaving right away as the representatives of members whose interests conflicted with those of the board and who were sceptical about the proposals. The meeting room seemed to have become immune to fun and humour.

The circumstances of the meetings differed in just one respect. Three were held around a couple of square tables that had been joined together and covered with a table cloth – much like a dinner table, with participants seated for a family meal. For the fourth meeting, it was impossible to replicate this setting because the meeting room had a fixed table and seating: a large, wooden, oval design table that was open in the middle. Each participant had his own seat, with a microphone and a set of controls and there was a clearly designated position for the chair.

Guess which setting produced the high-viscosity meeting? At the very least, this example strongly hints that certain features other than the mental state of participants may have far-reaching consequences for content and outcomes.

A similar example is the one in Chapter 1.6 about safety on oilrigs. The outcome of that meeting was an alliance between (often competing) contractors, involving the voluntary exchange of employee safety measures. Would that alliance have taken shape without the horror story of the Norwegian operator who had fallen victim to a gruesome accident? Inviting him and putting him at the start of the programme was a conscious design decision. It contributed to an unprecedented level of commitment of participants in the course of the day. That commitment materialised in the alliance. Coincidence? In this case, too, there appears to be a relationship between a specific feature of the programme and essential content-related dynamics and outcomes of the meeting.

Let's quote one of our favourite examples: the meeting of the Association of Municipalities, mentioned in Chapter 2.1 and again in 2.3. In previous years, the congress had lost a lot of its appeal to members and part of our remit was to rekindle participant involvement. It became an electrifying meeting, full of vigorous debate about powerful opinions. We witnessed a revival, a rebirth even, and the congress regained its role in the association as a moment for decision-making and alignment. It is impossible to demonstrate conclusively that this was caused by the careful design of that edition, but once more there are strong indications of a relationship between design on the one hand and meeting dynamics and outcomes on the other.

One of the best stories is the one of the merger between the two banks in Chapter 2.1. Here, the bank director literally told us a couple of years later that the meetings flanking the merger process had avoided all the usual troubles he had experienced in previous mergers.

Admittedly, all these examples do not provide irrefutable scientific evidence. To obtain that would require a rigorous study with a number of meetings attended by matching samples of participants, going through two different formats: one traditional (the control group) and one with a tailor-made design. Such a series of meetings would need a number of measurable outcomes along the lines presented in Chapter 2.2, which could then be compared. A noble task for a Meeting Lab or Meeting Research Institute we will advocate at the end of this book.

However, having designed a myriad of meetings in the course of over 15 years, ranging from small-group conversations to conferences with thousands of people, from fun-focused get-togethers to conventions about organisational survival, we feel that often it is enough to look at the results with a bit of common sense to recognise that well-designed programmes produce better meetings.

Good. Having said all of that, we can now move on to the actual design process.

Sceptic:

Our conversation partner is Jack Collins, a 53-year-old veteran meeting planner with a large insurance company in Ohio. Jack is responsible for all the meetings his company does.

J: Brilliant, guys, that definition of a meeting design! Knowing what each participant does at a given point in time. Would never have thought of that myself.

M/E: Well, sometimes you need to say the obvious to move ahead.

J: Move ahead, going where? This meeting design stuff is a typically European idea. All a lot of boloney in my opinion! Talk, talk, talk.

M/E: So how have you been handling all those hundreds of meetings you have planned in the past – what it is? – 25 years?

J: 28, to be precise. Of course, me and my team, we know what is going on in our organisation. You pick up the signals in the corridors, at the water cooler, listen to the top guys for the big picture and then use your common sense to get an effective programme.

M/E: And never any surprises? Either for you or for the participants?

J: Are you telling me that my meetings for the past 28 years have been crap?

M/E: Never! You work things out far too professionally for us to say that! What we're saying is that, like in all industries and professions, things develop.

J: Another observation of mind-boggling intelligence! Of course we read about new architecture in meeting venues, technological innovations, new systems and so on.

M/E: Come on Jack, give us a break – give us a chance to explain!

J: OK, spill the beans.

M/E: In fact, we acknowledge everything that has been achieved so far by the professionals in the meeting industry. Many organisations recognise the importance of meetings in their communication mix and meetings are organised with great expertise. And so, now the world of meetings is ready for the next step.

J: And what is the next step, according to you guys?

M/E: Well, let's repeat the question we just asked. Never had any surprises during your meetings? That things that went somewhere else than you had anticipated?

J: Well, I guess sometimes, yeah.

M/E: A recent example?

J: About six months ago, we had a two-day meeting of sales reps. The original idea was to have them exchange best practices about their sales strategies of the product portfolio on day one. For day two we had invited a couple of Berkeley people to discuss the sales-purchase process for insurance. They had done specific research on this for our products.

M/E: And what happened?

J: Halfway through the exercises on day one, this guy from Wisconsin takes the floor and starts doing a good bit of policy bashing. I mean, his point, you know, was that the whole work plan was useless because since the financial crisis, customers had started responding in a totally different way to what we were offering. He did a quick straw vote before we could stop him and about 80% of his colleagues agreed with him... We hadn't seen that coming.

M/E: You didn't find that funny, did you?

J: No, not at all. The VP for sales' idea was to counter things by changing the plan for the meeting and cancelling the panel. Instead, we quickly brought over a couple of guys from HQ for day two, to work on new products. Cost us $ 5,500 just in air tickets. Without even mentioning the cancellation for the Berkeley professor and his crew.

M/E: Great solution! Quick on your feet and adapting to the new situation in accordance with the need that emerged.

J: Yeah, we managed to pull off the second day pretty well, arranging all the changes in everybody's schedule.

M/E: We don't want to rub in the message, but did you do any pre-meeting interviews with the future participants?

J: No, as I said, we normally pick up the signs at the water cooler.

M/E: We feel many people who now work as meeting planners could well make good meeting designers. For that they would probably just need to add some notions and techniques that have emerged in the industry in recent years. We're not preaching revolution (although sometimes people make us feel like that); we want to give the industry some stuff to chew on, allowing meeting professionals to develop meetings into an even more effective means of communication.

J: You say, huh.

M/E: Some of those things are predictable and rational and some aren't, because meeting design is about people's behaviour and that is not always rational.

J: I was a bit irrational.

3.2 Designing Meeting Programmes

The Design Process

his chapter is hopefully like a Christmas gift for a 5-year-old: waiting forever for it to arrive and fearing that it never would. When are they, the authors, finally going to explain how Meeting Design actually works? About what they do when designing? Well, that is what we're going to talk about, at last, in the next pages.

To discuss the design process in a useful way, we prefer to start with an example. The "good conversation" we introduced in the previous chapter is a conveniently simple and controllable design request, so we shall use that. We'd better do it in some detail so as to make the various stages in the design process quite clear.

For the sake of argument, let's assume that the conversation mentioned in Chapter 3.1 is initiated by Stewart Hinks, CEO of the Acme Corporation. He wants a person from a partner organisation called Leon to meet two senior Acme managers, Stephen and William, and he wants them to talk together about a joint project in Hong Kong in order to get it unstuck. The project is evidently important for Stewart and for Acme. Details needed to make the design will be provided as we plough through the case and draft the basic elements of a programme.

We shall allow ourselves the freedom to come up with design solutions, without significant budgetary restrictions or 'social boobytraps' (see Chapter 2.1). We shall add or invent circumstances that one might realistically expect to occur when dealing with a request of this type; and we shall limit ourselves to a design in which the three characters conduct the conversation without a facilitator.

Where to Start?

A logical first idea would be that a good conversation requires a suitable environment. So we could start by imagining the setting: three comfortable chairs in welcoming surroundings: a wooden cocktail table, low lights and some decorations on the walls, perhaps a fireplace, a couple of book cases and a dog, a golden retriever, asleep. In the mind's eye of the Designer an image is conjured up of three gentlemen, perhaps British aristocrats, conversing about the latest political developments or price swings in raw materials for manufacturing industry. This image is well-anchored in Western collective memory and seems to fit the idea of a good conversation. The question is, is that the image the meeting owner has in mind? Because here is another solution that could work equally well. The Designer could place three bar stools around a high table so as to obtain a more active attitude, with notepads replacing glasses of vintage claret, a plasma screen sunk into the table showing graphs and tables, and so on. This looks more like a top-drawer intensive working conversation, with rolled-up shirt sleeves and regular breaks for coffee from a machine. Hmm, that looks attractive, too; it might be the right answer to the meeting owner's initial request.

So now, we have at least two viable options. But the list is almost inexhaustible. How about a long walk in the woods, with the good conversation happening while the three sit on a wooden bench overlooking a quiet lake? Or staring into a campfire together on a warm beach, late in the evening? Two parents sitting with their son at the kitchen table, meticulously going over his school grades? The good conversation a bishop might have with two priests in the safe intimacy of his sacristy, surrounded by art treasures, because they are both suffering from doubts about their religious vocation? The diabetes specialist and the dietician grilling an obese patient about his lifestyle? You can see that a myriad possible images readily pop into the Designer's mind as a first vision of how the 'good conversation' could be styled.

How should the Meeting Designer choose from all these possibilities? Is it a matter of pure analysis or does it involve creativity? Is there only one possible solution or are there several? What information does the Designer use to make the right choices? And what is that magical moment in which the right idea does take shape and he knows what participants are supposed to do and experience?

What Does a Design Look Like?

In line with the definition of Meeting Design given in 3.0, the programme description needs to take a distinct form. At its most informal it could be a sketch on the back of a beer coaster; the other extreme is a script containing verbatim texts for every second of the meeting. In general, the purpose of the design process is to obtain an understanding of what is going to happen during the meeting at what point in time. This understanding can be an overall description, a story line or a timetable. The commonest form is a script containing details about presentations and supporting media, such as music, images and staging. In this chapter we will describe how such a script comes into being, using our example of the good conversation.

Starting with the Meeting Owner

So now let's return to the start, and the start is never to think immediately of things like tables, chairs, lights and catering. These are design details that propose themselves naturally from a comprehensive, coherent and fruitful idea about the meeting at a more fundamental level.

It all starts with developing the meeting backbone that emerges from the desires of the meeting owner. In this case, Stewart's desire is to have a good conversation. This means he needs to tell us two things: what does he understand by a conversation and what makes it good, in his opinion. It goes without saying that both views are totally subjective: there is no such thing as a universal notion of 'a good conversation.' It is all in the perception of the meeting owner who may have thousands of reasons for wanting things a certain way, fed by thousands of previous experiences and thousands of mental images produced by those experiences. As far as the design is concerned, that subjectivity is fine, because we do not want just any good conversation. We want to design exactly the conversation the meeting owner wishes to have.

As a first step in the design process, the task of the Meeting Designer is to make that subjectivity transparent. In Chapter 2.2, we have already introduced the two main tools that will create this clarity: Content Flow and Experience Concept.

Content Flow and Experience Concept in Practice

Suppose the Content Flow drawing the meeting owner makes looks like this:

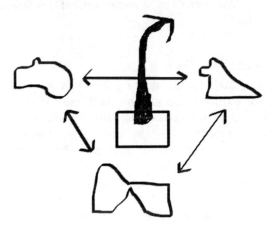

We see three blobs, connected by bi-directional arrows. From a square in the middle, a thick arrow rises up towards the outside; and here our 'fictitious' example becomes almost factual, because this content flow drawing is very similar to one we actually once obtained.

According to the meeting owner who drew it, that drawing meant that all three participants would contribute their own ideas to the conversation, and in the course of a discussion arrive at a common viewpoint – represented by the square in the middle. That viewpoint should lead in an unexpected direction, and that explains the big arrow with its abrupt turning. The direction of the arrow is the direct consequence of the good conversation and the frank exchange of views between the three participants.

This explanation of the drawing already provides a pretty neat image of what the meeting owner considers a good conversation and what he does not. For instance, the idea is not for the conversation to give one of the three people a special position. Excellent, that means we can skip the image of the bishop faced with the two Doubting Thomas's, and also the confrontation between the parents and their son at the kitchen table. Neither of these situations produces a shared new insight that goes into the outside world. The wavering believers and the underperforming son are just expected to listen and then draw their own conclusions. Neither the bishop nor the parents have any intention of departing from their initial fixed positions. So that type of situation is not what the meeting owner is looking for. The meeting's final conclusion needs to be something all three have contributed to and hence agree about.

The drawing has another interesting feature: no content is introduced from any external source. The three participants to the conversation arrive with their three blobs of content, and that's it. That content is modelled into the square in the centre. So there will be no contribution from outsiders (e.g. guest speakers). The three partners in the dialogue will come along with all the necessary information in their heads.

Let's suppose we have also pinned down the Experience Concept, thanks to the methodology described in Chapter 2.2. After some prodding, the meeting owner has listed a set of verbs and worked them into a recognisable meeting experience. In this case, the outcome is an informal chat after a good dinner. The conversation takes place in a gentlemen's study in the same premises where the three had the meal. The room does not belong to any of the three participants; they are guests there.

As already underlined in Chapter 2.2, the idea is not to copy or simulate the situation described in the Experience Concept. That would mean we confuse the means with the goal and it would turn the meeting into a kind of little stage play, which is embarrassing. The point is that the design should capture the emotional value of the EC. It is how the meeting owner wants the participants to feel during their chat. In this case, a feeling of being well-fed and completely at ease as they process the content in accordance with the Content Flow.

Having obtained this input from the meeting owner, the Meeting Designer rolls up his sleeves and rolls out the design process.

The Timeline in the Experience Concept

The EC indicates that the participants are relatively important people, who withdraw after a having dinner together. We discern immediately that such an after dinner talk has a specific timeline. By defining the EC, the meeting owner implicitly also expresses his views on the meeting's desired timeline. A meeting owner who had in mind a joint brainstorming session lasting two days would never have come up with the EC of an after-dinner talk. What we are looking at is a conversation in a stately room of a substantial house and such a meeting never lasts less than 25 minutes and never more than two hours. It is our experience that by intuitively defining the EC, the meeting owner has in mind the corresponding duration and a number of events on the timeline.

The events taking place in that time frame might be something like this:
- preparatory stage: a fine dinner with a somewhat larger company;
- end of dinner: host (for instance the home owner) invites the three participants to withdraw to his study, leaving the other dinner guests to amuse themselves. From then on, no other people are present;
- host briefly shows off his collection of curiosities, for instance paintings, books or musical instruments;
- a professional waiter, with deference, serves a digestive;
- the host leaves and one of the three men launches the topic of the conversation, motivating it with a short personal anecdote, a meaningful passage from a book or a picture or painting;
- the conversation develops, interrupted just once by the quiet waiter who offers some further refreshment;
- after about 75-90 minutes, the waiter announces that transportation will be arriving in a couple of minutes or another cue signalling that time is up. This is an invitation to formulate the joint conclusion;
- the three participants leave in a quiet, friendly atmosphere.

The working method based on this timeline description involves an investigation into how elements from the Experience Concept relate to the desired Content Flow and how they can be put at its service. A simple way of conducting this search is by describing the connections in a table. In the left-hand column, we note Experience Concept characteristics; on the right you will find the corresponding meaning of these for the Content Flow. At this stage, the choice of ideas that goes into the columns is still relatively broad; the Meeting Designer imposes few restrictions on things that might enrich the design, such as the possibility to allow the other dinner guests to offer extra content. Formally, this would fall outside the CF but it may prove a valuable addition to the design, so it does not fly out of the window right away.

EC, translated into activities on a timeline	CF, impact of activities on content
Meal with other dinner guests, followed by withdrawal to study.	Ensures a relaxed beginning, followed by a feeling of exclusivity at the moment of withdrawal, which helps to focus on the content. At the same time the meal can be used to add input from outside, without Interrupting the good conversation itself (see MO briefing).
Enter the appropriate space, a room with its own 'presence'.	This is a place where people address the core of issues – no fooling around. This corresponds with the three clearly outlined blobs that represent the content each participant brings along. They are expected to go to the core of the issue together.
Together examine and discuss art treasures.	Appreciating fine art has an inherently cathartic effect. This will carry over into the depth with which the exchange about the content will take place, as represented by the three bi-directional arrows.
Conversing for about 75-90 minutes.	Provides indications on the conversation dynamics and the breadth of the discussion. There is no time for a 30-minute introduction by one of the participants, nor for taking the content into non-productive realms. Time is a constraint.
Structure is provided only by the duration of the conversation itself and by the moments at which the waiter enters.	There is no agenda with a sequence of topics; the focus is on the one issue and on the conversation partners listening to each other carefully.

Seating is not facing each other, but centred on an element in the room, for instance a fireplace.	With three chairs facing a fireplace, there is no natural position for a chairperson. This is an important inference from the CF drawing. It is a delicate point, calling for careful direction, because even a small misalignment of the seats could create a feeling that one position differs from the other two, giving the person sitting in that chair a position of primus inter pares. The angles between the chairs should be exactly the same. Even better would be a small round table with three chairs.
The conversation is exclusive; you cannot have children in there, nor wives, archaic as this may seem.	The CF excludes any content from a fourth contributor, so the three people enter the study and then the door remains closed. This results in an inescapable focus on the participants' own content, as per the CF drawing.
There is as little disturbance as possible.	No external presentations, no external chair, just the catalytic presence of the host at the start and perhaps a clock ticking and producing a noise after 75 or 90 minutes.
There is no need for modern AV facilities. At the utmost, someone may show a meaningful picture from a book or read a section or paragraph.	The Meeting Designer can make this explicit during his briefing with the participants. He will ask them to condense their contribution into its very essence, and invite them to look for a passage from a book, or a relevant illustration expressing that core.

The three conversation partners have total autonomy over how to conduct their conversation. However, there is a host who takes care of them and who tells them when it is time to leave the room.	The Meeting Designer can choose the host, thus creating an opportunity to steer the process. The CF shows that this role may not include a contribution of content. At the same time, the EC calls for an owner of the premises. CF and EC need to be reconciled here.

You may think that up to his point, the Meeting Designer has not yet done a great deal of creative design work and you are right. This first stage is essentially an exploration of the relationship, the resonance, between the EC and the CF. It produces a set of issues and images that need to be further elaborated in order to make this particular conversation into the 'good conversation' the meeting owner is looking for. This first semi-finished product is the backbone for the programme, or – with a similar metaphor – a skeleton programme.

In addition to immediate design solutions, the analysis also produces possible weak spots that require extra attention. In this 'good conversation' the autonomy of the participants is such a point of attention. The Meeting Designer has little opportunity to steer the conversation once it has started. This is Stewart's desire and it is necessary to have the participants' full commitment. However, as we will see, there are opportunities to provide steering in an indirect way.

At a later stage we will also check how the design solutions score in a hypothetical test of the inevitable characteristics of meetings as a means of communication discussed in Parts 1 and 2 of this book. For instance, does the design lead to a programme with activities that are acceptable by the standards of the national cultures of the participating individuals? Is the design in line with the organisation's culture? Possible frictions tend to emerge naturally during the design process, on the basis of past experience. In any case, if we do expect frictions in these respects, we look for the 'Third Way' as described in Chapter 1.4. Before we can do so, though, we need to flesh out the skeleton programme in a bit more detail.

Fleshing out the Programme

The logic of the timeline, suggested by the EC, and the connection with the CF as outlined above, actually gives us the blueprint of a script, which is another way of calling the skeleton programme at this stage. The script specifies the order and the rough duration of each of the programme items: an hour for dinner, moving over to the study, accompanied by the host, talking for

5-10 minutes about art, bringing in coffee or other refreshment, broaching conversation topic (5 minutes), part one of conversation (35 minutes), bringing in second round of refreshments, interval of 5 minutes, second part of conversation (30 minutes), waiter announcing that conversation must draw to a conclusion (5 minutes to go) and host inviting participants to join rest of the group again or to leave.

Now is the time we turn our attention to the study (the room where the conversation will take place). It needs to have the right 'feel.' It should contain the art objects for the brief introduction of the first couple of minutes, the atmosphere has to be 'intimate,' with a central focal point, such as a fireplace, the lighting will be soft and diffuse, external noise will be kept to a minimum. In the same building there has to be a room for a dinner with a limited number of people who know the three participants.

All of this is pretty straightforward, but there are two points of concern. One is the role of the owner of the premises. Our design includes this fourth person on purpose; the three men must not meet at the home of one of the participants. That would give that person a dominant status in the conversation that the other two could never overcome.

The Briefing

There is a second, more important concern. Leon, Stephen and William are autonomous, but as a result, once the conversation starts there is nothing to steer them in the right direction. (There is of course the brief entry of the waiter, but that won't be much help.) The only option is for the participants to be briefed very carefully, each individually, in writing as well as verbally before the meeting. The briefing will specify the reason for the meeting and why the three of them have been invited. It will establish that, while each is entirely responsible for what he says, they need to remember they have a shared interest in the outcome. It will also allow for the preparation of moments that can take place during the meeting, slipped in by the Meeting Designer. In our example, such moments are the reference to the personal anecdote, picture or the passage from a book the participants are asked to bring along. This helps to make the meeting as self-steering as possible.

The written briefing has to come directly from the CEO of the Acme Corporation, Stewart Hinks as you will recall. It is a personal message, and the best choice is sending a letter on unmistakably expensive paper, with Stewart's letterhead, written from a personal perspective and signed by hand. An e-mail is possible, but it would need to be followed up by a phone call, adding weight to this more impersonal means of communication. The text could read as follows:

Dear Leon,

On behalf of Acme, it is my personal pleasure to invite you for a conversation with two people you know well: Stephen from our planning department and William from our operations department. It will not come as a surprise that the reason for asking the three of you to meet is the state of play in our joint Hong Kong project – a project we all passionately believe in and that is in need of a powerful impulse at this point in time.

There is every reason for me to create the best possible circumstances for your conversation, as you will appreciate. That is why I have engaged a meeting design company called "Please, Stand Up" to design this meeting. We have worked with this company several times in the past and once again they have come up with a programme and setting that is to my full satisfaction. One of their managing partners, Edwin Spitz, will contact you today to illustrate in more detail what is expected of you and to answer any questions you may have.

The conversation will take place in Studio "Otto e Mezzo", on Thursday, 23 September. It will be preceded by a business dinner, starting at 6.30 p.m. For dinner there will be some other people present; Edwin will tell you who and why. Subsequently, a room is available for Stephen, William and yourself, for a conversation of about 75 minutes. The people who have dinner with you will stay on until about ten minutes after your conversation finishes, so that you can tell them what conclusions you have reached.

That means the session will be over by about 9 p.m. May I please ask you not to plan any other engagements for that evening? Afterwards taxis will be provided to take you home, where I trust you will further digest, not just a very good meal, but a really fruitful conversation!

I shall leave it up to your wisdom and experience to decide the best way of reporting back to me.

Warm Regards,
Stewart

Rationale for the Briefing

This letter to Leon speaks volumes. By opening with "On behalf of Acme, it is my personal pleasure..." Stewart immediately gives Leon a very strong signal that the interest in the conversation goes beyond that of the three participants and that he, Stewart, attaches great importance to it. Leon also knows that Stewart wants results and that he gives the three men every opportunity to jointly develop new insights, in the interest of this important project. The implicit message is: here is a chance to jump over your own shadows and if you don't, things in Hong Kong will not take the necessary turn for the better.

The briefing underlines the special identity of Acme. It implies that if problems crop up, this company is not afraid to use special innovative ways to solve them. Also implicitly, the letter testifies to Stewart's very strong commitment to the project.

Intentionally, but again implicitly, the letter gives status to the Meeting Designer. This licences him to further mould the participants' mindsets in the personal briefing, making him a natural extension of Stewart's communication tactics. As a person from outside and with this endorsement, the Designer is unlikely to meet with any serious resistance.

In allowing Stephen, William and Leon to decide for themselves how to report back, Stewart further strengthens their feeling of independence, but at the same time stresses that he expects some sort of report and therefore a concrete outcome.

The letter shows something else, albeit more to the readers of this book than to the meeting participants. The Meeting Designer has seen an opportunity to increase his influence on the dynamics of the conversation: during the meal that precedes the actual meeting. It offers the chance to invite a number of people who contribute content about the Hong Kong project as input. The Meeting Designer can use this opportunity to zoom in on an interest William, Leon and Stephen share. Stewart and the Meeting Designer decide this together. It makes quite a difference, for instance, if the other dinner guests are the three men's wives (Hong Kong is an expatriation project), 4 HIV patients from Hong Kong (it is a project to set up a care centre for patients suffering from AIDS) or 3 hip Hong Kong DJs (upmarket and innovative chain of restaurants aiming at a clientele of young professionals). It goes without saying that this fictitious letter is the result of an interview the Meeting Designer had with Stewart as the meeting owner. He has made the importance of the conversation abundantly clear and the two have addressed the 'tone of voice' for the conversation itself, as well as for the invitation. It is likely for Stewart's communication advisor to have played a role in this.

The Oral Briefing

The written briefing paves the way for direct contact between the Meeting Designer and Leon, Stephen and William, as well as with the invitees to the dinner. The oral briefing is arranged for the day the three men read Stewart's letter and it allows the Meeting Designer to execute the next step in the overall design and its realisation.

During the briefing, he illustrates the programme, adding that four employees from Hong Kong will join them for dinner – all colleagues with whom Stephen, William and Leon are familiar. During the meal, these four dinner guests will deliver a short speech, off the cuff, revealing what the project means to them personally. Each will focus on some aspect that for him represents its beauty. The Meeting Designer asks the three to simply listen to what these colleagues have to say and not to start the conversation right away. He also invites each of them to bring along a book with a picture, a poem, or something similar that seems to capture the value of the Hong Kong project. They are instructed to use this input when they feel it is the right moment in the conversation.

The host is charged with setting up a small collection of art treasures in the meeting room, or – preferably – a specific room is chosen that already contains these.

The Meeting Designer adopts a very personal style of address and encourages the three participants to enter the conversation without preconceived ideas, or prepared presentations and to just surrender to the interaction.

The briefing call takes place very shortly before the actual conversation, in order to prevent all sorts of prior consultations and to keep the first impressions fresh. In practice, this means that the agendas of the participants have had to be blocked quite some time before, without this leading to any questions.

The four dinner guests need to be briefed, too, after having been informed by Acme about the invitation. Edwin Spitz, the Meeting Designer needs to think about the right tone and the correct information around their role and the importance of their speeches.

All this work belongs to the responsibilities of the Meeting Designer and is part of the overall 'architecture' of the meeting. The Meeting Designer carries it out in close co-operation with Stewart. Where necessary, it may require further exchanges of views between them to get things spot on. In spite of all this detailed planning and execution, there is still one valid question to answer:

Is This Going to Work?

It is not very likely that Leon, Stephen and William will simply dismiss a meeting that has been prepared so meticulously. In any case, the litmus test for a successful design are Stewart's insights into the three men's characters. He needs to assess whether the programme stands a good chance of achieving the desired objectives. Naturally, this assumes a fair dose of trust between Stewart as the meeting owner and the Meeting Designer. Both need to feel free to express any reservations, without questioning each other's integrity.

At this point, the Meeting Designer needs to carry out two final checks. The first is to verify whether the design is culture-proof from the point of view of national cultures; the second if it is with respect to the organisational culture of Acme.

In this invented example, we have assumed that Stephen, William and Leon come from Western countries. In practice, the need to address cultural differences generally occurs earlier in the design process than in our description of the example. The translation of the Content Flow and the Experience Concept[1] into programme features often already calls for the 'Third Way' approach we described in Chapter 1.4. It is beyond the scope of this book to explain in detail how to find such solutions. What we can say, however, is that the knowledge of cultural differences implies that the Meeting Designer tests all possible solutions for the programme as the design process unfolds – as if it were a parallel stream of consciousness. A bit like parents who walk through a holiday home where they are going to spend two weeks with their toddler who has just learned to walk. The risks in the environment flag up because they observe that environment through a particular set of eyes.

The second test is a check against the identity of the organization. Since we made up the example ourselves, we can continue to provide further details. If unconventional solutions are not white raven in the Acme Corporation, and if Stewart as the CEO has a habit of giving this kind of trust to the people he works with, then the design will work out OK.

Things change considerably if, on the other hand, Stewart heads a charity or another NGO funded with donations from the public at large. In that case, is this dinner in line with the image of an organization that takes care to spend donated money only on charitable activities? The answer to that question is an outright "No". Sooner or later a story about spendthrift activities might hit the tabloids which would do damage beyond repair. That does not mean the whole idea has become useless, though; the basic concept holds, it is just that the actual execution needs to be more sober and frugal. Adjustments are required. For instance, it will be impossible to pick a venue especially dressed up for the occasion. Justifiably that would be seen as squandering donations. So, no outside caterer to provide the meal.

---

[1] Actually, especially the Experience Concept the meeting owner chooses tends to be highly conditioned by national culture. As we explained in Chapter 1.3, many Elementary Meetings hinge on meetings that are 'archetypical' in certain countries. However, it is often possible to recognise a more general type of meeting in culture-dominated ECs. A group we worked with chose as the EC for its meeting 'The Quest for the Holy Grail' – not an experience concept a group of Asian participants would have been likely to hatch. Nevertheless, 'The Quest' is similar to stories in many countries of a group of 'The Chosen' travelling in search of a holy object and the symbols of wisdom. That analogy is good enough.

Instead three participants doing the cooking together. No set dresser hauling in props, but asking a colleague institution to make available a room with the necessary art objects. No flight tickets for the Hong Kong four, but a Skype connection or teleconference.

It is our experience that it is always possible to adapt a truly functional CF and EC to the identity of the meeting owner's organisation. As a matter of fact, it is their knowledge of their own organisation which provides the necessary input for those adaptations. They know what is acceptable and what is not; they know who to call for resources; and better than anybody else, they know "How we do things here!"

Scalability

The example we have used in this chapter to illustrate the design process is a good conversation between three people – an example taken from normal daily design practice. We have chosen it because of its relative simplicity and the easy logistics. Naturally, a 2,500 people convention is physically a different kettle of fish. When scaling up meetings, though, the lion's share of the changes affect the production of the meeting, done by a PCO, a meeting planner, an independent producer or the communication staff of the meeting owner's organisation. They ensure that the actual 'performance' takes place, involving suppliers ranging from parking guards to make-up artists and from sound engineers to caterers. Cooking a meal for 2,500 people is a huge professional challenge and the Meeting Designer is only too happy to entrust that challenge to a professional caterer! He leaves registration to the PCO, lighting to the AV supplier, and so on.

From the angle of design, however, there is not a big difference. Even a mega event has all the characteristics we described in Part 1 of this book and the processes of Part 2 remain just as relevant. It is a matter of scale, not of essence; the actual process of designing the programme remains the same: establish the relationship with the meeting owner, obtain their input on objectives, analyse the content, create the programme features, develop the script, do the briefings and direct the implementation. The logistics may be more complex in a large meeting, the quintessence of the design process stays the same: directing participant behaviour in such a way that the desired outcomes are achieved.

The Script Is a Score

The outcome of the design process is a script: a detailed description of what person X does with content Y at time point Z of the meeting, as in our definition of meeting design.

A meeting script is like a musical score; and just as a score is not the same as a musical performance, a script is not a meeting. A score only becomes music when musicians of flesh and blood start playing the notes; a script becomes a meeting when participants of flesh and blood live out the temporary ecosystem. The implementation of a script can never be the same twice: the script is a blueprint that leads to a unique experience. The circumstances will always be different and, even more importantly, with their unique behaviours, the participants play an essential role in its enactment. Each group of participants is unique; they influence each other through unique relationships; they respond to a unique set of circumstances in unique ways. This makes each meeting a one-off and it is the task of the Meeting Designer to make the most of that uniqueness.

Competences of the Meeting Designer

The above description of the design process harbours another piece of information: it shows how the Meeting Designer deals with all the information he gathers during an assignment. That input is processed (carved, sawn, cut, hammered out, glued, welded, baked – you name the process) into the building blocks with which to construct the programme. In addition to professional know-how, that requires guts, an analytical mind, sharp wits, and a little bit of creativity. We do not believe creativity is the talent that most distinguishes what a Meeting Designers has to offer. Creativity is a means to an end – Meeting Design is an applied art. The really distinctive skill a Meeting Designer possesses is his grasp of connections – rationally as well as intuitively – and understanding what features in the programme will produce specific behaviours. And that requires above all a lot of common sense and human experience.

The remaining chapters of Part 3 address the practical implications that influence what happens when the 'score' is performed, that is, when the scripted design is put into practice. In succession, we will discuss, firstly, the venue, because the venue provides the backdrop for all meeting processes. Then we shall turn to technology, which provides the means to overcome our physical limitations. Facilitation, next, describes the attitudes and styles of all those who play a role in transforming the score into music; they are the musicians in the orchestra. We shed some light on the content providers, such as speakers, workshop leaders and experts, who enrich the meeting with specific input and who could be considered the soloists in the performance. And finally, we have a chapter on outcomes: what should meetings produce.

Meeting Design: Designing an Ecosystem

Above we have described the design process of one meeting. In this case, the design produces a good conversation between three men. The number of meeting programmes in any set of circumstances is potentially infinite. That begs the question whether there is an approach that reflects how meetings work and what that means for the design process, from a more theoretical viewpoint. We feel there is. In order to unfold that approach, we need to introduce the notion of receptivity.

Receptivity is the implicit or explicit willingness or ability for something or someone to change their state (their being, their essence – call it what you will) as a result of a stimulus. The stimulus and the ensuing change create a new situation with other, slightly different receptivities. As events unfold, this process repeats itself countless times, working as fast as the human brain and causing an infinitely varied kaleidoscope of ever changing, ever new possibilities and impossibilities, of needs and capabilities, of open and closed minds, of choices and obligations, under the influence of an equally infinite number of external stimuli. You could say that a meeting is a complex, temporary ecosystem of evolving receptivities. Many of those stimuli and many of the developments are predictable. That is the domain of Meeting Design. But all human beings are capable of surprising others and themselves. Therefore, no meeting ever follows a course you can entirely plot in advance.

As the Meeting Designer works with this ecosystem and creates or develops his design, he is constantly on the alert to notice changes in overall and specific receptivity. This awareness is like an anticipated representation of the future meeting. It is as if the Meeting Designer has a somewhat scrambled preview of a documentary that has been made of the meeting. While watching the footage, he constantly juggles and balances all the thoughts and notions we have described in this book so far. Which is the reason why we could not present this view on meetings at an earlier stage.

In this understanding of the design process, the Meeting Designer sometimes receives signals that do not feel right, a warning light that flashes, a shadow, the hunch of an unsettling presence behind some corner. These warning signs mean the design is not ready yet and that it requires further analysis and 'fleshing out', i.e. different ways of activating and managing the sequence of receptivities. A good design achieves an optimum fine-tuning of the receptivities of the meeting owner and his representatives, of the meeting participants and of everybody else who has a role during the meeting.

That is Meeting Design.

Sceptic:

We have a chat with Aileen, who is in her second year of a London-based B.A. degree course in Tourism and Events.

A: It's interesting to read your views on creativity and its role in your work.

M/E: That's nice to hear, though it may depend on why you think it's interesting. What exactly do you mean?

A: I find it interesting because you are so utterly wrong,... No, just joking...

M/E: Hm, every wisecrack contains a hard core of wisdom that needs to be cracked. So let's have it.

A: Well, in a way it hurts to see that in this profession, too, rational analysis comes first and creative freedom is just a follower.

M/E: Things are not quite that clear-cut.

A: I don't get what you're hinting at.

M/E: What do your fellow students think about this? What is their motivation for doing your course?

A: They chose this course because events management reminds them of all the times when they were swept thoroughly off their feet by a festival or some major happening. You know, being close to the performers, the vibes of the crowd – that kind of drive.

M/E: And what about yourself?

A: Oh, that applies to me, too. But what about you? Especially at this stage – after having gone through so many meetings?

M/E: To some extent it's the same for us, but it has changed in the course of the years. Initially there was the thrill of coming up with something special, a temporary work of art, the enthusiasm of creating the ultimate moment. Now, in addition to that there's the surprise, actually a kind of astonishment about how things go on in the world we enter when we work with a client – the relationships, the strategies.

A: And do you need that, the astonishment? How does that relate to the analysis and the creativity?

M/E: Difficult to put it into words. We feel it is an integral part of what we do, because if a topic or a situation no longer arouses your interest, if you lose your curiosity as human beings, if you have only the professional outlook, you lose your edge and with that goes the energy you want to breathe into the design, right from the start. It goes beyond mere feeling. As if it synthesises passion and the ability to be ruthlessly lucid and rational.

A: Right, that is interesting: if a client commissions something from you, how do you manage to infuse the right intensity in your work?

M/E: Do you have a background in arts?

A: No, not really, at least not professionally. For a couple of years I studied really hard to play the oboe, when I was about 16-17. I actually entered a couple of those international competitions.

M/E: So you understand the difference between a musical score and the execution?

A: Of course. A score is only the first half of a piece of music. The musicians provide the other half.

M/E: It's the same for meetings and events. The designer provides the script, the score; and the producer, the AV people, the speakers, the moderator and above all the participants supply the other half.

A: Do performances sometimes go wrong?

M/E: It's important for the designer to carefully monitor the execution, be present, insist on the 'purity' of the design. And that requires analysis.

A: You've lost me.

M/E: Whenever you need to defend an idea or a choice, analysis is more effective than passion. Passion is not good enough when working with organisations, either corporate or not. You need the persuasive strength of reason. Without that, you'll lose your battles. You won't convince a CEO that his managers need to – I don't know – play along getting married to some person from the company they are going to merge with, as in one of our examples. When explaining to him which of his problems will be solved by that ploy, you need sound arguments, not just a feeling. That's not credible.

A: So when you pit yourself against event idea agencies, you win?

M/E: We're not so arrogant as to answer that question with a simple "Yes." More importantly: organisations in today's economy want to see results, based on credible analytical models and a proven track record. That's what we have learned.

3.3 The Venue Message

Growing Small

ave you ever visited Saint Peter's Basilica in Rome? It is interesting to observe what happens to people when they enter this impressive building. They are overwhelmed by a range of emotions, and although that range is broad, people's emotions rarely fall outside it. Exactly the same thing happens when you go into the Aya Sophia in Istanbul or the Oslo City Hall where the Nobel Peace Prize Award Ceremony takes place.

Practically all visitors suddenly experience some variety of *littleness*. Due to the immense surface area and especially the height of these buildings, it is as if people instantly feel their bodies shrink to the tiniest of proportions. The effect of feeling suddenly exceedingly small is actually visible. Initially people go quiet, their bodies slow down, their shoulders curve slightly forward, then they start talking again, but in a low voice. The interaction between church and visitor goes beyond that. There is also an impact on group behaviour, on the way people who are together relate to each other. Children seek the hands of their parents; couples on the other hand let go of each other; groups of tourists stand closer together without actually touching; many gaze up and around, captured by an unsettling mixture of awe and devotion; every now and then they exchange a meaningful look. It is as if the building issues commands and they obey; it speaks to them, its voice soundless but irresistible.

It is remarkable that hardly anyone shows a different reaction. No one bursts out laughing, people never move around busily (actually, you can immediately recognize the clergy working there because they are the only ones who do), there is no exuberance, only the odd group of twelve-year-olds may call out to each other, the same way they might in front of the lion's den in a zoo. Evidently, Saint Peter's dictates a certain kind of behaviour and its demands are so insistent you simply have to listen to them.

Buildings and People

Would Saint Peter's be a suitable venue for a creative and interactive congress about worldwide problems in providing potable water? The question is purely academic, of course. The Catholic Church may have had some headwind in recent decades, but they are unlikely to rent out their main stronghold to congress organisers. However, the essential meaning of the question is not academic at all: are certain buildings more fit for certain communicative purposes than others? And if so, what makes them special? It is not a major intellectual discovery to ascribe to Saint Peter's an influence on the mental state and behaviour of its visitors. That is arguably one of the main reasons why it was built the way it is: big and imposing so as to impress visitors – believers and non-believers alike. However, from the point of view of Meeting Design, a more general reflection on the influence of buildings on human communicative behaviour is worthwhile. Meetings always take place in some kind of building and the impact of that building on the behaviour of participants needs to be addressed in the programme design. Even if meetings are virtual or held in the open air, there is a 'building.' In the latter case it is the sky, the trees and the land surrounding the specific spot, the access route and the weather. But why complicate things unnecessarily? Let us focus on meetings that take place inside buildings; let us explore how those buildings influence meeting behaviour and how the Meeting Designer needs to deal with that influence.

Part of a Community?

A medium-sized international association organised its annual convention in one of the largest conference centres in the world, somewhere in the US. According to the centre's specs, the 632,321 square metres of surface area can accommodate 125,000 visitors at any one time. To cover the roughly 2 km from one corner of the centre to its opposite, you could do with a bike or a moped which would whisk you past restaurants, fair halls, book shops, and umpteen coffee corners on your way. Big times big.
During the convention's opening session, the 1,600 participants were invited to network and connect. The appeal was based on the conviction that the members felt part of a living community in their industry and so one of the – predictable – goals of the meeting was that of creating and strengthening relationships.
What a pity that the building had already delivered a different message: "I am big and you are small." It had already impressed the feeling on participants that in relation to its size, individuals and most groups were insignificant. In this immense structure, their number literally took up only a tiny corner. The room available for networking was so enormous that the groups of seats were several feet apart, leaving participants in a de-personalized void. As a result, halfway through the programme, the networking moments saw single participants hunched over their phones, texting to the world outside, whilst sitting ironically underneath banners several metres over their heads that carried lovely phrases about building a community and co-creation.

Both Saint Peter's and this Conference Centre have an impact on their visitors. They broadcast a message about what it is like to be a human being in that environment. In Saint Peter's, that message strengthens the religious experience which was the reason for building it. The building conveys an appeal to its visitors which is coherent with its function. That was not the case in the US conference centre. The goal of forging community bonds between congress participants was frustrated by the building's message. The dynamics of people who "belong" did not get off the ground; instead, people kept apart, in conformity with the building's message.

The voice of buildings like these is silent but at the same time almost deafening. In issuing their instructions they are very dominant. The instructions exert an influence on how people share the space together when inside, on what we called the *togetherness environment* in Chapter 1.3. As a result, that voice is automatically relevant to Meeting Designers and to the readers of this book. A Meeting Designer needs to hear the voice, he needs to listen to what the building says – or rather: commands – because it directly affects what happens during meetings.

The Voice of Less Dominant Buildings

Do only massive buildings have this domineering voice, because they were built with the express purpose of imposing a certain kind of behaviour on their visitors? Is the message from less overbearing buildings less loud? Can we place buildings on a sliding scale according to how they speak to people? Are there modest buildings that do not seem to say anything?

We will investigate these questions by beginning to appeal to your imagination. Let's start from the shop where you do your daily shopping. Those few lucky mortals who shop in a place with a powerful 'aura,' such as the world's most beautiful square (arguably Saint Mark's Square in Venice if not the Red Square or the one in Isfahan) or the world's largest shopping mall (in Dongguan, China) have to think of a more mundane environment: just an average supermarket where you 'hunt and gather' for your daily needs. Now imagine that all the staff have left that shop. It is completely empty and you are all on your own, as in a teenager's dream. You look around and now you allow yourself to undergo the shop environment. What does it say to you? Does the shop deliver a message about what behaviour is expected from you? What is the effect of all those colourful groceries, waiting there like silent orphan children for you to save them from their shelf life? How do you experience the entrance with its trollies, the aisles, the check-out area? Does it say anything about how you are to relate to other shoppers? What hidden invitations does the shop hold out to you? Does the environment propose movement or immobility, openness or reticence, focus or relaxation, encounter or solitude? All these questions serve to identify a latent message. For you as a customer. Naturally, in shops messages of that kind are the result of research and purposeful design – purposeful because shops exist to sell things. Therefore, professional shop designers build them with a keen awareness of what will happen in the minds of vagrant shoppers. For instance supermarkets, like casinos, have no clocks. A clock tells shoppers how long they have dwelt in there already and the shop prefers to keep that to itself. Also, many shops have a layout in which the shelves in the back seem to hold especially attractive items (detergents and toilet cleaning products are in front). And so the buyer is drawn deeper into the timeless spender's paradise.

Maybe the shop in your mind's eye is not a supermarket and things go differently there. But now try to formulate a statement the shop is saying to you. Can you, in a single sentence, capture what the shop tells you about the sort of behaviour that is expected of you? Perhaps it comes easier to you if you mention a couple of actions that would definitely be 'inappropriate' in the building's eyes. Done? Good, then you are ready for the next step.

The Message in Your Home Environment

Let's move on to a building that has no public function: your home. Suppose you want to have a conversation about a moot point with one of your family members. That requires a safe environment, a place that says: "It is OK to talk here." Which room in your house would you choose? The choice will depend partly on the room's functionality, for instance whether it is easy to close a door so that you will not be disturbed. But other considerations will also play a role. Naturally, you will give thought to the influence the environment exerts on your family member's willingness to open up in the conversation. The room needs to be useful both in terms of functionality and message. Could you formulate the message of the room you have chosen and of other rooms in the house that seem less appropriate? You may notice that the messages given by some rooms are relatively similar. In that case, functionality criteria make the difference. In the end, you pick the room that provides you with the best chance of achieving your particular goal for the conversation.

Can you specify your decision criteria? Good, if you can, you have just – in your imagination – gone through the same kind of process a Meeting Designer carries out during each assignment: the mental test whether a certain meeting venue is suitable for the meeting that will be held there and for achieving its objectives.

Venue Message

Travelling from Saint Peter's to the US conference centre, your supermarket and finally home, we have illustrated that buildings, or physical environments, convey various messages. For meetings, we call such messages simply the Venue Message: the message that the surrounding environment gives us about how we are supposed to relate to it and what patterns of behaviour are appropriate. In Meeting Design, everything that influences human behaviour during meetings is relevant. Therefore, it is essential to establish what the exact Venue Message is and how it influences the togetherness environment (See Chapters 1.2 and 1.3). The definition of the Venue Message as it should be understood by Meeting Designers is:

> The Venue Message captures the influence of a building and its surroundings on the behaviour of those who are in it.

Hear it, Capture it

In order to include the Venue Message in a design, you first need to hear it and grasp its meaning. This is one of the main reasons for a site visit. During such a visit it is not enough to just walk around a bit and get some measurements, possible seating plans and the location of wall sockets. When physically in the venue, you need to change the default setting of your senses and turn the volume up. Then you allow the building into your system. This starts from the first moment you set eyes on it. Even the parking lot may send out its own message, a message which colours your perception of the building as such. You continue to absorb impressions until you have taken in all the parts of the buildings where the participants will go.

Once you have taken in the building's sensory impressions, you find a quiet place to actually formulate the message. You do this by imagining the building having a mouth – yes, a mouth, literally somewhere in a wall, just as in a Harry Potter film. The mouth speaks to you; it pronounces a sentence, directed at you personally. This sentence describes your role in the building, in combination with an indication of proper behaviour there. Often it contains a reference to some crucial detail in the building, viewed naturally from the perspective of the building itself. While doing this exercise, and this is essential, do not think of the meeting you are working on or its objectives. Just focus on the building itself.

Formulating the Venue Message, in fact, means that you listen to the commanding voice of the building. Generally, this works particularly well when done with a small group of people, who – together – gradually refine what the building says. Does the sentence contain a specific message, rather than a generic one? Does it appeal directly to the participant? Does the sentence say something about roles and behaviours? If so, then you have captured the Venue Message. Preferably you want it to start with I or you: "I'm a bit shabby, so acting mediocre is OK." (a hotel past its best), or: "You want to play, don't you?" (science museum for children).

The Conference Hotel high in the Swiss Alps can only be reached by means of a special rack and pinion railway. Travellers literally rise up above the world. The short walk from the train stop to the hotel entrance is a feast of silence, pure air and grand, unobstructed views. When stepping in, guests are welcomed as if they had just escaped from savage hordes (which to some extent, they have, of course!). The hostile world with its daily humdrum and busy-ness is far away. The peaceful, tranquil surroundings, the unadorned luxury of the rooms and facilities, the views from the meeting rooms, the wooden walls and furniture say: "You are safe here, so please enjoy each other's company."
The implication of this message is that no one refuses to have a chat with a fellow guest. Meetings in this venue have an instant intimacy and guests feel free to be more open than elsewhere. We experienced this with a team that met in order to discover its hidden powers and coherence. That voyage of discovery already started in the carriages of the funicular train.

You may have noticed that the sentence capturing the Venue Message sounds a bit like a small piece of theatre dialogue. That is correct. Good dialogue in plays shares with Venue Messages the ability to stimulate action – whether on stage or in a meeting. "At this point in time, I can clearly discern a remarkable level of affection vis-à-vis this person in front of me," sounds a lot different than: "Sweetheart, I'm madly in love with you!" The first sentence is an observation without any immediate implications; the second is the prelude to some sort of action.

It is crucial to formulate the Venue Message as the command issued by the building itself. Having it as a description makes it a lot harder to process, as in the theatre-style example we just gave. As for the Swiss mountain hotel, "The building emanates a feeling of safety," is a lot less direct and 'naked' than: "You are safe here!" Conceived as a sentence in a possible dialogue, the Venue Message is much more powerful.

The Wrong Venue Message

In many design assignments, the meeting owner contracts a venue early on. In such cases, the Meeting Designer does not have a free choice of venue and the Venue Message may not suit one or more of the meeting's objectives. For example, there may be a misalignment between Venue Message and

Experience Concept. Or the venue may impede achieving other meeting goals. Fixed seats in conference halls are a frequent challenge in this respect. For whatever reason, sometimes a venue simply has the wrong Venue Message for a certain programme.

If the Meeting Designer meets with impediments like this, his job is to propose adjustments. We can illustrate this by returning to the example of the sensitive conversation in your house. Maybe you do not have a room that entirely satisfies what you are looking for. In that case, something somewhere needs be changed. Maybe you can increase the intimacy by partly closing the curtains or by adding or moving a piece of furniture. All over the world people use mechanisms to slightly adjust rooms and space: from placing a bowl of fresh fruit or flowers on the table, to a small chocolate bar on a guest's pillow.[1] It is the task of the Meeting Designer to pinpoint the needs for such changes; set dressers and producers can then work out solutions.

Return to the Association Meeting

The Association who organised their meeting in the outsized conference centre clearly had the challenge we just outlined. The Venue Message proved a handicap in achieving some of the objectives of that meeting and it would have been necessary to adapt the venue in a number of ways.

The area intended for members to socialise lacked a natural central spot to which participants would be drawn as if by a magnet during 'spare' moments in the programme – the way a village square with a small café does. All participants will naturally gravitate towards such a central spot, so if you wait a bit, sooner or later you will bump into that person you were looking for. This is less likely to happen in spaces with more than one centre, let alone in ones without any centre at all.

So, in order to induce better networking, the venue should have been provided with some central spot. That 'village square' could have been made more intimate by screening it off, reducing the available number of square metres per person. That makes it simply easier to find one another. The seats could have been grouped in small corners, facing one another, so that people would automatically have looked at each other, with the possibility of making eye contact, instead of being tempted to look away into the far blue yonder.

The banners could have given the place a clearer identity, if they had been hung down to maybe 2 metres from the ground, instead of 6. That would have brought them closer to people's hearts, reinforcing the shared values. Being as high up as they were, they reminded people of their smallness – not really an incentive to muster up the courage that is always needed to start

---

[1] In many German hotels you will find on your pillow the utterly incomprehensible 'Gummibären,' cheerfully coloured gum candy in the form of a teddy bear with outstretched arms.

talking to perfect strangers.

All in all, these modifications would have involved a different use of existing elements or decorations, plus the rental of about 25 metres of screening. A small investment for a big result! Actually, the book stands that were already there, together with the banners, could easily have functioned as partitions between sets of chairs. Just a change in the system for hanging up the banners would have done the job. Even cheaper.

Using the insights of a Meeting Designer could have optimised the networking outcome of the association's Convention. And who knows how many more registrations that better atmosphere would have brought in the next year?

A peculiar paradox is observable in circumstances like these: the paradox of inverted efficiency. Of course it is nice for people to have a lot of leg space, as was the case in the 'mixed zone'. It is also nice to get your cup of coffee without waiting in a Soviet-style meat-shop-queue. However, the drive for efficiency makes it less likely for people to have a chat without having to decide to do so on purpose. And having to decide to go and talk with strangers is always a barrier.

The Venue Message and the Six Reasons for Having Meetings

Knowing how to adapt meeting spaces requires a sense of human proportions and some talent for improvisation. Sometimes it is enough just to change the seating; in other cases you need to refurbish and redecorate more radically. Budgets are always an issue, because builders and materials come at a cost. So in order to establish the border between what is necessary and what is nice-to-have in meeting venues,[2] let us pinpoint some guidelines, working from basics up. The six reasons for having meetings (see Introduction) provide us with the direction of thought about meeting spaces. We will briefly touch upon them, one by one.

- The Association example has already emphasised that good **networking** venues should have a centre. A centre that offers a sense of safety and security, with no more than 2-3 square metres of floor space per person at peak periods of use, a varied choice of standing and seating arrangements and many sight lines for viewing and spotting people. What you need is a togetherness environment that offers many spontaneous opportunities to literally bump into people – the ones you know and the ones you don't know yet. People should be encouraged to stay on the move. Tables, for instance, usually impede spontaneous movement. Loud music is a taboo, as well as dim lighting: you want to see people! Incidentally, lengthy interventions from a central space are not a good idea, either; so: no extensive speeches

---

[2] We are referring here to the venue in general, whether it is a complete building, or just a single meeting room. In each case, the relevant Venue Message is the sentence participants hear in the space they experience as the place of the meeting.

by board members, sponsor presentations or performances.

- If **learning** is the main reason for having the meeting, venue needs are dramatically different. Check out this quote from the website of a venue where the architecture is focused solely on optimising learning: "The sensory stimulation theory tells us that effective learning occurs when the senses are stimulated. The vast majority of knowledge held by adults is learned through seeing. By stimulating the senses, especially the visual sense, learning can be enhanced. If multiple senses are stimulated, learning can be even greater. Stimulation through the senses is achieved through a greater variety of colours, volume levels, strong statements, facts presented visually, use of a variety of techniques and media. The architecture of the UniManagement Center follows this theory and you can see it in each room of our premises."[3] That covers the requirements neatly! What we would like to add is that the floor of a meeting room should be flat. This increases its flexibility. Seats bolted to the floor are anathema, because different learning formats require different seating arrangements. Rooms with fixed seating are almost invariably set up in theatre style, which invites frontal teaching and suffocates interaction or peer exchange. In pedagogy, it has been known for decades that frontal teaching is the most ineffective form of learning. Frontal teaching is teacher-centred, not learner-centred.
Also, learning is more effective if the members of a group can focus entirely on the specific processes they are experiencing. This means groups should be isolated – exactly the contrary of what we just described for meetings with a networking purpose!

- **Motivation** demands venues where people can share stories. If a meeting owner chooses to have a meeting to stir up motivation, evidently he wants to reach a whole group of people. If not, he would have chosen a different means of communication. So the meeting should develop a sense of community. A meeting room that fosters this must have a lot of reciprocal visibility and opportunities for exchanging and sharing experiences and feelings in plenary. This makes a round room more suitable than a rectangular one. In a rectangular room, some people are closer to 'the action' than others and in meetings that need to motivate, that is undesirable. Backbenchers are less likely to be touched by the emotional content of the meeting: the inequality in physical distance has an impact on how involved people are, as everybody who has ever been to a rock concert or an opera will acknowledge (and as expressed in differences in ticket prices!).
There is a second desideratum. The meeting owner will want the duration of the motivation achieved by the meeting to last as long as possible. This means

---

[3] Taken from the website of UniManagement in Turin (Italy), a venue with a mission expressly focused on learning. Its architecture and interior design incorporate state-of–the-art insights on didactics and adult learning.

that the meeting should leave a strong and lasting emotional effect. The more the venue acts like an 'emotional anchor', the stronger the emotional imprinting in the memory of participants. Buildings can accomplish this by being special, by hitting home. A distinctive identity helps, while flexible multifunctionality does not (remember St. Peter's? Definitely a single-purpose building!). Or a similar anchor: you will never forget who was with you the first time you walked through a tropical rainforest.

Be careful, though! If the building's special characteristic is merely some quirk in its design, with little or no bearing on the content, its effect is greatly diminished. A well-designed programme hangs together and its parts reinforce each other.

- Venues that host meetings with **rituals** as their main reason for existing require a high degree of adaptability. There is endless variety in the symbols and gimmicks different meeting owners cherish. Consequently, there is a great need for meeting rooms to be 'dressed up' differently each time. This means the venue needs to be multifunctional in a specific way – not so much in the sense of different activities it is able to accommodate, but rather in the sense of being able to take on different faces: redecoration of walls or scope for hanging things on them, enough space to set up special display features, technical amenities, etc. Maybe one meeting requires 15 life-size human figures hanging from the ceiling, the next, two days later, may call for 600 chairs with headset connections and a stage in the centre. Maximum technological flexibility and openness are the maxim here, and that includes the openness of the staff that work in the venue.

- **Decision-making** as a reason for having the meeting calls for a venue with inherent beauty, style and little hogwash – much more so than for the previous categories. Ideally, the venue offers safety, demands concentration and surrounds participants with the lofty and sober atmosphere that gives importance to what is happening. In line with Chapter 1.2, the decision-making inevitably involves something that will be carried out somewhere else. Therefore, the space should allow participants to connect mentally to that other reality. A somewhat solemn and stern environment helps, because in pondering decisions participants need to consider factors, opinions and thoughts for what they are, without being influenced or disturbed by invasive but unintentional signals from the surrounding environment. This is a vital difference compared to venues equipped for learning which benefit from a high intensity of stimuli.

Board rooms in up-market hotels often exemplify the sober stylishness that facilitates good decision-making.

- And finally, venues that support **Alignment**. In practice, for this type of meeting, we favour relatively large rooms, with a flat floor, but also some focal point to hold everyone's attention: a stage or a lectern, say. This makes sense: the meeting owner wants to steer the alignment in a certain direction, so it is useful for participants to have a reference person to point out that direction. Participants need a natural focus on this reference person, who appeals and explains, steers and coaches. An absolute necessity is having additional spaces, such as break-out rooms, where participants can experiment with either alignment or non-alignment. This provides the level playing field for a true process of making choices.

So we often use several meeting rooms, one of which is a central reference point. It contains an easily accessible stage, allowing aligners and non-aligners to take it, preferably somewhere in, or close to the centre.

The Ideal Venue

It is obvious that the perfect venue, able to respect all six requirements equally, does not exist. As a consequence, the Meeting Designer will often propose adjustments, sometimes even in the course of the meeting, in order to alter and optimise the Venue Message.

During a 2-day conference on priorities in the medical treatment of the elderly, we used four different room set-ups. This was necessary because the somewhat scruffy, old-fashioned hotel did not express a sufficiently powerful appeal to participants to develop innovative ways of working out solutions together. The Venue Message we registered was: "I'm a bit shabby, so acting mediocre is OK" – you may recognise this as the Venue Message we used as an example earlier on. Here is a brief summary of our thinking and our choices on that occasion:

The start was a plenary, with seats directed towards a screen, flanked by a lectern, placed on one of the longer sides of the rectangular meeting room. Participants came from many different countries and this lay-out offered them the safety of a start that was in everybody's comfort zone. It also facilitated the alignment around the main content issues for the conference, illustrated by a keynote.

*Next we switched to a set-up with discussion groups seated around relatively small round tables. We wanted participants to exchange viewpoints and **learn** from one another. Moving them to a different place in the building helped to create a different perspective and offer them new stimuli.*

Meanwhile, in the main meeting room we had put up a low stage, with space for five experts in a row. The participants were placed in semi-circles quite close to the stage. During this phase it was necessary for them to develop a shared motivation while actively working on issues tabled in the opening session. We kindled that motivation presenting a short video that had a universal appeal to all those present, before starting the panel.

The last layout was a large circle. In this formation the participants became a community, supporting each other in the decisions they took. It was a final moment of decision-making and renewed alignment, needed to ensure that the policy-making process after the meeting would have continued support. Throughout the two days of the event, participants were reminded visually of the meeting's objective: using available health care resources for elderly people in the best possible way. To this end, the conference room was lined with large boards, displaying pictures of senior citizens. Each had a caption, just a sentence or two, with some personal story about the person in the photograph.

In this event, we modified the Venue Message as a function of the meeting owner's objective: get participants to agree on policy-making in the specific field of healthcare for the elderly. That is why alignment layouts played such a prominent role at the beginning and at the end of the conference. A sound analysis of the Venue Message gives the Meeting Designer opportunities to make changes – sometimes simple changes – in the meeting space that can have a significant impact on the process the meeting owner envisages.

Decision Latitude on Venue Message

The possibilities for change are not limitless: organisational culture and national culture of the participants determine the leeway the Meeting Designer can allow himself – in addition, of course, to the boundaries of the venue itself.

A Meeting Designer can come up with a host of brilliant ideas, but one of the things that makes the profession so fascinating is that, at the end of the day, those ideas need to be 'done' by people of flesh and blood. 'Done' here takes the meaning of what is done or not done within certain organisations. For instance, can a group of chartered accountants have a meeting in a zoo? The answer depends on the objectives of the meeting but also on the resilience of the participants. People react to our ideas and proposals from their personal convictions and from their feelings about the reputation and identity of their organisation (see Chapter 2.1). For the Venue Message these reactions tend to be particularly strong. The reason is probably that the Venue is so physical and its impact so immediate. Just as in our example about St Peter's, people cannot simply shrug off the Venue Message. Its voice is simply too loud.

Our considerations put forward in Chapter 1.4 are highly applicable to this topic. Just as people from different countries watch the world through different glasses, their ears hear different things when spoken to. For instance, they receive different messages with regard to: the status of a building, the meaning of its sheer size, acceptable service levels by staff, and also about such things as innovativeness and the extension of comfort zones, as well as the degree to which people are willing to let themselves be taken out of these. People from more formal cultures, for example, easily have the feeling that conferences are automatically a serious affair. This means that if a venue is too 'jolly', they feel treated disrespectfully. As usual, cultural differences are best solved not by looking for a compromise, but for a differentiated 'Third Way' that satisfies the needs of all participants.

The theme for the annual HR Conference of a multinational company was "Building the HR Community." That community counted 20 odd different nationalities. All over the world, communities tend to decorate the spaces they use for shared activities. How they do that and what they use is, of course, vastly different from one place to another.
We asked each participant to bring along something that they would normally use in their home country to decorate the room or square where the members of communities meet. The first activity on the programme was that of decorating the room together. The participants from less formal cultures helped their more formal colleagues to overcome their initial hesitation. Those from more extrovert cultures did the same for those who tend to start by listening instead of speaking. In the end, together, they created their own Venue Message: the message of their community.

The Venue Message's Sustainability

How long does the Venue Message hold? Is it only heard when people come in? Or is it a constant undertow? Is participant behaviour not mainly a function of such things as the power of the programme, the single participant's personality and a further, wide range of almost random circumstances? This is a relevant consideration, because naturally the longer the message reverberates, the greater its impact on their behaviour. Unfortunately, there is no one-off answer to this question. A major determinant is how overpowering the building itself is. St. Peter's again. Apart from that, we can only say that the message tends to be weak but persistent. This may not look like particularly helpful information; the truth is that we can do our utmost to describe and predict human behaviour, but it will never follow a purely mechanistic paradigm. The Venue Message is an integral part of the complex system that drives participant behaviour. Like the meeting conventions that emanate from the Elementary Meetings we discussed in Chapter 1.3, all the perceptions amalgamate in the mind of the participant and generate the stimuli to display certain behaviour. We cannot make it any easier than that. To a large extent, this unpredictability gives Meeting Design its distinctive character as an applied art form. The task of the Meeting Designer is to strike the balance between rational considerations and human intuition to produce a workable system that generates just those behaviours that will help participants to achieve the desired outcomes.

Apparently trivial details can play a decisive role in this. Remember our example in Chapter 3.1? About the effect the shape of a table had on the outcomes of a meeting? A table shape and seating that generate antagonism will influence what happens during a meeting. A specific feature of a venue that influences participant behaviour in the final stages of a meeting can have an overriding impact on that meeting's outcomes. Here is the last example of this chapter:

A zoo is the venue for this symposium about safety at work. The small flock of HS&E managers are impressed by the tiger keeper's presentation on the meaning of safety in his daily routine. Straight after this presentation, they walk back to the plenary room where the meeting had started to conclude the programme with an informal exchange of views. This room is underground, slightly cramped, yet feels safe and snug.

For about 20 minutes the 40 participants stand around 10 bar tables. The moderator catches the mood and asks each participant to share a personal reflection. These final 20 minutes turn into a particularly meaningful finale. In the intimacy of the room people speak freely, address the fundamental questions, and say things that shed a new light on how to work with safety. When the moderator winds up, those present are impressed with the sincerity that emerged, suddenly and spontaneously. Was that a coincidence?

Sceptic

We have a conversation with João Schmidt Nunes, policymaker in São Paolo (Brazil) and special advisor to the mayor for innovative projects.

J: In São Paolo, we have three huge Conference Venues. The São Paolo Conference and Exhibition Centre, and well, two more – the actual names won't mean much to you, right? The biggest hosts meetings up to 50,000 people. We'd like to develop a fourth, capable of handling meetings up to 100,000 participants.

Now, I would like to have your advice. Thinking about the things you explain in this chapter about 'venue speech', what should it look like? I mean, we want to make a statement: São Paolo has something to prove, we are not the third world any more. I trust you don't see us like that!

M/E: Thanks for asking us, João! Two things in your question cause us to reflect.

J: Wasn't I clear enough, then?

M/E: Oh yes, certainly! You are very clear, crystal clear! Allow us to share some ideas with you.

J: Sure go on. That's what I'm here for.

M/E: For a start, you mentioned the name of a Venue you already have. This new centre, is that also meant to be a multifunctional building, for conferences and exhibitions? Is that what you're saying?

J: Yes, it is. It should be big, very big, a bit like the centre in Atlanta you mentioned. You know São Paolo is one of the biggest cities in the world.

M/E: And like the ones in London, Singapore, Bejing and Sydney.

J: Right, and in Boston, Macão and Cape Town.

M/E: We could easily go on for another while, mentioning venues that are just like the São Paolo Conference and Exhibition Centre you would like to build, couldn't we?

J: Yes, and I am proud that we are a city that can stand its ground against all the others!

M/E: So do you want your new Centre to broadcast as a message? Something like: : "Welcome to London, oops – sorry: Welcome to São Paolo, of course! You're lucky to be here!"

J: You're pulling my leg, aren't you? Of course we want the conference visitors to recognise the place they're in!

M/E: So it should be different from all those other buildings?

J: Of course!

M/E: Fine, our plea in this book is a plea for identity.

J: Yes, but we cannot afford to lose functionality!

M/E: Well, that sounds like a great assignment for an architect! You have quite a tradition for that in Brazil.

J: Careful what you say! Praise like that makes architects put their fees up. We don't want to be priced out of our dreams!

M/E: We have seen many Venues built on budgets that did not allow for good architecture. After a few years the same people who initially kept a tight hold on their purses, later had to pay for the operational losses generated by their multifunctional but unsympathetic concrete. They do not attract enough meetings to make a profit. We say: "Identity pays." Every marketing expert will tell you the same. No branding without identity and no competitive advantage without branding. Otherwise you end up competing on price only.

J: So you are saying we should concentrate on the Venue Speech? Try to make it a powerful speech?

M/E: Exactly, in this book we call it the Venue Message, but Venue Speech sounds great, as well!

J: Ah, so that must have been the second thing that triggered you? Sorry, but in Brazil we do not deliver messages, we shout them! We yell a lot here!

M/E: The Venue Yell! How should this yell sound, from your new Venue?

J: Something like "Hi friends, welcome to a place where meetings and good business are also full of warmth and fun

M/E: Starting to sound like a samba!

J: Yes, the Samba Centre for meetings with joy. That is Brazil and that is São Paolo!

M/E: What does a samba look like?

J: Well, of course colourful, sensual and full of movement, with an irresistible rhythm.

M/E: To us that sounds like a very promising start for a rich and powerful brief for an architect. Multifunctional designs lack the power of the heart, João, we are sure that as a Brazilian you know what we mean by that.

J: OK, funny to hear such words from Northern Europeans! But what if someone wants a meeting that is not joyful at all?

M/E: Like the annual Conference of Undertakers? Major meeting! But not with much samba in it, eh? Just kidding. You mean a meeting to commemorate a well-known Statesman who passed away or something like that?

J: Yes, good example.

M/E: That would be one of those meetings that revolve around rituals as their driving force. A space that hosts such a meeting should allow for easy transformation. It should allow for using the symbols that somehow belong to that kind of meeting.

J: I guess that must be possible. But it won't be a Samba meeting. No joy.

M/E: Isn't it the Brazilian spirit that should surface, even in a meeting as sad as the one we are thinking of now?

J: Do you think it is possible to design a Samba Funeral?

M/E: Well, as you said, it would not have the sensuality and the joy. But it could still inspire people with a good feeling of energy.

J: I'll have our architects read your book, as part of their brief before they start sketching. I like this idea of identity instead of plain functionalism. And I think our fellow Paulistanos will like that as well. They might embrace the building, instead of protesting... like they did when we built the new Market, a heartless building, for sure...

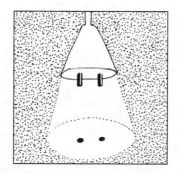

3.4 Technology

Technology and Communications

y grandmother used to tell me how her father, my great-grandfather, refused to take the telephone seriously. Indignantly, he would make it known to her in the plainest of terms that it was impossible to communicate by means of 'that thing' because you could not see each other.

My great-grandfather was right, of course. If you cannot see each other, you cannot communicate. But what he could not foresee was that one day people would learn to 'show themselves' when talking on the phone. By means of subtle pauses, changes in the tone of voice, rhythm, and a variety of hmms and ahs they would know how to 'show' their facial expressions when using the phone. My great-grandfather did not know these conventions yet and so he felt hopelessly helpless.

What would have been even further beyond his comprehension is that just about a century later a very similar debate would rage over cell phone texting. Many complain it is impossible to communicate seriously using this medium. But young people know better! They have learned, for instance, that the timing and frequency of messages can be turned into meaningful ways of conveying information. If you text "lov'u" to your loved one at 3 o'clock in the night, followed by "4ever" an hour or so later, you will have sent a message as powerful as a perfumed billet doux, borne to her bedside by a maid some two centuries ago. And so we gradually learn how to make use of the – sometimes very limited – bandwidth of yet another new medium.

All technological innovations follow such a learning curve in their implementation. For technology to mature requires time, the time to adapt ourselves, to discover and develop new conventions, and also the time needed for natural selection. Some technologies eventually establish themselves after a troubled launch, others start out with great promise but quickly wither away, yet others remain forever in the shadows and end up as orphans in Wikipedia.[1]

It is no different with technology in the meeting industry. In 2012 we find ourselves on the steep upward slope of the learning curve, for instance trying to find out how to make virtual presentations work best. How can you stop distant participants doing something else while you are delivering your presentation? A lot of potentially useful technology floods onto the market; the Meeting Designer needs to find his bearings and make the right choices about whether, when and how to use all these novelties. The aim of this chapter is to provide some guidance.

---

[1] In 1943, aviation publicist Harry Bruno wrote: "Automobiles will start to decline as soon as the last shot is fired in World War II. Instead of a car in every garage, there will be a helicopter." Yeah, sure...

Speed of Change

Technology is hot. Ever more new products and possibilities hit us ever more quickly. It remains to be seen whether all of these inventions are really useful in general and in particular at meetings. Is the launch of a new type of smart-phone really such a staggering moment in the history of mankind? Is it comparable with the opening of the first Paris metro station (1900), transatlantic radio telephony (1901), the electric vacuum cleaner (1902), or the aeroplane (1903)? These were major technological strides in a span of just three years, all with a lasting impact (although, admittedly, the importance of the first vacuum cleaner for the meeting industry may be limited). And the list of inventions later in that and the following decades continues: synthetic plastics (1905) neon lighting (1910), sonar (1916), television (1923).

Our primary task as Meeting Designers is to steer the elementary processes in the meeting room in the right direction. In the course of meetings, a fine selection of technology is always in use. There is light and sound, air conditioners and hygrometers, fridges for drinks and microwaves for snacks, computers with WIFI and more or less sophisticated registration systems, participants are phoning, faxing, mailing, blogging, tweeting, pinging, or -inging whatever did not exist yet when we were writing this chapter.

In our view, all this technology can be brought to bear on the task we defined in the previous paragraph: how can technology help to steer the essential processes that take place between meeting participants. The stress here is on the word help. We do not want to hand over the helm to technology; rather, in the design process, we need to understand the added value of technology with a view to achieving the meeting's desired outcomes. Therefore, the basic question to address is: to what sort of questions or difficulties do technical solutions provide an answer?

To help us gain that understanding, let us do something we have not done yet in this book: a bit of archaeology.

The Greeks

The Greeks gave theatre to the Western world; a highly successful innovation, for Greek plays are performed up to this very day. Historians presume that Greek drama developed from rituals in the cult of the god Dionysos.

Meanwhile, Greek social life became familiar with orchestrated meetings in public places: the dissemination of important information by town criers, generally standing on carts, rocky outcrops or small stages, to shout their messages at the tops of their voices. (Actually, this social process is probably older than Greek civilization.) In the course of time, these messengers discovered that they could transmit their communications more effectively by giving them a story line. Groups of people would flock to public places to hear travelling story-tellers, who gradually spiced up their official announcements into catchy stories. At some point, the two types of aggregation – Dionysean rituals and public storytelling – must have merged into theatre plays.

When the numbers of theatre-loving Greeks increased, two limitations became apparent: one was the maximum size of audience; the other the duration of the performance. To allow people standing at a distance from the stage to hear the town crier's message, the Greeks developed the first sustainable technical solution for meetings: they started building theatres with exceptional acoustics.

By locating these early theatres on mountain slopes, the Greeks solved both problems in one go: hundreds of people could sit and see the performance while the natural acoustics allowed them to hear it.

We still experience the almost religious tension when the lights in a theatre are dimmed and it is "curtain up" – whether what comes next is Shakespeare or a keynote. We have maintained this sensitivity for scripted rituals that convey a message.

From Rome to Verona

The Romans perfected the Greek half-natural venues into amphitheatres featuring all manner of technical amenities that allowed them to mimic live battles, organise combats between gladiators and ferocious animals (or equally ferocious other gladiators), and address huge crowds.[2]

In the first centuries after Christ, the largest multifunctional venue[3], the Colosseum in Rome, could hold crowds of over 50,000 people watching events that could easily match the opening ceremony of the Olympic Games in modern times, or a European Cup Final. The Colosseum's technostructure allowed a sun blind to be pulled over the entire building. It was held up by 250 masts and required 1,000 gaffers (probably slaves) to raise or lower it. More than 30 lifts hauled gladiators, big cats, slaves and props up and down. One of the most stunning feats the Romans achieved was to replicate complete naval battles, which meant pumping in millions of litres of water. Up to this day, it remains a mystery how they pulled that off. Also, until this very day, the Roman arena at Verona in northern Italy each summer hosts a series of opera performances visited by music lovers from all over the world. It is fair to say that the Romans had a way with event technology.

---

[2] Check out the movie Ben Hur (MGM, 1956). There, addressing the crowd seems a piece of cake; in practice, despite their phenomenal acoustics, this was probably less obvious, considering the size of these theatres.

[3] With a capacity of 300,000, the Circus Maximus was bigger. However, it was not multifunctional but mainly used for horseracing. According to an American study, in the 42 years of his life, the Roman horse cart driver Diocles totalled almost 36 million sestertius in prize money. This equates to around 15 billion of today's dollars, making him the best paid sports personality of all times.

What does Technology Solve?

Essentially, technology offers solutions to satisfy a wide range of human desires, in particular the desire to experience more than we physically can. This also applies to meetings, where the role of technology has not changed fundamentally since the ancient Greeks' first solutions in their theatres. The human limitations for which technologies provide solutions during meetings include:

- Wanting to see in the darkness: artificial illumination powered by oil, gas, electricity and recently in the form of computer-controlled, integrated systems.
- Wanting to hear and understand the spoken word to large audiences and other languages: sound amplification, floor and roving microphones, induction loops for participants with hearing impairments, live subtitling, wireless interpretation.
- Wanting to see something that is too far away: the "laterna magica", slide or overhead projector, electronic video beamer, mega screen.
- Wanting to speak to and see people who are somewhere else: telephone, radio, video satellite connection, skype conversation.
- Wanting to illustrate a story with images and props that are not physically present: slide projector, PowerPoint projection, film projection.
- Wanting to know who is in a large audience: badge, Spot-me device[4], electronic tagging for smart phones.
- Wanting to discover the whereabouts of a person you want to talk to: electronic identification and signalling systems.

Since the Industrial Revolution all kinds of technical innovations have made meetings easier, longer, more comfortable and more efficient, but more importantly, they have allowed people to overcome the above limitations. The basics for most of these technologies date back to long ago; we stand on the shoulders of giants like the Greeks, the Romans and brilliant individuals like Thomas Edison and Alexander Graham Bell. The decades around the last turn of the century have brought us two major technical breakthroughs.

1. Microelectronics: a host of information-related applications have become small and manageable. Today's mobile phones and tablets are a combination of a telephone, a photo camera, a video recorder, a computer, a television and a database. That as such does not make the device unique, but the fact that it is so small and works everywhere does. All these appliances already existed in the late 60s, but making them available in a meeting room would have required a small van for each participant. They now fit comfortably into a trouser pocket and everyone at a meeting can make use of them.

---

2. The Internet. Obviously. The Internet potentially connects everybody with everyone and everything. That connectivity has burst into every meeting room, board room and lobby. People all over the world are constantly fingering their mobile devices. We saw how the smart phone has gained its place in one of the poorest countries in Africa, Mozambique. Today, the outside world can be an integral part of meetings, interacting with participants and providing information.

In short, technology allows meeting participants to do things they are unable to do by themselves. This awareness gives us the *meaning* of technology for meetings in general and, therefore, for Meeting Designers:

Technology enables physically impossible desires

In meetings, technology follows the desires and needs of the meeting owner and meeting participants. The two major technological breakthroughs we have just described happen to have a major impact on meeting dynamics thanks to the power of their combined effects. The fact that their impact on communications is so huge means we need to investigate their implications and their use for meetings in-depth. The introduction in 1902 of the first electric vacuum cleaner has clearly had less of a sway.

Technology and How to Use it during Meetings

There is a basic principle that guides us when deciding on the use of technology; how we deploy technical devices depends on the purpose of meetings as put forward in our introduction, and at the same time, on the general meaning of technology as defined in the previous paragraph.

The meeting needs to achieve the objectives formulated by the meeting owner and satisfy (or preferably exceed) the expectations of the participants. Technology exists to overcome physical obstacles and to create ways of communication that go beyond the participants' normal means. Either there is an expressed need or desire and the technology works and helps to achieve the objectives; or there is not, and then there is no place for it. For the Meeting Designer it is as simple as that.

A meeting is not a technology laboratory and it is not the place to try out interesting novelties. Naturally, it may be fun to experiment with something out of curiosity, but the essential criterion we apply to choosing any kind of technology is: there must be a need or desire to achieve something useful that is physically impossible without that technology.

Knowing What the Technology Does

New possibilities and new devices come onto the market so fast that it is becoming almost impossible to keep up, let alone deciding whether they have any useful applications as meeting technology. Of course, there is the fun and sometimes an untapped potential in working with good meeting technology. It stretches the Meeting Designer's imagination. We will give some examples of this in the next couple of paragraphs.

Nevertheless, we have also discovered something else: programme items directed essentially by the wish to be technically innovative almost invariably fail. The utilisation of technology is a demand 'market', not a supply one. Pushing the limits of our guiding principle is a risky venture. Here is an example:

At this meeting on teaching, the university professor used a smart little system that allowed participants to send him text messages which were displayed in real-time behind him. The idea was that this would spark off a dynamic question-and-answer session involving the floor.

Sounded like a good idea, but unfortunately, the audience had different desires. At the end of the day, they were ready for some light-hearted fun. And so it didn't take long for the first witty text message to appear on screen, soon followed by a marriage proposal... An unstoppable string of funny remarks followed and the moderator had to intervene in order to save the professor's contribution. The audience had a ball; clearly the professor less so.

This example shows that the audience's wishes are the main determinant whether a programme item works out or not. In this example the opportunity to send anonymous messages triggered mischievous behaviour and sabotaged the professor's best intentions. The programme item had not been designed right. The Designers of that meeting (we, in fact) should heed the lesson and the lesson we got from this small disaster was:

> **Never allow a technical solution to promote itself into a programme unless there is a valid design reason.**

A 'valid design reason' means a desire of the participants to do something which is physically impossible, in pursuit of the meeting's objectives, and so there has to be recourse to some sort of technology that is additional to, and beyond, the physical capacities of humans. Some choices about technology are non-issues, such as the need for good microphones in a large auditorium; others are less obvious, as shown by the above example.

Source of Inspiration

Technology does not only teach harsh lessons, however, it can also provide inspiration. A good example is the new type of platforms that allow for dynamic voting. Meeting participants do not just vote, they can follow the dynamics of the vote as they are cast and preferences shift to favour one option rather than another. By projecting the votes as a swarm around options, and by permitting participants to change their votes, attendees can actively influence the voting process. They may decide to come to the rescue of options that risk being lost or further strengthen options that emerge as winners. This can be interspersed with rounds of negotiations, lobbying, alliance forming – a dynamism within and between groups that would be impossible without the platform.

Here, the technology enables a participant desire, even one that was initially no more than latent, to emerge during the process of casting votes, turning it into a dynamic process rather than a static poll. This technology works for the reason that it adds a dimension to a familiar process, in this case the dimension of time to voting. Votes can be reviewed and re-cast. Once people have participated in this method of voting, they recognise, with hindsight, the latent desire. Many other technical novelties tend to disappear for the same reason: they do not resonate with a real desire. The Meeting Designer can draw from inspiring technical novelties to his heart's desire, as long as he is able to properly assess the impact of that technology on participant behaviour.

Meeting Technology and Participant Behaviour

The speaker asked the technician to dim the lights a little to improve the visibility of his presentation on the screen. The participants responded in unison, agreeing this reduced lighting was much more effective.

However, there was a side effect to this little technical intervention which went almost unnoticed. The speaker himself became poorly illuminated. Sometimes, part of the presentation briefly lit up on his face or belly, after which he would quickly sidestep, thus reducing himself to a minor presence. As a result, the participants felt more connected to the screen than to the person talking to them, and in the background there was constant muttering. That makes sense: chatting in the twilight is fun!

Which clever inventor will come up with an ingenious form of spotlight capable of following a presenter who doesn't want to be eclipsed? Even after so many years of PowerPoint (since 1987!) eclipsing still happens. Another solution would be to have a projector with enough light capacity, but these do not come cheap.

Just like all factors in the environment, technology inevitably has an impact on the way participants behave at meetings, and this can be used to great advantage. For example:

During the opening ceremony of an office building, we set up a number of 'attention stations.' Each station offered guests a moment of special attention. In one of them, we would ask visitors to tell us something about an eye-catching feature of their appearance, such as a coloured scarf or a brooch. The replies were fascinating: little gem stories that laid bare a small piece of participant's personal lives and perhaps of their identities. Visitors were remarkably relaxed when telling their stories, probably thanks to the fact that we used the video camera as a friendly catalyst of human warmth and not as something alien. We would zoom in closely on the garment or accessory, without showing the rest of the person. This created an atmosphere in which interviewer, guest and camera were all fully and intimately focused on the object and its story. The interviews were taped and shown later on a large screen, attracting large groups of viewers.

Human behaviour in front of a camera is broadly predictable. As in that well-known TV show for which a fake camera crew would gain access to all kinds of quarters, simply by stating: "Yes, hi! We have come to shoot an episode of X..." That simple sentence and the presence of the camera opened doors. This kind of predictable impact on behaviour can be used in Meeting Design to obtain a desired result. The impact of technology on behaviour may also be counterproductive, though:

The association conference promoted a new, clever device: a little box that was to enhance networking. It allowed meeting participants to exchange messages and business cards, receive organizational announcements, reply to polls and... spot who was sitting close to you. Most of this functionality was very useful, but with an embarrassingly counterproductive sidekick: During presentations and workshops, about 25% of those present were watchfully following their device so as not to miss any of the "buzz" on screen. As a result, and as you can guess, 75% of the buzz created by the people in their session was lost upon them.

The desire to know who exactly is sitting in the meeting room is a legitimate curiosity, but here, the solution decreases rather than increases togetherness. That is perverse. Probably in due course the users of such devices are likely to develop an alternative to this counterproductive behaviour, the way my great-grandfather needed time to learn to talk to other people on a telephone. If no alternative develops, the device will end on a shelf and something else will allow meeting participants to satisfy their curiosity about who that good-looking person in row 2 is.

Technology and the Meeting Designer's Own Know-how

When choosing technology and fitting it into the design, the Meeting Designer needs to be aware of available technical options and their impact on behaviour. Access to technical options means having a network of informants. Technology is moving too fast and it is impossible to always know what is available in order to satisfy legitimate desires participants may have. Literally hundreds of companies are producing various forms of voting technology. So rather than knowing all the options by heart, the Meeting Designer needs to be informed about novel technological developments: visit trade fairs, ask for demonstrations and nurture a network of diverse people and organizations: suppliers, friends, nerds, whom we might label together as 'tech spotters'.

For any specific meeting, the ability to properly deploy all the boxes, booths and beamers depends on their contribution in achieving the results of the meeting. The criteria to judge that positive impact can be found in the Experience Concept. If the EC is a birth visit, a Kraambezoek, then constantly checking out data on some little screen is not a good fit. If, on the other hand, the EC is an intercontinental flight, it is!

There are three different methods a Meeting Designer uses to find out how compatible any form of technology is with an EC:

1. Experimenting himself with the chosen device, preferably under the same circumstances as in the meeting itself. The experiment should allow him to establish not only to what extent the technology satisfies the desires of participants, but also the more general impact it has on behaviour.
2. Keeping his distance and staying well away from the actual operation of the technology. Standing too close risks causing the *button syndrome* – a special form of tunnel vision. If the Meeting Designer starts to meddle with the buttons, he risks losing a proper perspective on the participants' behaviour. Time and again we have seen speakers and moderators joining in with technicians in a frantic fiddle with wires, buttons, jacks and displays, totally oblivious of the context within which they were acting. The Meeting Designer should stay away from the buttons and leave the technology with the technicians.
3. Questioning whether some device or other needs to be provided just as a 'given'. Whenever you find that certain technologies have become a given, extra vigilance is called for. The best example is, of course, the widespread use of PowerPoint. This presentation programme has enormously improved the possibilities of illustrating oral presentations with visuals. It has become a given to the extent that "My presentation

is ready" today means that someone has finished putting their PP slides together. The real meaning of the sentence — the performance of a presenter in front of a group of participants – seems to have eroded into nothingness. This can be perceived strongly in many presentations: yes, the PowerPoint file is ready, but the live presentation is not ready at all. Actually, it has often been given remarkably little thought. Just having the slides ready seems to be enough – a highly counterproductive view of live communication. Solutions are not hard to find, though:

The CEO's desire was to put his vision about the company's future across to his 1,000 employees. He asked us for advice about his PowerPoint presentation, aware of his limits as a speaker and the culture of his organisation. His audience would be made up of no-nonsense workers, not accustomed to sitting on their behinds for more than 15 minutes.
We suggested he let go of the PowerPoint as a given and designed the following opening sequence for the meeting: when the 1,000 people had filled the meeting room, the lighting was dimmed until only a narrow light beam from a moving spotlight was left. While the beam slowly moved through the room, the CEO's crisp voice depicted the future of the company in firm, measured tones. Finally, the beam came to rest on one person, somewhere in the centre of the room. There he was, the CEO, standing up amidst his people and looking around. Unplugged this time, he said: "That is what I would like to achieve, together with you!"

In this example, we discarded the given and used relatively simple technical solutions to put the CEO in the position he desired. By recording his message in advance on tape, he had all the time and tranquillity he needed to turn it into a cry from the heart – which was exactly what he thought was needed. The lighting supported the message in a visually attractive way. We used technology the way it is meant to be used: to enable things that are desired but physically impossible.

Technology in the Design Process

What sort of desires might the Meeting Designer himself have in the design process, desires that cannot be realised by normal physical means? With around 30 to 40 designs required from us every year, a number of things are indeed impossible. For instance, the participant interviews the Designer has to carry out number several hundreds, so it is physically impossible to meet all these people personally. Combine that with the site visits to hear the Venue Message and the sessions to extract the EC and the CF from the Meeting Owner and it is obvious that the Meeting Designer cannot manage this workload without highly effective ICT connectivity.

A second point is the desk research required for a robust content analysis. This may involve going through book titles and summaries, but far more frequently rapidly scanning annual reports, project plans, stories in the press and reports of previous meetings. The time when you had to retrieve all this from your snail-mailbox is fortunately gone. Meeting Design as a discipline comes with savvy Internet use and the ability to quickly dig up directly relevant, but also indirectly utilisable, data from the internet.

Today's web-based applications offer a further series of aids, such as shared project planning, integrated meeting invitation and registration platforms, etc. However, most of these applications are especially useful for meeting production and less for content-related Meeting Design.

One option worth mentioning is crowd sourcing, with a view to obtaining input, solutions and opinions from large groups of (future) participants. Surveys submitted in advance of the design process allow participants to suggest themes, recommend speakers and express views on the proposed content. Real-time assessments can lead to on-site adaptations of the programme, or even to participant-led processing of content:

The conference started with a one-hour session with all 800 participants seated at tables of 10. Each table was to identify the most urgent question in the field. The ten would appoint a questioner, who would send their table's question by e-mail to an 'Editorial Board.' It was this Board's task to collate and order the questions, and choose the ten most relevant ones.

Meanwhile, a panel of experts was waiting eagerly in a room backstage. The Editorial Board brought them the ten selected questions and each of them took one for a first round of discussions in breakout rooms. Displays all over the venue announced which expert would be tackling which question in which meeting room. The original questioners received a text message, asking them to join the relevant expert and ask their questions. All this was done with a swing while participants were drinking their coffees. Then off they went to the appointed rooms to engage in the programme they themselves had co-created.

The essence of this design solution was the meeting owner's desire for the conference to be driven ultimately by demand. It is easy to rise to that challenge with ten people, but on this occasion technology made it possible to do it with as many as 800. The desire came first – the technology enabled. And that brings us back to the real role of technology in meetings. Meeting Designers use technology to realise the physically impossible desires of meeting owners and participants. When doing this, it is essential to integrate into the design the human behaviour that the technology is likely to prompt.

The Sceptic:

Oona is a project manager who works for Google in India. She is a self-employed professional, based in Bangalore.

O: Eric, Mike, both of you, I see some sort of paradox in what you've been saying, and I wonder if you could clear it up for me. If designers do not incorporate new technology in their designs, how can people ever develop a desire for it?

M/E: Good point, Oona, thanks for raising it. Is your question really about design in general and not just about meeting design? At least, that's the feeling we get.

O: Yes, I guess you're right.

M/E: So, could we just concentrate for a moment on meeting design, because that's the area we know something about?

O: Of course, although any analogies with other industries will be interesting.

M/E: OK, then. Well, as far as meetings are concerned, wishes often emerge from meetings that are not purposefully designed: private meetings, meetings in our personal lives. Actually, the wishes rarely spring from the technology itself.

O: You mean things like Facebook, based on a certain technology, but actually satisfying a non-technological desire: the wish to feel in touch with other members of society?

M/E: Right. Differently from many other industries, ours – the meeting industry – has a product that is quite fuzzy at its edges.

O. Two people meeting in a shop and talking briefly is a meeting, but not a product of your industry?

M/E: Right, and in practice, things can be even more complicated. A firm in the Netherlands designed a marketing campaign in which their staff went to pubs, so they could start talking to other customers and promote a certain drink. All done in an indirect, low-key, informal, perhaps even sneaky way, but very effective!

O: So that was the contrary: a designed meeting that looked like an un-designed one.

M/E: Right again, so the dividing line between 'Meeting Industry Meetings' and just people meeting is fuzzy.

O: In India that line doesn't exist. Just look at our streets. They look like an on-going meeting all the time.

M/E: Using smartphones as well?

O: Sure!

M/E: OK, so people experiment with technology in all kinds of settings. That can breed desires, as well.

O: Do meeting participants experiment too?

M/E: They do, massively, and this influences meetings everywhere. But strangely enough, there is no such thing as a Meeting Technology Lab.

O: Do you think there should be a Meeting Technology Lab somewhere?

M/E: Yes, definitely! In fact, it's amazing that nobody has set it up yet! What would happen there should go far beyond technology, by the way. We think technology is only one of the fields worth experimenting with. There's lots more.

O: Such as?

M/E: Oh, participant dynamics, the influence of hormones and chemical substances on participant behaviour, the psychology of decision-making, learning styles, communication drivers, etc., etc...

O: Sounds like a budding industry

M/E: It is. And at the same time it isn't. People have been meeting since ancient times, but only recently have we started to ask ourselves what happens when they do so. The logistics is well developed, but the rest is very young – like us! Joke!

O: Like India too. Old culture but young at heart. Thanks, and may God bless you.

3.5 Facilitation

The Clumsy Photographer

he intention was for the meeting to be a bit nonsensical, but with serious undertones. It was on the verge of reaching its climax with a theatre sketch about the organisation's past, when the photographer tripped over the wire of the CD-player. The plug popped out of the power socket, the music evaporated and the actors stopped in the middle of a scene, stunned. The audience looked at the main character in great expectation, both the technician and the photographer cursed just a bit too loud and the coffee lady called out: "You moron!", startled at hearing her own voice. Gone was the magic which had been palpable just seconds earlier and nobody had the wits to improvise a solution. The meeting collapsed like an amateur cheese soufflé.

Everything was set for a spectacular meeting and in one second Murphy's law blew it to smithereens. It was not just that the music stopped, but in an instant it seemed that the whole event had gone sour. What had caused this? It took us a while to get to the bottom of this. One might think: these things happen – just bad luck; which is true. What we failed to grasp, though, was why *everybody* seemed to do precisely the wrong thing (or nothing). In the end, our interpretation was that people who had a role in executing the meeting had little idea of its essence, of why ultimately each of them was there. And so, when something went wrong, the only thing they could come up with was the natural, primary mode of just focusing on their own little task, with no concern for the overall outcome.

The catering lady, who should not have been in the auditorium in the first place but behind her coffee counter, considered herself a spectator because in that moment there was nothing going on in terms of coffee. She was not aware that participants could perceive her as something other than a person pouring coffee into cups. The photographer was in the meeting just to take snapshots – not as a part of a greater whole in which everybody contributed to an end. The actors failed to improvise because they just saw themselves as the enactors of a text written by someone else and not as partners helping to fashion the dynamics during the meeting.

And so, the whole group of people giving shape to the meeting, to the experience of the participants, were not a team with a shared mission. They saw themselves as being at the meeting just to do their own task and had no vision of adding to the meeting as a means of communication. The trivial accident with the cable brought all this to light.

A situation like the one described is unlikely to produce a meeting with good outcomes. Essentially, the tipping point was not a poorly taped electric wire – that too. More importantly, there was something wrong with the perception of the design of the meeting by the people involved. There was something missing and it is a task of the Meeting Designer to provide for it. This chapter will illustrate what and how.

The Score and the Meeting

We have already compared meetings with musical performances in Chapter 3.2. Expanding on that, the design of a meeting corresponds to the composition of a piece of music. In music it materialises as a score: a stack of sheets with pentagrams on which the composer has dotted which notes to play, when to play them, in which time and rhythm and by which instrument. The execution of the score is in the hands of the conductor. Depending on his musical ideas and taste, he instructs the musicians on the colour, the accents and the intention of the performance. He cannot do so entirely at free will because the composer has added code words to the score to guide him. There are hundreds of these and they come from Italian. Legato means that the notes are played connected, while staccato is just the opposite, each note on its own. They vary from *affrettando*, an increasingly hurried pace, to con brio — with vigour and spirit. All these indications help the conductor to grasp the composer's intentions even though the latter may have passed away centuries ago. It is all to the benefit of the audience who get to enjoy the work the way it was meant. What do we see if we compare the 'execution management' for music with that of meetings? What guidance do the 'performers' during meetings receive? How can their behaviour assume the desired tone or colour? The steering mechanism appears to be a type of common law, based on received practice – not because it is the most effective but because there is nothing else. The support vocabulary – known by all practitioners in musical performances – is simply missing. There are no specific words to indicate that at some point the support services should slowly fade out, or that the moderation needs to become more energetic. What we have is a limited offering of terms true to the hospitality roots of the meeting industry, such as "service-oriented," "pro-active" or "correct," with a topping of terms like "interactive" and "inspiring" from group dynamics. That, however, is a meagre vocabulary, insufficient to perceptively direct the complex dynamics of large groups of people in meetings, insufficient to clarify to the meeting performers of our initial example what exactly was expected from them. Of course everyone knew their tasks and which actions that involved, but they had no idea of the coherence and the harmony in the programme. And that is where things went wrong when the wire-tripping incident occurred.

The Notion of Facilitation Style

Like a musical score, the design of a meeting programme is carried out by a diverse group of people in a ratatouille of roles: from chairman of the day to catering person and from light engineer to cloakroom attendant. They all shape their roles according to the know-how and customs of their profession. The composer who writes music assumes that the musicians in the orchestra are capable of playing their instruments and equally, the Meeting Designer sees no point in meddling with the technical details of catering, sound amplification or participant registration. But, as we already argued in the final paragraph of Chapter 3.2, what the Meeting Designer does interfere with is the overarching connection between all these support functions, the relationship between what the light engineer is doing while the chairman is opening the day and while the last coffee cups are being cleared away by catering. All these people need to understand what tone to generate together in their work. In order to direct that connection we need a specific notion that avoids any misunderstanding between all the professionals, a notion to which we have given the name of Facilitation Style.

Defining Facilitation Style

In the execution of a meeting, the Facilitation Style provides the same guidance as the musical terms do when playing a piece of music. The individual performance of the instrumentalists corresponds to the individual behaviour of the meeting staff and just as the musician is sure to play the right notes, the catering lady will ask: "What would you like to drink?" The point is not what these professionals do or say, the point is how they do it. It is the subtlety of the tone and the behaviour when speaking the simple sentence about the drink. The Facilitation Style describes and gives direction to the basic attitude, the 'vibes' of the staff, indicating the way in which they should manifest themselves during the meeting. The attitude is a desired way of being, rather than a description of their actions. And so, our definition of it is as follows:

> **The Facilitation Style describes the desired state of being of all those who give shape to the meeting during its execution.**

The state of being in our example was "somewhat nonsensical but with serious undertones." If all the people involved there had been thoroughly imbued with this attitude, the wire trip-up could have fitted in perfectly. The actors could have improvised and poked fun at the photographer, the coffee lady could have commented later from behind her coffee stand that the photographer's clumsiness was hilarious – the incident could have turned into a positively memorable moment! Getting these reactions, though, required a different presence in that moment, an attitude planted into the staff's mind beforehand, a state of being for which we feel the Meeting Designer is co-responsible. And that is exactly the difference between Facilitation Style and the common hospitality-industry-friendliness-cum-professionalism on the one hand and general good teamwork on the other. The latter have a bearing on how people act, Facilitation Style is about how people are. As a result of how they are, they also act in a certain way, but their actions grow out of something that has been implanted, taking root at a deeper layer.

So that explains why we have formulated the definition the way we have. It does not, however, explain why we have chosen the particular word 'Facilitation.'

Making Things Easy

We consider Facilitation as everything meeting staff do to make the meeting go more smoothly. Facilitating and facilitation derive from the Latin 'facilis/e' which means 'easy'.

Traditionally, the term facilitator has been reserved for the person who structures the interaction between participants and not for all the other professionals involved in making things during the meeting 'easier.' In our view, however, the welcome desk hostess or the sound engineer do play a facilitating role with their work. Strictly speaking, and to avoid confusion, we could call this 'support facilitation,' but let us agree for our purposes that facilitation includes the totality of people-generated support during meetings. In order to turn the correct execution of tasks into the necessary building blocks of the intended participant experience, the facilitation needs to hit the right tone. Here is an example of what happens if one of the support functions plays out of key:

When the Ministry of Health was organising a small-scale international conference for policy makers concerned with innovative care, we asked a small PCO to provide organisational support. The PCO was a company just consisting of a married couple who did everything themselves. In the preparatory phase their work was impeccable; and during the conference itself a pleasant and relaxed relationship developed between the couple and the rest of the small conference team. They manned the registration desk, ran the logistics, meals and hotel contacts – all flawlessly.

Content-wise the meeting was a distinct success and when we went to the Ministry for the evaluation, we thought we were in for a party. We were indeed, with one exception: the PCO's work. Their casual manners and informal style and way of dressing had not gone down very well with the organisers and many of their foreign guests.

A loose and informal style is generally acceptable in the Netherlands. In fact, in social exchanges it is desirable as an expression of equality and 'no fuss.' However, after having read Chapter 1.4, it will not come as a surprise to you that in the international arena reactions to this attitude may vary significantly. For some of the participants the PCO couple's loose attitude had seemed a lack of consideration and respect, and was on the verge of being actually offensive. This had irritated participants and made them less receptive to the innovative meeting content. As a result, in the eyes of the meeting owner, the PCO had made it more difficult to achieve the outcomes of the meeting. That is not good facilitation.

How should the Meeting Designer have described the way he wished the PCO staff to present themselves, something more in tune with the expectations of the international audience? To answer that question, we need to establish how the Facilitation Style should be expressed, what kind of language is necessary. Let's think of an unlikely example: a serial killer talking to a captive audience. It may seem strange, but this example will help us clarify the practical application of Facilitation Style.

Hannibal the Cannibal

In the film 'Silence of the Lambs' a rooky female detective (played by Jodie Foster) meets the serial killer Hannibal the Cannibal. Our first impression of Anthony Hopkins' throat-gripping performance is that the character is strangely subdued. He is almost gentle while at the same time his presence is overwhelming, because beneath the gentleness you feel a possible volcano of violence. Foster's acting as FBI agent Clarice equally mesmerises the audience. Her interpretation of the role is striking as a peculiar combination of someone with great determination, in spite of being inexperienced.

Describing Hannibal's way of being as merely gentle would miss the mark totally. It is the combination of being so calm with pure evil that makes Hopkins' role blood-curdling. The quiet evil Hannibal evokes is brilliantly mirrored by Jodie Foster who infuses Clarice with inexperienced determination.[1] Either role cannot be captured in a single word. To describe it you need the combination of a state of being (in this case 'evil' or 'determination') with a qualification ('gentle' and 'inexperienced').

The reason why we quote this example is this: describing the way actors interpret their roles helps us to understand how to describe Facilitation Styles. We specify a certain way of being and combine it with a qualifying

[1] Both actors were awarded an Oscar for their interpretations.

characteristic. The two notions together produce an effective description of the desired behaviour for the meeting staff. The precise characterisation of that behaviour makes it possible to steer support staff. Language-wise the Facilitation Style takes the form of a noun representing the way of being and a qualifying adjective for the specification.

What happens if we apply this approach to the PCO with the loose style mentioned in our previous example? Some participants complained that they were too informal style but a strictly formal style would not have been effective either. That would have stifled the innovative mood participants needed to find novel solutions. Therefore, the style should have been light-footed formality, or nimble formality – formality with the legroom for a small joke or witticism, a slightly different solution, an uncommon context. For the reception desk support this would have meant a special, stylish presentation of both the people (their attire) and the desk. In combination with the formal attitude, that would have allowed the programme design to be carried out with the right tone. A precise description of the Facilitation Style would have made it possible to guide the PCO couple towards this behaviour.

The Meeting Designer's Role

Achieving congruence between the style of those who facilitate, including the support facilitation, is one of the things a Meeting Designer does. The reason is that the way participants perceive the programme – in the broadest possible sense – depends on how they are treated. That, in turn, has an impact on the outcomes of the meeting, for which the Meeting Designer is responsible. It is part of his work to establish the togetherness environment that is necessary to make the meeting a success and the Facilitation Style is an integral part of shaping that environment.

The Methodology

The next point is of course how it works. The formulation of the Facilitation Style is generally the result of a bit of level-headed analysis. It is definitely not a sudden brainwave that hits the Meeting Designer from the depths of his subconscious self. It is a deceptively simple task, structured by an overall awareness of the meeting, its subparts, its objectives and its participants. This is how we do it.

The starting points are the Content Flow and the Experience Concept. The Meeting Owner wants the content to move in a certain way and to do so within the context of a defined participant experience. Therefore, the question the Meeting Designer needs to answer is: what kind of behaviour from the realm of the EC will cause the CF to happen? Paraphrased: What is a way of being that is part of the EC and that will make it easy for the CF to materialise? What type of supporting behaviour from professionals is helpful with a view to achieving the dynamics between the participants? All of the above formulations may sound a bit California-dreamlike and theoretical, however. So why not make it practical and revisit the example used in Chapter 3.2 so that we can see how the methodology works? Here we are again with the good conversation between the three people involved in the Hong Kong project.

Applying the Methodology

Would it help that conversation if we used a sharp interview style during the initial dinner? A tone that clarifies and zooms in on any possible differences? The answer is pretty obvious: no, it wouldn't. We do not think such a style will make it easy to get to the shared insights and position Stewart, the CEO, is envisaging as the meeting's result. Stewart wants the three men to understand what connects them in their views on the Hong Kong project. Consequently, a 'connecting' style will work much better. That yields the noun 'connectivity.'

The EC Stewart has in mind is that of a quiet conversation after a fine meal. He does not want any additional excitement around the topic of conversation which is probably electrifying enough in its own right. He wants the men to make a step change and he wants them to do this in a constructive atmosphere. The adjective we are looking for should come from the world of after-meal talks and it should express the way of being that will help the CF to take its proper course. An excellent candidate is 'tranquil.' Taking the noun and the adjective, we obtain a Facilitation Style defined as 'tranquil connectivity.' That is a clear description of what the Meeting Designer would expect as the basic attitude of all those involved in facilitating this meeting. In this particular case, there would only be support facilitation because, as you will recall, there is no moderator guiding the conversation. The FS imposes a ban on commotion and fidgeting, it excludes polarisation and contrasts and a whole lot of other things – enough for everyone to be able to act coherently.

The Meaning of Congruence

'Tranquil connectivity' describes the togetherness environment Stewart wants the three conversation participants to enjoy. In practice, this is probably not what he will say, but the Meeting Designer proposes the formulation, based on EC and CF. Thanks to these words, from the very first briefings onwards, the entire project can proceed in this style and tone throughout achieving the desired environment. So does Stewart's introductory letter effectively create the right spirit? We let the reader decide, but if it does, it means that Stewart's communication staff have done a good job. Incidentally, with regard to support facilitation the communication people in all organisations are a Meeting Designer's regular dancing partners. We will return to this point in the next section.

What does this example mean for the cooperation between the Meeting Designer and the facilitators, whether in a primary facilitation role or in support functions? In any case, it does not mean that the Meeting Designer establishes the facilitators' way of working. The point is not what technique the moderator uses when conducting a session or what technology the PCO deploys for participant registration. What it does mean is how these techniques impact on the participant.

A nice illustration of this comes from a world outside meetings: sales. Apple has understood the communicative value of a specific Facilitation Style. Arguably, customers visiting Apple stores may be considered as having a meeting with Apple shop assistants. The Facilitation Style in Apple stores could be characterised as 'patient competence,' patient as in 'with patience.' There is one and only one criterion that determines when the contact in the shop is finished and that is when the client is satisfied. This style is congruent with Apple's product: conceived to be at the user's service even if (especially if) he knows zilch about computers. The user experiences comfort (Apple's EC) and the IT knowledge the shop assistant expects him to master is limited to what he needs to know to simply run the thing (Apple's CF). At least, that is the prevailing situation in 2012....

Communication, Venue, Technical Services and Others

Over the years, experience has taught us the vital importance of involving the people responsible for communications very closely in the practical application of the meeting's FS. It is only natural that all of the communications around the meeting should bear the imprint of the desired FS. Also, first impressions tend to stick and so the tone of the first mail, the first letter, the first briefing with a speaker will strongly influence the dynamics that develop around a meeting. There is always a risk of communication staff wrong-footing participants but that risk is smaller if the Meeting Designer manages to convey of the required communication style successfully.

In our example, Leon and his colleagues would have come to the Otto e Mezzo restaurant very differently disposed if Stewart's letter had begun like this:

Leon,

Project Hong Kong worries me. Also your position in project Hong Kong worries me. Time for action...

That does not breathe 'tranquil connectivity.' That breathes concern and opposition, with the likelihood that participants start off in a defensive mode. A letter phrased like this might have led to a list of action points, but not to a good conversation.

The venue is another variable that calls for the Meeting Designer's undivided attention during the design stage, as we have seen in Chapter 3.3. There we introduced the notion of the Venue Message which depends essentially on the physical environment. In addition to the building itself, it is essential to ascertain whether the venue staff are capable of adapting the way they normally work and approach participants to the FS. Unless these mesh, the Meeting Designer may need to advise the meeting owner to consider a change in venue – an excellent way of making yourself unpopular! Since the venue is often chosen early on and irrevocably, quick action may be called for.

A third party playing a decisive role in attaining the FS are the suppliers of technical services. Their support may include AV equipment, room layout and all sorts of other amenities. It is easier when this relationship starts early in the process, but even at a later stage it is possible to influence the way these partners operate and to foster adaptability.

On the evening before a two-day conference for ICT professionals, the Meeting Designer gave a final briefing to the operators responsible for video registration, sound, lights and special effects. The ten-man crew listened attentively to the explanation about the programme which did not limit itself to what they were supposed to do, but homed in especially on what the whole team was going to achieve for the participants. It provided a clear insight into what the Meeting Designer, on behalf of the Meeting Owner, had in mind for the two days and the goals the whole team had to reach. Apart from encouraging them with his passion for efficiency, he described the Facilitation Style as 'helpful innovation.'

The technicians listened attentively and reacted with remarkable enthusiasm to the briefing – remarkable because there was a lot of pressure on them to complete the conference set-up.

Halfway through day one an emergency message came in: the organiser's external software supplier had failed to put together a small application. It was a clock that needed to be visible on the screen during a crucial session with audience participation. During this session, participants would be given exactly 1 minute of speaking time and would be videoed onto the central screen. The clock was a tool for implicit time management, avoiding embarrassing interventions by the chair. Cutting off participants would stifle the atmosphere of 'helpful innovation' needed for a successful programme. One of the technicians immediately saw the implications of the missing clock and volunteered: "Don't worry, we'll get that sorted out. I know what you want."

The next morning, the crew proudly demonstrated a circle-shaped clock that was placed in the upper corner of the video images. A little train choo-chooed the circle perimeter in precisely one minute. It was even possible to stop it midway and push it back or shorten its course. The train was exactly what we needed. Two of them had been pottering almost the whole night and got it just right. The afternoon's intervention round was a great success.

The clock-train materialised not because it was someone's task or out of commercial interest but because the engineers had understood the dynamics needed to make the programme a success and which Facilitation Style would enable that. Therefore, they were perfectly capable of thinking up the specs for the clock by themselves. Their professional pride gave them the drive to finish it, in spite of the lack of sleep. Instead of being just a bunch of people who had a job to do, the technicians had become part of a conspiracy: a conspiracy to make the meeting a success. They acted in harmony with the desired tone of the meeting, something the Meeting Designer had made them aware of: helpful innovation. That was exactly what their contribution was.

Participants were guided through the main auditorium of a prestigious conference centre along a succession of carefully arranged, compact stands. The international audience were deeply involved in short interview conversations at each stand, exactly as we had envisaged in the programme design. The interpreters accompanying each group provided perfect communication support. Then the lights went out. Literally.

The unthinkable happened: nobody panicked. The programme was quite innovative for organizers as well as audience and the Facilitation Style had been carefully tuned to that: 'controlled innovation.' And that was exactly how all the professionals behaved. Nobody lost control. The session continued in the diffuse darkness almost as if it was all part of the game. Meanwhile, the technical company – who, as it turned out later, were not to blame for the problem – tried quickly to restore the lighting and the interpreters carried on unperturbed translating for the participants.

After 14 minutes the lights came on again. Astonishingly, the guided tour of the stands was still on schedule.

All the people involved in realising that meeting brilliantly stood up to the test of making it a success. Professionalism? Certainly. But also something else: the understanding that the meeting's objectives could be achieved more easily with the right behaviour from everybody, guided by the right wording for the instructions.

Istanbul

An international manufacturing company hauled its top 80 executives to Istanbul to discuss its new strategy. With the shifting weight from West to East in industrial relationships, Istanbul was spot-on for this dialogue, right on the crossroads of Europe and Asia.

In this shift, it was important to carefully cope with the sensitivities of many operating companies about their autonomy. Their interest in the strategy needed to be kindled and any resistance appeased so that implementation would become a shared commitment.

In order to strike a balance between stimulating debates and control, between diverging interests and shared loyalty, the moderator's FS was carefully plotted out as 'thoughtful curiosity.' In the course of the three-day programme that proved an inspired choice. The very first moments on stage with the CEO embodied the exact mix of the two FS aspects. It produced a minimum of tension and a maximum of exchange. After the meeting, many participants expressed their surprised satisfaction with the sensitivity of the facilitation, which had produced a safe environment allowing participants to engage in high-quality, open dialogue.

In a qualitative evaluation the participants expressed that the wrong style could have caused serious communicative problems. Confrontational curiosity, for instance, a useful style in circumstances that call for more external stimuli, would have been risky. For this meeting, it would have brought things to a head too soon, creating uncertainty about the company's future. This kind of strategy meeting is not something a company does every month. With people from over 30 different countries, a corrosive togetherness environment would have been hard to redress. Reconvene the meeting? The shareholders would not have been amused.

Conclusion

We have observed that meetings with a congruent design and facilitation benefit from a clear FS that guides the behaviour of all the 'staff' involved. Every restaurant owner is aware that his guests can only appreciate the quality of his food if the waiters behave towards diners in the manner the menu seems to suggest. In an Italian restaurant it is fitting for staff to show Italian courtesy and gallantry. Only then will the diners feel the space to experience the untold pleasures of Italian cooking. If, on the other hand, the waiters are not aligned with how the food is 'meant,' then the dining experience will be below par. In their behaviour individual waiters should stay close to an established norm. Otherwise visitors may feel insecure and distracted from the essential pleasure of enjoying good food in the company of others.

The suppliers of content who are the topic of our next chapter play a different role, more like that of a restaurant chef. They may be a bit more eccentric – literally a bit outside the centre, although in yet another paradox, they take centre stage.

Sceptic:

We meet Keith, an old friend who runs a sheep farm in New Zealand. Former world traveller, experimental musician and now the producer of fine sheep's cheese.

K: Damn good CEO, this Stewart guy. Must be a Kiwi like me. Of course you guys made him up.

E/M: We are designers. Our passion is to give shape to the world – well, at least temporarily to a small part of it.

K: Yeah, you give shape to the world, I give sheep to the world. Some pun that, eh? What is more useful, food or thoughts? Food for thought, I should think...

E/M: What do you think about this chapter?

K: Well, when we last met, in our 20's, we made great music on great beaches, with great girls around. Since then, you have turned into a bunch of old Fascist farts.

E/M: Trust a New Zealander to give you a straight opinion...

K: I mean, the two of you think everything can be controlled, measured and steered, even the style in which people react to other people. You must be out of your minds! I think you are fundamentally wrong, it's a model that gives the world a depressing predictability. Full control, despicable! Thanks to ideas like that we live in a plastic world, man. No spontaneity. None at all.

E/M: So what do you see as an opportunity for the Meetings Business?

K: Well…, what about un-conferencing? I went to a meeting like that in Sydney last year. Good fun, great parties, too. No plastic people there. Why don't you use formats like that?

E/M: Did we say we didn't?

K: But your book breathes big business, not the human scale…

E/M: We sometimes work for big business, but you are wrong about the human scale. Our job is to translate meetings, also big business meetings, into encounters with a real human scale. That is the shape we want to give to the world and our clients and participants appreciate that.

K: So what happened to anarchy?

E/M: We have never been true anarchists. Neither have you, and you know it. Big business yearns for improved relationships and meetings between true human beings, meetings with a soul. Just structuring meetings and organising them isn't good enough for us. We want to put some heart into things.

K: That sounds better. Here are my old pals again!

E/M: If un-conferencing is the thing that brings out the essence, that's what we will go for. But to be honest, most companies think in terms of more traditional and palpable results.

K: Here we go again, result is the only thing that counts. Financial results of course! Money. Capitalism is eating you alive, you clowns.

E/M: So how do you yourself cope with harsh economic realities? Do you dish out your cheese for free to anyone who happens to pass by?

K: No, in all fairness usually I don't… I market it well! But occasionally I do – my own type of charity. I put together parcels with cheese and some other stuff, for poor people in the village nearby and drop them in their yard at night, without letting on who it was. That gives me a lot of satisfaction.

E/M: There are many ways in which one can do other people a service. It hurts, though, when you say we took a wrong turn somewhere, because we honestly believe we did not.

K: OK, respect, man... I was just joking about you being old Fascist farts. At least about the Fascism I was, not about the fart bit.

E/M: Some control for the good cause?

K: No kidding! Let's go and have a beer.

3.6 Providers of Content

It Goes Like This. Should It?

his chapter is about the thing meeting organisers tend to think of first when picturing a meeting in their mind's eye: the role of speakers. Typical thoughts that generally travel through a meeting owner's head right from the start include: "Let's secure a couple of catchy names, so that we will get early registrations and some income." Or: "The Chairman of the Board must address the company's top 100." Or perhaps: "That lady has an interesting story. Let's ask her for our annual management retreat."

Although this approach may produce valid reasons for deciding who to invite as speakers, it tends to be ad hoc. In our experience, the vast majority of meeting programmes are crafted this way: think of a topic; think of someone who knows a lot about that topic; invite that person as a speaker. It will not surprise you that as Meeting Designers, we feel that the deployment of speakers is an integral part of a broader process: What speakers have to say and how they put it across is subordinate to the overall programme design, and a good design is built on stated objectives and desired outcomes. Except if a meeting is perfectly dove-tailed to the message of just a single speaker, building a programme on the basis of one or several speakers' specific content makes it much more difficult to achieve the meeting's objectives. It is like buying furniture before you've constructed the house: doing things in the wrong order.

The meeting owner may well come up with a different set of initial thoughts, such as: "A powerful programme, with top-notch speakers, will produce registrations and income." Or: "By the end of the day I want our top 100 managers to be thoroughly informed about XYZ." Or: "We want some powerful messages for our annual management retreat." These thoughts come in the form of objectives for the meeting and the desire to obtain an overall high-quality programme. They stay away from the knee-jerk reflex of immediately starting to invite speakers, jumping all the intermediate steps in the design process. Evidently, meeting owners have widely different ideas of what speakers are about in their programmes. So let's explore how we as Meeting Designers deal with the role of speakers during meetings.

Speakers and Content

We know of an institute for leadership development in Great Britain which has started to put on sessions during their conferences with no presentations, no keynote speeches, no PowerPoints, no panel debates, no rapporteurs and no chair. What these sessions do have is a specified duration, and so-called Gatekeepers and Passers. A session lasts for four hours and no one can leave during that time because the Gatekeepers ruthlessly prevent it. The task of the Passers is every now and then to inject a fresh statement in the proceedings.

There is no doubt that the organisers want to offer participants a successful session, yet the only thing they write in the agenda is a theme and the only structure is the erratic input from the Passers. The responsibility for obtaining good outcomes rests unconditionally and almost entirely with the participants. The conference and this session in particular have been extremely popular for several years now.

Does the session described here have speakers? Clearly, it does not in the traditional sense of the word 'speaker.' Normally, a speaker is a person who addresses a meeting's audience with the intention of putting across some kind of content. This is what distinguishes speakers from chairpersons, facilitators or moderators. They, too, address the audience, but what they deliver is structure or process, not content. In our example, therefore, we can safely say that there are no speakers. So, what happens with the content in this session?

In Chapter 2.3 we have already argued: No content, no meeting. In each meeting and each session something needs to happen with content. Interestingly, there is a lot of content at the British Leadership Development Conference. The difference is, the participants don't receive this content from speakers – they provide it themselves, prodded into doing so by the Passers.

In our opinion speakers are merely a special type of Content Providers; they inject content in the meeting by speaking. But speakers are not the only ones who can provide content, nor is 'speaking' the only way in which content can be injected. The Passers in our example provide content as well, and in this participant-driven session, the same goes for the participants themselves. In the remainder of this chapter we will base our discussion on this broader notion of Content Provider rather than on speakers.

How Effective is Speaking?

Most meetings provide their content much as Henry Ford preferred to deliver his T-model Fords: "Any customer can have a car painted any color that he wants, so long as it's black." The approach to choosing speakers we described at the outset of this chapter ("We have a meeting, so who should we ask as speakers?") is much like the salivation reflex of a Pavlov dog to the sound of a bell. Of all the aspects about meetings we discuss in this book, this one is probably most in need of a drastic overhaul.

Content Providers are almost invariably cast into the role of speaker and asked to deliver a monologue. We are convinced that, in many instances, that is not their most effective contribution to meeting programmes. Monologues and frontal teaching are notoriously poor as forms of didactics or inspiration. An important reason for this is that, unfortunately, few speakers possess the gift of truly captivating an audience with their content. Although this is not an easy thing to admit, many speakers would contribute more to meetings if they went about things differently.

For this reason, this chapter will propose many examples of doing things differently, in addition to a description of the process that explains what alternatives you may come up with. To get started, here is a first set of cases taken from our working practice and involving different roles for Content Providers.

Palette

The sage

During the meeting, the poet sat quietly in his corner, alternately listening and scribbling. After the chair had wound up the debate at the end of the afternoon, he was called on stage, duly introduced and asked to close the programme. The audience pricked up their ears. In a 7-minute poem he summarised the development of the content in the course of the day, reflected on a number of special moments and got some hearty laughs when he recounted three comical incidents. The warm applause he received meant more than just admiration for his poetry. It expressed the audience's appreciation of the kindly wisdom which had helped them to see the day's proceedings in a broader perspective.

The wisdom contained in the poet's words makes him a Content Provider; there is no doubt that he adds content to the programme. Thanks to the form in which he casts his message and the compactness of his language, the poet – the wise old sage – makes a sudden appeal to a different area of the participants' thoughts and emotions and deepens the insights they acquired during the day.

The outsider

The airline pilot was facing the participants with his hand on an impressive pile of manuals, check lists, maps and route descriptions on the table next to him. "When flying a Boeing 777 from Frankfurt to Manila, do you know what I need most?" The audience called out the obvious: "The checklists?" "The maps?" "The aircraft manual?" The pilot shook his head at each suggestion and then pointed to his head: "This, ladies and gentlemen, clear thinking and common sense."

Sometimes, the dialogue during a meeting needs input from an unexpected angle. This is particularly effective with groups who are strongly internally focused, use a lot of in-speak and have difficulty opening up to a different line of thought. In such a group, a Content Provider from a completely different industry can unblock the processing of the content.

In the above case, the pilot's comment immediately caught on with the audience: collected professionals from the oil and gas industry. Their sector, too, is flooded with rules and regulations, gathered together in copious manuals. His appeal to common sense as the solution to most of his problems with safety invited the participants to reconsider theirs.

One of the most penetrating characteristics of this role lies in the fact that the outsider does not try to make his content 'fit' the world of the participants. He focuses on his own story leaving it to the audience to translate it into their own circumstances and think of applications or analogies. This gets their brains going. To help the participants do that, time has to be allowed to process the outsider's input. On the other hand, there is no great need for interaction between outsider and audience; it would make little difference to the impact he has.

The fictitious character

Dolores Chu is a special lady. She always fits the meeting's content! The facilitator introduces her to the audience with a number of pictures taken from her life, like in a family photo album. Her bio and her life choices always contain questions that invite participants to reflect on the content of the meeting. Dolores is the ideal personification of countless issues: she comes from the real world and instils the personal touch that helps to deepen and intensify discussions between participants. There is one small detail participants only learn at the end of the day. Dolores does not exist...

Dolores Chu was invented by us at the interface between play and reality – a fascinating source of inspiration for providing content. Meeting participants do not meet her and cannot interact with her in any way. However, as long as her story is credible and participants get the time to understand how she connects with the content, Dolores can help them to look at that content from a practical, yet unforeseen angle. Once they get the hang of discussing Dolores's issues, whether she exists or not has become irrelevant.

The maverick

The youngster clad in T-shirt and jeans was a conspicuous presence at the meeting for people in the insurance business. "Money sucks," read the T-shirt. During the first breakout on high-level strategy he gave a relaxed account of his views on risks and future prospects. Initially, his partners in the conversation were cynical. "Right," you could hear them thinking, "here is yet another smart alec who's unwilling to come to terms with the fact that he will one day be old."

But when he proceeded to analyse the connection between traditional economic models, sustainability and knowledge sharing, he caught their attention. Especially when he connected that with the increases in world food prices and the relationship with immigration into Western countries. When in the end he produced an inedible loaf of bread made from compressed used banknotes, he had caught everybody's attention and the discussion between the others at the table took off.

Sometimes the Content Analysis brings out the need to sharpen up the content, to shine a spotlight on paradoxes and moot points. Under such circumstances, the Meeting Designer will try to enrich the programme with a Content Provider capable of opening the windows in people's minds and letting in some fresh air.

The maverick is just such a Content Provider. He overturns the accepted wisdom in an industry or an organisation and startles participants into leaving habitual paths by presenting unfamiliar or provocative viewpoints. Maximum interaction with the participants is required in order to obtain a thorough clash of ideas. The maverick's contribution is generally relatively short; after fifteen or twenty minutes he has served his purpose, catalysing a more intense mental chemistry in the meeting.

These examples give you a flavour of what is possible. It is obvious, though, that ideas like these on how to deploy Content Providers do not magically materialise from thin air. They arise from the design process. So let's now zoom in further and see how.

A Cookery Book?

You might have expected us to discuss Content Providers earlier in this book. Clearly, the choice and deployment of people like speakers is vital for the success of a meeting. This topic has been held back till now because, in order to use Content Providers in the best possible way, we need some grasp of all the notions we have been dealing with so far.

It would be convenient if there were simply a palette of possibilities, a number of hard-and-fast rules for dealing with Content Providers, a book of rules the Meeting Designer could learn by heart and then apply, adapting them as necessary to the needs of the moment. As with a cookery book. Of course there is no such thing; working with people is nowhere near as easy as working with flour, currants, an egg and margarine.

As in this book, in reality the choice of Content Providers comes quite late in the design process, although they are an integral part of it. The basic considerations for the use of Content Providers are actually quite simple. They are: "No Content, No Meeting"; and "Meetings inevitably give participants an experience." In line with this, all considerations about the delivery and the development of content – i.e. what the participants do with the content – as well as about how that content is brought to them, take us into the very heart of the meeting.

Chapters 2.2 and 2.3 have laid the foundations for the design of meetings: Content Flow, Experience Concept and Content Analysis (CF, EC and CA, respectively). Choices about the programme and what participants need to do are essentially governed by these three notions. During the first stages of designing, CF, EC and CA provide the building blocks for an initial skeleton version of the programme (as outlined in Chapter 3.2). That skeleton programme contains rough timeslots for providing content, what needs to be achieved in each of these slots and, consequently, a profile of the person concerned – overall a pretty clear idea about the function of each of these moments in the programme. So the broad design is there first and the specific Content Providers are fitted into it, as with the examples we gave in the palette earlier in this chapter.

What Input, When?

Content Flow and Content Analysis provide quite specific insights into what participants should be doing with the content in the course of the meeting. Remember the drawing Stewart Hinks made for the 'good conversation' in Chapter 3.2? Content Flow drawings reveal if and when meetings need content input and what type of input that should be. The Content Analysis tells you whether the content should be given a specific angle. The combination of the two also indicates when a certain Content Provider should be up there and just about for how long to be effective. There is always a compelling logic underlying these decisions, a logic that can be gleaned from CF and CA. That same logic also articulates whether participants should be given time to process the content that has been provided during the meeting and if so, when and for how long. In carefully designed meetings, we often see that participants get a lot of time to work together and process the content.

In the end CF and CA come together:

The pay-off for the Global HR Conference of a multinational corporation is: "HR leading the way." Interviews with participants reveal that at present, in their organisation, HR are not leading yet. The combination of CF and CA yields a 3-day programme with workshops on company-wide strategic issues for which HR should take the lead. In between, participants use group work to process that input.

However, after interviews with the CEO and the Global HR director the CA also shows that as HR professionals, the participants need to become better at convincing their business partners of HR's strategic importance. They need to be able to actually work with HR's strategic position in their own environments. Therefore, the content should be made hotter, less abstract, more challenging, out of the participants' comfort zones. It should be closer to their skins and even get under it. And so we decide to include two sessions that train personal competence, one on 'Boardroom Politics', the other on 'Convincing People through Presence.'

In this example the CA brings to light the opportunity for a valuable enrichment of the programme by adding Content Providers from an unexpected angle: that of strengthening the participants' competence in two specific areas. Finding competent people able to deliver these two sessions turned out to be relatively easy, because the profiles and objectives for their contributions were crystal clear.

A Finger Exercise in the Heart of a Meeting

Let's try to work out a programme choice for an imaginary but realistic meeting to get a feel for how we would go about designing a contribution involving Content Providers. And let's use a different example from the good conversation.

Suppose the meeting owner draws a Content Flow consisting of a line going straight up with three large black bulges in it, one after the other. After each bulge, the line emerges out a bit broader. "Those bulges are substantial speakers who sharpen up and deepen out the content," he explains. "The impact of each of the speakers is strengthened by the next ones." And what is the content? A mini-module on statistics during an annual conference on cardiology, as part of a broader one-day seminar on epidemiology.

We get the challenge (sometimes Content Analysis goes surprisingly fast), for statistics is not exactly the topic that quickens the average cardiologist's heart (or almost anybody else's). Statistics' lack of appeal is a serious threat to the meeting owner's objective, that of a sharpening up the content in a succession of presentations.

We get down to business. There are three slots available for the Content

Providers. The Content Flow and the initial Content Analysis tell us that especially the first speaker has a great responsibility. If he does not succeed in sharpening up the content for the cardiologists immediately, if his bulge falls flat, the two colleagues after him are faced with an impossible task. The first shot has to hit the bull's eye: the line has to broaden out right away. The speaker needs to establish a powerful connection between statistics and the cardiologists, and he needs to do it at once. So what input does this require? What specific angle of attack on the subject of statistics can produce such a connection?

These are the kinds of questions a Meeting Designer racks his brains about when reflecting on the heart of meetings. So what would you propose? How would you frame the content for that first slot? And who would you invite to deliver it? It is worthwhile to chew on these questions a bit before reading on. And don't worry that you are not a statistician; the issue here is not statistics, but the perceptions of cardiologists. And probably you find statistics just as fascinating as they…

Writing this paragraph we were reminded of the striking novel Bonita Avenue by the Dutch author Peter Buwalda[1] in which the main character is a professor in statistics. He starts the first lecture of his undergraduate course by inviting his students to tell him an unlikely story from their own lives. He will then analyse that story statistically and draw conclusions from it, using the theory of probabilities. Each year his students follow him breathlessly because the calculations are about the life of one of them. In the mean time they learn about statistics: how one can use a data set to find out about the probability of future events.

In the book one of the students tells the story of a trip he made to Norway with his girl-friend. Driving along a frozen road in the barren arctic plains, a large lorry is coming towards them. The very moment the two vehicles pass each other, the lorry's shaft accidentally breaks loose, swerves across the road and smashes the windscreen of their rental car. When they come to a stop, the student finds himself unhurt; his girl-friend has been decapitated. When the professor confusedly clears his throat and starts to scribble his first calculations on the whiteboard, you can hear a pin drop in the lecture room.

This is the kind of input that would in all likelihood do the job of producing the first bulge of the Content Flow drawing. The first Content Provider could introduce the topic of statistics in this manner, with the cardiologists as co-

---

[1] The idea about the novel and its powerful story materialised after our choice to use a case about statistics and teaching in this chapter. We can imagine the reader's slight doubts about this but can only give our word for it. You may still object that we may have chosen the example because we had read Buwalda's story some time before. Of course, in all honesty there is no way of telling.

In any case, the example illustrates neatly how analysis and creativity interact in the brain at this stage of the design process: the recollection of the statistics professor and the student came drifting into the conscious mind from somewhere and while writing, we picked up the story. That is how creativity works. Something drifts by and you pick it up.

creators. The idea from the novel points us in the right direction. It provides the appropriate combination of participant involvement and 'hotness' the meeting owner would be looking for. In one of the next sections we will go into possible sources of inspiration for these brainwaves, such as in this case Buwalda's novel. For now, the next question to answer is: "Who can we find that would be able to deliver statistics content in this particular way?"

Choosing Content Providers

Choosing Content Providers is a delicate task. The process many meeting owners follow is to set up a reference group (called conference committee, sounding board, scientific committee or something analogous) with the task of recommending speakers. In the majority of cases, these recommendations are based on the candidate's content knowledge and reputation, or – much worse – as a reward for personal favours. In our experience these procedures rarely lead to superb meeting programmes.

It is a rare content expert who is able to carry the full weight of the programme on his shoulders, alone. Naturally, many speakers are good and capable of providing fascinating insights into their knowledge. But what happens with those insights in the course of the meeting? How can you manage and optimise its impact on participants? And – even more importantly – what happens with the content afterwards? In the absence of a proper design based on desired outcomes and a choice of Content Providers stemming from that, good results are just a hope at best.

In our way of working, the actual choice of the Content Providers is mostly the outcome of mutual cooperation between Meeting Designer and meeting owner. The skeleton programme presents itself with a number of time slots that must be filled; and to fill them, somebody has to answer a question that runs roughly like this: "We need someone who can deliver/do/present/catalyse X or Y. Who do you know?" If the profile is biased towards pure content, the meeting owner often knows the right candidate. If you are looking for something more ludic or outlandish, it is the Meeting Designer who has to come up with the solution. This means Meeting Designers have to have an extensive network of Providers with the experience and know-how to put across their Content in a professional manner. That network includes people we may not know directly but whom we approach through a shared relation.

A slightly different option, often resorted to, is using a person proposed by the meeting owner and asking him to deliver his content in a different format. A good example of this is the design solution for the former Philips president who took the confessions of young entrepreneurs, described in Chapter 1.2. He delivered his content in a specific way that suited him perfectly and that aligned well with the intended experience of the participants. And that brings us to the third basic ingredient for designing the role of Content Providers after Content Flow and Content Analysis, the Experience Concept.

Formats for Delivering Content

The essential experience with a traditional speaker monologue is that participants sit and listen. Is that all there is...?

Draped in many-coloured scarves, three actors, using mime, performed a scene taken from the working life of a man who was sitting right in front of the stage. Just beforehand, this person had told the session director the story he would like to re-experience, because it had had a major impact on a persistent problem in the organisation. Fully concentrated, his colleagues looked at the impact the issue had evidently had on his work and above all on him. The story-teller's eyes filled with tears as he re-lived his recollections along with the actors.

Playback theatre is a powerful medium to steer group processes.[2] In this case, the participant group was quite intellectual and sceptical. Just letting them speak about the content carried the risk of getting bogged down in abstract discussions and tripping up over words, while the objective of the workshop was to catalyse a number of specific changes in behaviours of people in the organisation. Overcoming the scepticism in the attendees required an intense experience that would go beyond words. Theatre suggested an effective form in this case.

"Is that all there is?" we asked just now. The palette and this last example make it clear that our answer to that question is a resounding no! We see lots of alternatives. Several forms of art work well when you want the meeting to offer participants an unexpected experience.

A firm of consultants to the life insurance industry wishes to show their clients that they are capable of coming up with out-of-the-box solutions for strategic, long-term issues. One of those issues is that the time horizon and 'rhythm' of traditional insurance companies is becoming ever more detached from the rhythm of society at large. After a general introduction by the chair, a classical guitarist takes the stage. He plays a specially composed theme that captures the rhythm of the life insurance industry. Later that day he plays a different piece with the rhythm of today's economy and at the end of the programme he merges the two in an improvisation. The 60 people in the audience are both fascinated and stunned.

---

[2] Playback theatre is a form of improvisational theatre during which audience or group members tell stories from their lives and watch them enacted on the spot.

Who said that content always needs to be spoken content? The guitar player unmistakably and effectively delivered content: he brought home the message that the organisers had the resources and the courage to come up with innovative and unexpected solutions – one of the objectives of the meeting, in keeping with the way they wanted the identity of their organisation to be perceived and expressed in their EC.

Sources of Inspiration

Probably more than in any other area of his work, the deployment of Content Providers calls forth the Meeting Designer's creativity. If Meeting Design is an applied art (and we think it is), it is so mainly because of the way well-designed programmes deal with the delivery of content.

Explaining art is like explaining why strawberries with whipped cream are delicious. Nevertheless, we can try to give you an impression of what we use to develop formats. As with all ideas, solutions for delivering meeting content pop into your head like inverted soap bubbles. But they don't get in there just out of the blue. Picasso once said: "Good artists borrow; great artists steal." And so we borrow, steal, combine, modify and sometimes invent things thanks to the inspiration we find in a number of different 'worlds'.

Many of our formats or solutions use art: music, theatre, dance, video, graphics, and so on. Our book is rife with examples built on various forms of art. Debating techniques also offer many interesting possibilities; the maverick comes from this world. Particularly rich is the whole world of large group interventions and group dynamics, which is closely related to that of facilitation techniques and coaching. These sources yield all kinds of design solutions centred on powerful questions. The world of sports and gymnastics is great for ideas on how to get things moving. Naturally, the world of teaching and didactics is a treasure trove, especially teaching methods for children. Thinking of children, simply the idea of letting participants play is a major source of inspiration: Design a game for them. Film and TV offer many options. Some TV formats can be very effective in meetings and there is no need to be ashamed of using them. And finally Mother Nature is one of the best sources of inspiration. Representing what happens with the content in a meeting as an organic growth process, for instance, offers many insights into the best ways of structuring the delivery of content.

Managing Content Providers

All of these lofty ideas come to nothing, however, if the people who need to deliver the content stubbornly resist complying. It is not enough to hatch a great idea for the Content Provider's role; he must also be cajoled into actually doing it. Remember the professor in didactics we introduced to you in chapter 1.5? The meeting owner invited him because he was a specialist in his field and would bring along the right know-how. When briefing him, he also accepted the challenge to tailor his contribution so it would fit in with the Experience Concept. As a result, he ended up doing a presentation that was different from any he had ever done before. Why did he accept all those changes to his routine? Was it just because he thought we were nice people, or was it the result of what Winnie-the-Pooh would call a cunning plan?

There are two set mechanisms we use to manage Content Providers. The first is transparency. The Meeting Designer needs to share all the basic ingredients of the design with the Content Provider. That means the meeting owner's objectives, the Content Flow, the Experience Concept, the Content Analysis – the lot. This way the Content Provider becomes the Meeting Designer's accomplice.

The second mechanism is to challenge the Content Provider just to the right point. Together with him you will want to explore his comfort zone and end up somewhere close to its edge. In other words, make sure the content and its delivery turn into a stimulating adventure not just for the audience, but also for the Content Provider himself. How much of an adventure will depend on his competence in his field and his experience of speaking in public.

Many Content Providers are grateful and take to the design as if it was their own. Time and again we have worked with speakers who literally tapped into a different kind of person within themselves when challenged to do things differently. Exploring the comfort zone also means that the Content Provider should not be asked to do something that will detract from his stature or credibility. Avoiding this involves a sound mapping of his and the audience's expectations about appropriate roles, formats and delivery. Culture is a dominant feature on that map.

And finally, if a Content Provider doesn't respond to one or other of these two principles, in the interest of having a good meeting, the best thing is to advise the meeting owner urgently to look for someone else.

After a thorough briefing, the experienced professional speaker promised that he would tailor his standard presentation to the specific objectives of the conference. He would send a proposal stating clearly where and how he would make changes to achieve this. When the outline arrived, however, it was almost identical to what he had submitted previously! In the following phone call the speaker argued that all of his previous 1,200 speaking engagements had been successful. There was no reason to doubt this, nevertheless the presentation outline did not meet the proposed objectives. He was evidently unwilling to commit to changes that would make his contribution more

compatible with the meeting's Content Flow. Meeting Design was something he claimed never to have heard of. He became increasingly irritated and accused us of wanting to put him into a straightjacket, which he found intolerable.
We gave our client a negative report on his proposed contribution and they agreed wholeheartedly.

Possible Frictions in Decision-making

You will have noticed that the Meeting Designer plays a prominent role in choosing and briefing Content Providers. For many organisers this is a novelty and it is a potential source of friction when working with meeting owners who, for whatever reason, want to keep the selection and management of speakers firmly under their own control. We have found, whenever we propose to involve a Content Provider or format that really fits the overall design, the meeting owner is apt at first to have some difficulty overcoming his resistance to the unknown. In the end, however, he tends to accept the undeniable logic of the design.

Many years of work in our profession have demonstrated that a sensible mix of challenge and trust helps to avoid unnecessary conflicts. That approach rests on a double foundation. On the one hand we keep on underlining that the presence and performance of Content Providers is an integral part of the overall design. On the other we stress that all considerations about Content Providers should be openly discussed. Sometimes this may lead to difficult conversations and sometimes even to clashes, but almost always there is a solution everybody realises will work. One of the reasons for this is that the CF and the EC have been formulated by the meeting owner himself. If the meeting owner sees the relationship between the desires he has expressed and the design solutions, most objections disappear. And if they don't disappear, the Meeting Designer needs to come up with a better programme proposal.

While many meeting owners respond positively to the approach we have outlined in the previous section, it is not infallible. Sometimes things simply do not work out the way you envisage...

The evening prior to the Conference, the meeting owner received a phone call from the Minister's office. The Minister, he was informed, had decided to attend the event after all and so would he kindly provide the necessary time – somewhere around 30 minutes – for him to speak. A lectern and good projection facilities would be needed, as the Minister would be showing forty slides. That the entire programme was ready, the setting was a catwalk and that a monologue was the last thing the 2,500 participants were looking forward to, seemed to be of no consequence at all to the Minister's staff. His speech the next morning was a disaster; it had a direct negative impact on the ratings of the conference. It also messed up lunch arrangements because he ran over time. No amount of Meeting Design could have prevented that.

Meeting Design as a Paradigm Shift

As you can conclude from the many examples we have given, there is an almost endless variety in the possible relationships between Content Providers and meeting participants. Why then are Content Providers so often relegated to the role of speakers?

In all parts of society, we have grown deeply accustomed to the paradigm of the *classroom model*. It implicitly states that the proper way of passing on knowledge and content is by means of a teacher-like figure who places himself in front of a group of people: the speaker. This paradigm rules the vast majority of exchanges of knowledge that take place at meetings. And often this severely stunts the results.

The point is not that we are principled opponents of speakers during meetings; we are not – we often use speakers in our designs. Our point is that speaker monologues with a couple of questions at the end should not be the only way, or even the main way, of dealing with content (viz. Chapter 1.5). As Meeting Designers we propose a different paradigm. In today's complex and less hierarchical society, knowledge exchange during meetings calls for a different road: co-creation. Instead of a one-dimensional movement from teacher or speaker to pupil, student or meeting participant, we see content emerging from many different angles and sources; we see the potential for new connections and insights as a result of the amalgamation of diverse input; we see unexpected results growing organically and much more rapidly thanks to the types of processes for which we have coined the term 'mental chemistry'. Internet-based platforms and social media are obvious signs of this paradigm shift. We will have fewer one-way speakers during meetings, simply because we can no longer afford to reduce the audience to mere listeners.

Conclusions

As with the chapter on the design process overall (3.2), the work process we have described for the choice and deployment of Content Providers sounds relatively clear-cut, linear and straightforward. In fact, in the real world it is not. Or rather, it is in part. At the same time though, it is multi-dimensional, intuitive and a bit messy, in the sense that initial insights change as you plod along and that certain choices are traded in for something better, sometimes even quite late in the process.

There is one thing we have not stated explicitly so far but which we think requires a last comment in this chapter. Designing the deployment of Content Providers has focused on CF, CA and EC. Nevertheless, everything discussed in Part 1 and Chapter 2.1 of this book applies to the design process without reservation. You may have concluded this yourself from the examples given and from the sources of inspiration we presented a couple of pages ago but it is appropriate to mention this specifically. If we take the maverick as an example and measure him by the yardstick of Chapter 1.4, it is clear that this Content Provider will work fine in some countries, but not in others. For participants from relatively formal cultures, or ones that respond very strongly to a bit of provocation, he is not the right choice. Based on our analysis of Chapter 1.6, it is obvious that the maverick only works at the very start of the middle part of any meeting. While the rightful position for the Sage is just before the end.

All of the above leads to the important conclusion that part of the Meeting Designer's competence is having at his disposal a truly vast range of choices for giving shape to the role of Content Providers during meetings. The deployment of Content Providers is crucial to the success of all meetings and the success of any design depends on how well the Meeting Designer manages to do just that: deploy Content Providers effectively. Being able to do so successfully means the Meeting Designer needs to apply all the knowledge we have set forth in this book. And so, from a one-dimensional line-up of experts in a certain field, the deployment of Content Providers turns into the quintessence of the Meeting Designer's interventions.

Although it may initially make meeting owners feel awkward, the meeting will have the quality he is looking for only if the Meeting Designer can fully integrate the selection and management of Content Providers into the design process.

Sceptic:

We talk to Miko, 25 years young, and responsible for speaker management and communication with a Japanese PCO.

M: Thank you, Eric and Mike. I found the approach in this chapter very new and inspiring!

E/M: Good, thanks, Miko. What is the part you liked most?

M: Oh, many parts are new and inspiring for me. Do you know the game of Go? It is a traditional Japanese game, very interesting for you.

E/M: Vaguely, maybe you can refresh our memories?

M: In Japan we call it I Go. It's a board game. The board is the playing field, with lines making a grid. There are two players, one having black 'stones,' the other white ones.

E/M: A bit like checkers?

M: Yes, a bit. But in Go the players do not take away the stones, they put more stones on the board, at the intersections of the lines in the grid. The player adds stones of his colour. Each turn the players decide where they want to place their stones and they think very hard. Have you ever played Go?

E/M: No never, unfortunately. How do the players decide where to put their stones?

M: The point of the game is that each player isolates or surrounds the stones of the other player. When he has completely surrounded a stone it becomes his prisoner. The player who takes most prisoners is the winner. So you put your own stones where they exercise the strongest influence, depending on the positions of the other stones on the board.

E/M: Sounds like a complex game!

M: Oh yes, very, very complex! In Go you must always try to work out what the other player is thinking. There is a given situation on the board, a status quo, and yet with each move that situation changes.

E/M: I guess we see what you mean... It's a game about strategic decisions, right? So, how can you tell if someone is a good player?

M: That's easy, a good player wins because he makes the right strategic choices!

E/M: Which is the whole purpose of the game, of course. Is there anything else that marks a player out as special?

M: Yes, in Japan we always recognise as a good player someone who invents original, strong moves. Maybe this player will not win with his new move the first time, but if he continues to use it in other games, it will be seen for the skilful move it is. We appreciate players who develop our traditional game like that.

E/M: Would it be an interesting new 'move' to play Go as a team?

M: Many people in Japan would like to think about that idea. I am sure they would.

E/M: Let's suppose for a moment they would be willing to give it a go; and we apologise for the poor pun.

M: No need to say sorry! It's a fun pun!

E/M: If you were to play Go as a team, how would the team decide on the moves?

M: The most senior person in the team would make those decisions. He would carefully weigh up all the suggestions offered by members of his team and then decide.

E/M: So he wouldn't decide all by himself, would he?

M: Only the last surviving bee in the autumn decides what to do all by himself.

E/M: How can you become a person whose advice the team captain will take very seriously. Will he only listen to other senior people?

M: He will listen to all the team members who come up with winning moves and he will listen to people who suggest some daring, powerful move.

E/M: As the senior member on the team, he knows that he needs the other team players to come up with the best moves, right?

M: Good teams have the wisest senior person. Against such a team, other teams will not win.

E/M: There seem to be many similarities between Go and the real world. Do you also see any important differences?

M: Ah, that is a good question. I believe maybe Go is the real world!

3.7 Finale

Back to Outcomes

 *ebruary is traditionally the month of the association's General Assembly. For this year's programme, the chairman wants the members to reach consensus on an action plan for a whole series of issues. It should also be more challenging than in previous editions and foster more contacts between members. Finally, it should trigger them to implement the action plan in the following months.*

From this description you will probably glean the six reasons for holding meetings we gave in the Introduction. 'Decision-making' is evident from the wish to agree on an action plan; 'Alignment' in the desired consensus on that list; 'Rituals' are recognisable in the annual recurrence of the meeting; 'Learning' in the challenging programme; 'Motivation' in the effort to stimulate implementation of the action plan; and finally 'Networking' in fostering more member contacts.

In Chapter 2.2 we discussed goals and objectives and how to establish these. In this chapter we will look at design solutions that help consolidate those objectives into sustainable outcomes. Outcomes – the word is self-evident – can only be recognised at the end of the meeting. Yet they gradually materialise as the meeting progresses, while the timeline draws nearer and nearer to its finale. The closing stages of the meeting are decisive in firming up those outcomes. Therefore, in addition to our general comments on order and sequence in meetings in Chapter 1.6, this climactic moment deserves extra attention in part 3 of our book where we deal with the design process. So, let's see how outcomes or results materialise and how we can imbue them with maximum value. And that expressly includes business value.

Bucket Production Machine

Suppose you have a factory with a machine dedicated to producing plastic buckets. The result of the input into that machine is clear each time it produces a plastic bucket: you can pick up the bucket, put it in a large box, together with other buckets, and ship it to supermarkets and DIY shops. A neat and tangible outcome of a process.

The chairman in our earlier example also wants to obtain outcomes, not as a result of a production process, but of the meeting process. The meeting goes about things in an entirely different way from the bucket-making machine and its results are not just something material. It produces both tangible and intangible outcomes, and it uses the interaction between people to do so. At the association's meeting, tangible outcomes include decisions about the action plan, or business cards changing pockets during the networking; whereas the desire to implement the action plan and a challenging atmosphere are intangible results.

Tangible and intangible outcomes are generated in fundamentally different ways. Intangible results arise gradually during the meeting. A thing like 'the desire to implement' or 'atmosphere' does not come about all of a sudden. Rather, it is like moss that grows and spreads over a stone, slowly but surely. The same applies to results related to motivation. Because intangibles 'grow upon' the meeting so gradually and because they are, well, *intangible*, it is in their nature that they are generally difficult to describe or quantify. It is also difficult to establish whether what has been 'intangibly' achieved is satisfactory. Chapter 2.2 offers methods and solutions for dealing with that. While intangible outcomes seem analogue, tangible results, on the other hand, are binary. If at a certain point during the meeting, the assembled participants decide to adopt the action plan, then that decision has been made and that's it. The assembly cannot make such a decision 'to some extent' – either they have made it or they haven't. Decisions are like pregnancies. Half a decision is no decision, as any business consultant will confirm. The machine in the bucket factory may be environmentally-friendly, make a pleasant noise or fit the company's investment policy, what counts at the end of the day is whether it turns out buckets or not.

The Relationship Between Tangible and Intangible Outcomes

The fact that we can distinguish tangible and intangible outcomes does not mean they are independent – quite the contrary, they influence each other constantly, the way different forces typically do in ecosystems (and as suggested earlier, one of the ways to understand meetings is to look at them as temporary ecosystems). A good example is the relationship between trust and decision-making – an intangible and a tangible meeting outcome. As in society at large, in meetings trust influences the way in which decisions take shape; and at the same time, good decisions inspire further trust.

Overall, intangible results need to start emerging first, before tangible results can be gained. And although the two types of results are interdependent, they cannot compensate for each other or be reciprocally exchanged. It is especially unlikely for a meeting with a dreary programme, a battleground atmosphere or a riotous debate (poor intangible results in terms of the togetherness environment) to yield neat tangible outcomes like action lists or inspiring petitions. As we shall see shortly, it is even more unlikely that such tangible results will have any serious impact after the meeting.

The contrary, intangible outcomes compensating for tangible ones, is more common.

The objective of the meeting was to generate a list of six innovations. When taking stock at the end, there were found to be only five. The meeting owner pointed out that nevertheless the atmosphere had been excellent and that people had worked together very positively, making the meeting a success. The Meeting Designer countered that the programme had not been an overall success because the tangible result had not been attained.

Here, the meeting owner weighed the tangible result on the scale of the intangible. We believe this is a flawed way of looking at outcomes, one which obscures the effectiveness of the meeting and its design.

Intangible results, as pointed out in the previous section, surface gradually. Once they start to develop, they tend not to disappear. Meetings that have a weak ending may suffer from a dip in their intangible results due to the anti-climax, but these results are not eradicated entirely. They are the upshot of the total collective experience of the participants and therefore, they develop inside the participants. It is as if they condense in their souls, like dewdrops on water lilies on a summer morning. Although perceptions may differ, everybody is able to distinguish a successful meeting from a poor one in so far as intangible results are concerned. One of the reasons why major conferences of international bodies such as the UN often fail to prove effective may very well be that their programming does not seem to take the need to produce intangible outcomes into consideration. Their formality represses true alignment which ultimately also chokes the opportunities to achieve tangible results.

Since intangible outcomes consist of the shared perceptions of the participants, nobody is their exclusive owner. Yet at the end participants take them away individually and automatically, and they normally linger on well after the meeting has concluded. The intangible outcomes are among the main *raisons d'être* of meetings; they are closely connected to the Magic we discussed in Chapter 1.7.

The situation for tangible outcomes is entirely different. They need to cross the bridge between the meeting and the outside world.

From Stage to Street

Though meetings are generally characterised by unity of time and space, their tangible results definitely aren't. In Chapter 1.2, Meetings are a Stage, we explained that meetings are by definition about something that needs to happen somewhere else and after the meeting is over. This applies in particular to the tangible results. It is as if they exit from the stage and enter the real world. The reason is that the tangible results are not borne away inside the participants, as the intangible ones are. Being tangible, material, they need to go somewhere; they need to find a place where they can have their intended effect. All tangible outcomes are to some extent co-created by the participants and so they have an interest in seeing that their output is taken good care of. It is like a prototype that hits the road for the first time; a hypothesis that witnesses its first practical test; a brainchild that takes its first steps. The passage into the real world is a precarious moment and for the results to be launched on a favourable course, they need a strong and clever push in the right direction.

The moment of launching the tangible outcomes into the world is the finale of the programme design (as well as the closing piece of this book). It requires an extra design effort, to ensure outcomes do not go to waste. We have found that a well-designed finale satisfies needs to address four basic variables: the ownership of the outcomes, the power of ritualisation, post-meeting communications and design impact. Working on these four requirements, the Meeting Designer can craft an effective final chord for the meeting, one that can be heard on the street outside.

Rule One: Ownership of the Outcomes

During the wrap-up session of a meeting for managers in health care the chairman of the day summarises the two days of intensive workshops and plenary group discussions. He manages to capture the main conclusion in a vigorous one-liner. The audience tacitly but unmistakably agrees. After thanking the speakers, the workshop leaders and the organisers, he hands over to the president of the association responsible for funding the meeting. The latter thanks the participants, expresses his amazement about the many insightful and creative comments he has heard and concludes by inviting everyone to join him for drinks. The small crowd replies with polite applause. Just minutes later, however, as the cocktails are downed, there is a low rumble of dissatisfaction among the audience. People are heard to sigh into their drinks: "Good meeting but, well, who is actually going to do something now?"

What is actually the missed opportunity here? The atmosphere, the togetherness environment, the workshop formats, it all seemed to be working. And yet at the very last moment, it feels as if someone has consigned the outcomes to limbo. The tangible results evaporated in the final addresses by the Chairman and the association President. Are there no tangible results? Of course there are! There is even a powerful and compact conclusion, shared by all those present. And yet the meeting ends with a downer. The participants are wondering who is going to do something with the outcomes and rightfully so! The programme of the meeting does not answer their question. Perhaps the chairman of the day was thinking that the President would take the initiative, while the President may feel that the individual participants are the ones who need to act. Meanwhile, the participants are left with the idea that no one is. In a word, nobody knows who is the *owner* of the outcomes.

What is clear is who produced the tangible outcome: the participants, under the guidance of the chairman. The programme, however, should also clarify who owns it after the meeting; the design should make this clear to the participants. It is up to the Meeting Designer to propose the first steps of the result beyond the walls of the meeting room, out there in the real world. The first thing that needs to be done, therefore, is to establish *who* is taking it with him. And so the first rule for designing a good finale is: Make sure that the programme design of the meeting tells participants who owns the tangible outcomes.

Most of the time nobody has thought about this, but often the solution is relatively simple. The flow of content during the meeting usually suggests a logical recipient for the outcomes and the meeting owner is generally aware of that. Such a beneficiary can come from inside the meeting, but also from outside. The Meeting Designer has to ensure that the meeting owner agrees about designating the appropriate person. It also means that there has to be a moment during which the selected person can actually take ownership of the result. Rules 2 and 3 give details on this. Often the right person materialises quite naturally from the hierarchy of the organisation: just give the results to the highest ranking guy because ultimately he calls the shots and so his actions are decisive in further processing them. In our earlier example, the association president would have made a good candidate. Here is another example:

At the end of the brainstorming session, the participants decide jointly which idea they think is the strongest. Once they agree, Harry, a member of the board joins the meeting. The facilitator reads out the idea from a specially made card which he then hands over to the board member. Harry thanks the participants and gives them an immediate, initial reaction to the idea. After that, he explains that the company newsletter will keep the group informed about what will happen with the idea. To underline this he actually signs the card in full view of all the participants.

That makes everything crystal clear, doesn't it: the board member is the new owner of the idea and he will take care of its future in the real world. The participants have handed him the responsibility for this and know through which medium they can monitor what is going to happen with their tangible result. The closing act provides the necessary transparency about who does what: the meeting participants have thought out the idea but they are not responsible for looking after its implementation. The board member is.[1]

In any brainstorming session in the future, the chances of cynical reactions from participants is a lot less likely than in the previous example of the meeting for managers in the health care institution.

Sometimes the participants themselves are the most suitable people to become the owners of the outcomes. Here is an example where that proved the right choice.

During the wrap-up of a conference on social policy, the Chairman cruises through the auditorium, followed like a shadow by a cameraman. He asks random participants to tell the audience, in just one sentence, what they are going to be working on during the week after the conference. After receiving a fair number of replies, he checks with the participants whether all the relevant issues have been covered. It takes him a further three mini-interviews before the audience is satisfied that this is the case. At that point, he purposefully removes the tape from the video recorder and hands it over to a technician who eagerly undertakes to upload the footage on a protected YouTube site within the hour. At the same time, all participants will receive a link to that site and the e-mail with the link will be in their inboxes even before they are back at work. Symbolically pushing a button, the chairman then opens a discussion platform, specifically designed for the purpose, where participants can post their experiences in the coming months. At the official farewell, everybody is told they will be invited to a follow-up meeting in twelve months' time.

Rule Two: Use a 'Ritual'

This last example is also helpful in illustrating the second rule for conveying the tangible result into the real world. Without necessarily being formal, the finale of this meeting is like a small ceremony which gives it a certain weight. You might call it a ritual. It may not be as dramatic as lighting the Olympic flame, saying prayers or some other age-old rite, but it is still a collective and slightly solemn moment. It is a designed ritual. Rule number two therefore is: Design the finale as a ritual that involves joint participation.

Rituals mark a point in time. That they are solemn helps to underscore the collective importance of events. Rituals connect participants to each other

---

[1] Note that it is not absolutely necessary for an idea to be actually implemented in order to give those who came up with it the feeling that it has been properly dealt with. A well-motivated decision that the idea has been considered and has proved impractical may be enough to create the necessary clarity. That means the idea has now dropped off the agenda and no longer needs an owner.

because they all feel that they are becoming part of something that is bigger than themselves. That helps them to let go of what is behind them, to hand over something they have accomplished and to move on to new (hopefully greener) pastures.

On their return from a school trip, the entire class gathers in front of the school to be re-united with their parents. "Gosh, what a lovely tan!" "How many hours of sleep did you get?" the parents cry. The teacher needs to cough only once to silence the chatter. They all know he is about to sum up the trip succinctly, with just the right mix of humour and fruity detail. His 'extroduction' has been part of the event for years now. Only after having heard his stories will everyone be free to go home, happy that their child is safely back (and less enchanted by the bags of dirty laundry).

An essential characteristic of a ritual is that it involves the transfer of something. In this case it is the transfer of responsibility for the children. In the conference on social policy it was the insights the participants had gained during the conference. The ritual in the finale of a meeting transfers the tangible results into the hands of a new owner, stressing its collective nature.

The sources of inspiration to design such rituals are all around us. Different cultures provide an astonishingly rich choice of transfer rituals: from gift-giving under all sorts of circumstances, to graduation ceremonies and from saying grace before meals to midsummer or midwinter parties. They all commemorate the transfer of something tangible (a diploma, a Valentine) or a rite of passage (the start or ending of a season, a new stage of life).

A collective finale is undeniably stronger than an individual one. If you have ever been in a theatre audience for a thumping farce, where 900 or so people all burst out in laughter at the same time, you know what we mean. The reason is probably, as we said earlier, that people experience greater awe over something they feel goes beyond their individual existence – but we gladly leave the subtleties of explaining the mental mechanism to psychologists. Relevant to us is that it means any final ritual should be designed as a group moment.

Rule Three: Deliver on the Follow-up

The effectiveness of tangible outcomes depends crucially on delivery. If the discussion platform from our last-but-one example does not exist, or the participants do not receive the e-mail, then the meeting will still turn into a failure, in spite of all the lofty design intentions and solutions.[2] The threat of a poorly executed follow-up annihilating all tangible results gives us our third rule: Encourage and assist the meeting owner to deliver on the commitments accepted during the finale.

Subsequent communications often take place through existing communication channels within the organisation. Meetings that break fresh ground or involve participant groups with no obvious access to a shared communication channel will benefit from a tailor-made solution. The discussion platform in our meeting on social policy is a good example.

In any case, meetings never stand alone and so the Meeting Designer must always look for ways that integrate the meeting with other communication efforts of the organisation. Finding these solutions together with the meeting owner and his communication staff is an integral part of the Meeting Designer's work and consumes a good bit of his time. We will comment on this issue from a somewhat different angle in the Epilogue.

Rule Four: Cater for Different Learning Styles

Each training session of this Swiss company starts with a peculiar activity: the trainer must walk to the emergency exit with his group. The company does not allow exceptions to this rule because they are convinced that this short march is an essential safety measure. Emergency situations are hectic by definition. When you have to run from a sudden blazing fire, a verbal explanation and a floor plan are not good enough. The body has to know the way out.

Different people grasp messages and meanings in different ways. In order to make their way rapidly to the emergency exit, some people want to see the route, others want to hear why a specific route is the logical one. We can recognise these groups as having either a *visual* or a *verbal/auditory* learning style, respectively. Yet other people[3] prefer to have a physical experience for maximum impact on their memory. The Swiss company is right that this last group are likely to have difficulty if they need to escape and their body doesn't know by experience where to go. Clearly, the objective is that *everyone* should be able to make their way quickly to the emergency exit. It would be sloppy to say the least to sacrifice one group because they pick up relevant information in a particular way. And so they have devised this particular safety drill.

Our observations of meeting participants in practical situations confirm the importance of catering for different learning styles. Consequently, a powerful finale should be effective for all, irrespective of their preference. These considerations allow us to formulate our fourth and final rule: When

---

[2] This point illustrates neatly why evaluations done immediately after the meeting inevitably give a limited view of the meeting's results. With hindsight, meetings may turn out to have been flops months after they finished!

[3] According to the literature, somewhere between 25 and 50%. There are many other models that describe preferred learning styles, but the distinction between visual, verbal and physical or kinesthetic is widely used.

designing the finale, make sure it includes verbal, visual and physical stimuli. To increase the impact of those closing moments, they should best be fun, surprising, varied and contain activities that appeal to the verbal, visual and physical perception of participants. This is one of the areas of design work where the Meeting Designer can have some fun cooking up creative solutions. Not just a declaration that is read out loud and confirmed verbally by someone, but also something people can see and that involves physical action.

At the end of the seminar, the facilitator instructs participants to arrange themselves in two rows opposite each other, like ice hockey players before a match. They find themselves standing in pairs, one in front of the other.[4] When he signals they shake hands, express a brief wish, and then step sideways to face the next person. In just a couple of minutes, all of the 64 participants have exchanged a meaningful goodbye.

An amusing and light-hearted closing ritual such as this will endorse the shared insights the seminar has built up. Verbal communication takes the form of expressing mutual wishes; lining up and being confronted with one different face after another caters for visual stimuli; shaking hands and moving about the room like a human caterpillar provide the physical or kinaesthetic part.

Rapid developments in technology for such things as graphics, video and video editing, projection, and their applications on relatively simple laptop computers offer inspiring opportunities. Here is an example of a closing ceremony that would not have been feasible before – let's say – 2000, when reliable video-editing software for laptops first came out.

The closing night of a 3-day strategic management meeting offered the participants a 'Souper Culturel'. Guided by tried and tested artists, in one hour each of four groups crafted an act they would perform for their colleagues during the farewell meal. The idea sprang from the fact that Creativity was one of the company's core values. The remit for the acts was to express 'The beating heart of Acme' (the name of the company).

In one group some twenty managers gradually laid bare their chests in a rapid series of stylised shots, culminating in a finale where an animation of the company's logo emerged from the human figures, beating like a real heart.

The showing of the video led to an almost ecstatic reaction in the audience, because it truly brought out everyone's idea of the company's heart. After the meeting, the video was sent to all participants as a powerful anchor for the results achieved in the three days.

---

[4] What happens in the case of an odd number is a small design assignment for the reader...

Tangible and intangible interaction revisited

Together, the four rules ensure a powerful and transparent closure: clarity about ownership of the outcomes and their destiny; 'substance' which is felt collectively thanks to a ritual; connection with the future outside the meeting; and communicative impetus through a combination of visual, verbal and physical stimuli.

Earlier we introduced the notion that tangible and intangible results influence each other and that intangible results precede the tangible ones. Conversely, though, a glorious finale can pay out an attractive intangible dividend. The video with the heartbeat had a momentous impact which instantly created added enthusiasm for the company's strategy (and that was what the whole meeting had been about). The YouTube clips and discussion platform for the social policy seminar led to commitment to keep the debate alive and worked as marketing tools for next year's event – a subsequent tangible outcome, closing one more loop. The ice hockey line-up created additional networking opportunities.

The examples show the connection between all aspects of meetings. They underline the depth and beauty of meetings as a means of communication and as a working environment which is inevitably multi-layered and pluri-dimensional. Returning to a metaphor we have used earlier, meetings are a temporary ecosystem. It is the task of the Meeting Designer to fiddle and tinker with that ecosystem, shaping it along predictable and unpredictable lines, and gazing in amazement (if he has a moment of time) at the unexpected interdependencies, the fascinating psychology and the astonishing wealth of human potential. More than anything, though, meetings uncover the capacity of humans for inter-connection and inventiveness. Working in that sort of environment is indeed a privilege.

Sceptic

We talk to Klaas, an old friend who – as you may recall – works for a Non-Governmental Organisation in Zambia. We met him earlier at the end of Chapter 1.1.

K: Congratulations, you claim that the meetings you design are not only less boring, but also that you get better results. Have I got you right?

E/M: Yes, actually, that's the whole point...

K: Suppose I want to buy that, I mean in a literal sense. Suppose I were a client, how can you substantiate such a claim?

E/M: Good point. Well, most of the time, our clients do.

K: Explain that for me, please?

E/M: Most of our clients come as referrals, so they have heard from other clients that what we do works.

K: So you don't even bother putting together the evidence. That's pretty conceited!

E/M: To be honest, you are quite right there. We do have a nice, perfumed folder with what we call our 'love-mail', you know, letters from clients who say nice things about us. But not a register of successful outcomes. Work to do!

K: Don't thank me for the idea. That's what friends are for, aren't they?

E/M: What about another one of those Belgian beers?

K: Sure, another thing friends should never stop to share! Listen, I recently heard this lovely new word that must interest you, a drone-athon.

E/M: Drone-athon?

K: Yes, as in somebody droning on for the duration of a marathon.

E/M: Where did you hear that?

K: New York.

E/M: Because somebody was busy delivering one?

K: Yeah, in one of those typical scientific meetings on public health.

E/M: So did you get anything out of that meeting?

K: Actually I did, because I used the time to visit the Apple Store in Columbus Circle! No, just kidding. But to be honest, in the US I would have expected a more 'modern' conference. Do you notice any difference in the willingness to adopt the kind of new ideas you advocate? I mean, what sort of people are ready?

E/M We do. It depends a lot on the type of organisation, but also on where in the world you go.

K: So does that also relate to the culture stuff you discussed in one of the earlier chapters?

E/M: Definitely! The forerunners are in North-Western Europe. Many meetings with 'ordinary people' in Africa use theatre a lot, but as soon as politics are involved, meetings there tend be very traditional. Have you experienced that, too?

K: Yes, I agree. And elsewhere?

E/M: It's mainly related to how important people think hierarchies are and how relaxed they are about trying something new – with the risk that entails. That's why the Nordic countries are such a good playground. Organisations there are very egalitarian and people tend to be quite laid back.

K: So in the rest of the world they will continue to expose the likes of me to drone-athons then... Silly, really, if you think of all the other things people could be doing in that same period.

E/M: Of course we couldn't agree more.

K: Any ideas on the future?

E/M: As good marketeers, we can refer you to our epilogue to find some ideas. Other than that we think that, in spite of the persistence of drone-athons today, meeting organisers will become much keener on effectiveness and on outcomes that add value. Achieving that will certainly involve more use of electronic media and virtual reality. Electronic media to cut back on travel cost, and virtual reality too, will also reduce costs. And still offer people a powerful experience. It'll take a while, though.

K: Virtual reality. That means simulations of real life. Hm, interesting. Do you do simulations?

E/M: So far that technology has made it into the meeting room only to a very limited extent. But what would you like to simulate?
K: Oh, I would definitely have some ideas about that. In a couple of months' time we need to do an internal meeting to evaluate our effectiveness in Zambia. I'm sure some simulations would be helpful there! But let's get that beer first.

Epilogue: A Bridge Too Far

Introduction

There was a serious risk this book would never see the light of day. The insights we have shared with the reader were constantly evolving and new material kept on spawning in our minds. Many writers struggle with this demon and usually they have an editor who helps them to overcome it. But in our case no editor was available, because no regular publisher was willing to take our manuscript on. There was simply no place for a book of this sort in their lists. Which isn't at all surprising as this is one of the first books ever about Meeting Design.

And so at some point we had to stop ourselves from adding stuff. We decided that a number of things were not going to be included in *Into the Heart of Meetings*.

This Epilogue is a compensation for making those sacrifices. In it we are going to touch upon a number of topics we believe we could have discussed more extensively. There are two main reasons why we resolved to talk about them only in passing and at the very end. One is that we realised that it would need too much time to develop these subjects to the point where we could discuss them in depth. The second reason is that as yet too little is really known about them. For the time being, they are a bridge too far for a serious publication or even for a chapter in its own right. At the same time, we believe these topics are ultimately relevant for professionals in the meeting industry.

So we end, not with another fully-fledged chapter, but an epilogue, standing rather apart from the rest of the book. The epilogue is also an invitation. We hope that in the near future someone will come forward (in a couple of years it could even be us!) and, after having done some serious research, write a book that will shed more light on the way these topics affect meetings and the meeting industry.

Earlier in this book we referred to Maarten Vanneste's book Meeting Architecture. In his final pages Vanneste issued a similar invitation for people to tackle a number of subjects relevant to the meetings industry. Writing and publishing Into the Heart of Meetings is a response to his appeal. Now, in turn, we are ready to pass on the baton to someone else.

The topics we will briefly introduce and that need further investigation are the following.

- The return on investment of meetings as a means of communication: what is the 'effectiveness' of meetings and how can it be measured?
- Meetings as a collective event and participants as individuals. What is the balance between collective and individual experience?

310

- Communications beyond meetings: what is the relationship between meetings and organisational communications overall?
- New types of meetings: are remote, virtual and hybrid meetings real meetings, or are they something else?
- Influencing participant behaviour: neuroscience is bringing to light many new insights about human behaviour. What is their relationship with behaviours during meetings?
- Meetings for the rising generation who have grown up in the network society: how does this affect the way they view physical meetings as a means of communication?

A few preliminary thoughts on each of these topics will, we hope, stimulate our readers to dedicate themselves to finding answers to some or all of these questions.

A. Meeting Effectiveness and Their Return on What?

In Chapter 2.2 we discussed meeting goals. We mentioned notions like Return on Investment and Return on Effort; we introduced Content Flow and Experience Concept; we suggested that they can be used as ways of measuring meeting effectiveness (in addition to their use as design instruments); and we proposed a method to make qualitative goals measurable. Yet we feel that the field of meeting objectives and effectiveness remains mostly unexplored territory. Nevertheless, it is vital to gain insight into the understanding and the measurement of meeting objectives. Without a framework of theory and practice, one that allows for the quantification of desired meeting outcomes, it is impossible for the meeting industry to prove it is able to add value to organisational processes. As things stand, any claim our industry may make in this respect remains tentative at best. Finding reliable methods of measuring outcomes of meetings (preferably of success, but also of failure, which is even more difficult) is of vital importance for the meeting industry's continued prosperity.

The main methodology fully developed so far is the ROI method advocated by Jack Phillips and his followers; we have referred to it several times in this book. We tip our hats to Phillips but the ROI method carries two genetic flaws: First of all it wants to express meeting outcomes purely in monetary terms. This neglects all the other valuable but intangible outcomes that meetings produce. Of course there are ways to quantify those intangibles in terms of money and yields. But for many meetings this is a cumbersome process, with many outcomes producing their returns long, long after the meeting is over. For smaller meetings we would go one step further: it is practically impossible.

The second deficiency of the ROI method is that it only produces a return on investment for the meeting owner. What about the meeting participants? Well, tough luck – they are in the picture only to the extent that changes in their behaviour produce a useful outcome for the organiser. Naturally, this is odd. Participants decide to attend a meeting or not and make their own assessment of the value it had for them. Who knows what that assessment is and how participants go about obtaining it? No one does! As pointed out earlier, there is a major objection to valuing outcomes in purely financial terms. Depending on the type of organisation, and the reasons for having the meeting, many other 'currencies' are thinkable. Generally, the main purpose of many association meetings is alignment or the performance of rituals.

How does one measure and express their outcomes in monetary terms? For lack of something better, the outcomes of such meetings are described in vague and wobbly language – just read any website...

The methodology we have proposed in Chapter 2.2 is a first step towards solving this problem, but a much more comprehensive approach must be hidden somewhere. Who is going to be first to find it?

B. How Many Meetings Are There in Each Meeting?

One reason why we were tempted to continue writing was that we sent our manuscript to a select group of pre-readers. Naturally, their comments sparked off new ideas. In particular, the CEO of a renowned world-wide association came up with a number of interesting follow-up thoughts. One of those relates to the following:

Part 1 of this book specifically discusses "principles of meetings" – the first bit of the subtitle. It approaches meetings from a particular perspective, namely that of the Meeting Designer who looks at meeting participants. In it, we have avoided to be prescriptive or normative – we just describe what we see. However, it is grand tantalising to imagine what happens if you do think through what it takes to be a successful delegate. The Meeting Designer tries to lure the delegate into useful behaviours, but what is the responsibility of the delegate himself in having a good meeting experience? Are certain types of professionals by definition better delegates? And why, if so? Is there such a thing as a good delegate, or does a successful meeting require a great variety in delegates? Would it be useful (or even possible) to offer training in becoming a more successful meeting participant?

On a different note, we have analysed and treated meetings essentially as a collective experience. Although in a textbook about Meeting Design we could hardly start anywhere else, there is no doubt that each meeting participant is an individual, who takes part in the proceedings for a series of reasons he himself only knows (although not even that is entirely certain). Each participant has his own expectations and objectives, his strengths and drives, his limits and peculiarities.

What can Meeting Design do in order to cater for the vastly different needs of all these different individuals? Many of the programme solutions described in this book allow for greater freedom of individual expression or content processing compared to traditional classroom formats. Nevertheless, without any doubt there are many more opportunities to facilitate the specific meetings between individuals within a larger whole. Food for thought!

C. Communications beyond Meetings

Meetings often seem a bit like church towers: they stand out but they stand alone. In this book we have treated meetings as a specific form of communication and at several points we have underlined the need to work closely together with people in the organisation such as communication advisors and departments. Why is this so important?

The main reason is that there is always a relationship between meetings and other communication efforts of organisations. Anyone who participates in a meeting is aware of these other efforts and perceives what happens during the meeting as a result of the sum total of signals that reaches them. When properly positioned in this overall communicative landscape, the impact of the meeting on any type of organisational process can be significantly stronger. At the same time, there is the risk that its dynamics suffer from poor positioning, as some of our examples in Chapter 2.1 show.

In the communication of meetings, other forms of communication often play a role in announcing them: a nice invitation, articles in magazines, announcements and flyers at other meetings, targeted (e-)mail shots and so on. Today, every self-respecting conference has its proprietary website. But that is only the smaller part of what we mean.

With the exception of events which are integral to neat marketing campaigns, most meetings do not live on beyond the final moment, when the chair wishes everyone a "Safe journey home!" Until the next meeting, that is. We may have seemed a bit sceptical about the impact of technology in meetings in Chapter 3.4, but we do see enormous potential for technological solutions to keep the buzz created by meetings going. All kinds of contemporary communication platforms can lend a hand in making that happen.

But there is more: In a meeting on strategy development for an international corporation, in collaboration with the corporate communications department we issued a daily newspaper — a ridiculously low-tech paper product that required only a pc and a printer. The conference secretariat not only placed a copy on every participant's chair at breakfast time, but also sent it to the next layer down in the organisation all over the world. Recipients were expected to send feedback to the secretariat, which was used as input during the meeting. The signal this conveyed was unmistakable: "We could not invite everybody over here, but you are definitely part of this process!" New technology opens up the possibility to tap into the wisdom of ever larger crowds. Meeting participants can be polled before, during and after the meeting. Websites can become on-going discussion platforms about issues raised during the meeting – the number of options is unlimited.

And the point is clear: harnessing a meeting in a range of other communication efforts makes it much more powerful. It exponentially supplements the added value of the meeting itself, which obviously centres around the physical presence of participants. There is a lot to be gained here by exploring further ideas, initiatives and research related to the connection between meetings and other modes of communication. Any volunteers?

D. New Forms of Meetings: Remote, Virtual, Hybrid

This topic is related to the previous one, but it is more specific. New communication technology is creating many new possibilities of enhancing communications through meetings: Teleconferencing, Skype, interactive websites, blogging, twittering and other platforms and applications for remote communications allow for the virtual presence of participants. Hybrid meetings, such as event camps and similar formats with live feeds and instant interaction with people elsewhere, combine physical presence and remote communications. It seems as though physical presence at a meeting might be becoming redundant.

As a first observation we see that the choices around programming meetings involving these new possibilities are often driven by technology. In Chapter 3.4 we expressed doubts about this. Reiterating some of the points made in that chapter, these new technologies do offer a solution for yet another human constraint: the need for people to be in each other's company during meetings. This has implications for one of the sacrosanct characteristics of meetings: bringing participants together in the same place. Evidently, some of the objectives for which meetings were traditionally held while participants were physically present can now also be achieved with people sitting behind their desks and logging in. Some, but certainly not all. These developments have so many implications that it is early days to assess their consequences in the longer run. But let us briefly mention a couple.

First of all, the need for meeting in person does not disappear. What these new communication opportunities do imply is that meetings need to become better. What can be achieved in the temporary complex ecosystem of people interacting in each other's physical presence is and remains unique. It is just that meeting owners will need to think through with much greater care what exactly is the added value of participants' physical presence.

Secondly, many of the principles we have discussed in this book continue to be valid even for remote meetings. For instance: the remote meeting still produces a physical experience. However, now the constraints on that physical experience are much greater than in live meetings. These meetings imply that people need to sit behind a screen. Everyone who has participated in remote meetings knows some of the consequences: you switch off your mike to answer a phone call, or talk to someone close by, you slip out to open the door or shout at your dog which is barking, you go to the toilet, etc. These are just some of the more obvious behaviours. Inevitably this affects how people enjoy or make contributions.

Much more subtle is the impact on communication processes we normally deal with effortlessly because of non-verbal signals. Turn-taking for instance. People who participate in remote meetings have not yet developed a smooth solution for this essential part of the communication process. As a result, remote meetings often seem to jolt from one excruciating silence to the next, interspersed with short monologues from the content provider. It definitely becomes even more difficult to involve shy people, or participants from cultures where it is not customary to take the floor, unless a high level of trust has already been established.

So, the principles apply, but their implications are different. That means that new codes, norms, behaviours, formats need to be developed. And guess what? If anything, this means that in order to have truly effective remote meetings, better preparations and more design work will be required.

We feel it is too early yet for these developments to settle down in the form of a book. Much more experimentation needs to be done around new formats and applications for remote and virtual meetings. We need to gain research-based insights into the behaviour participants develop under such circumstances, into what works and what does not. In all likelihood most information about these experiences, when it eventually becomes available, will disseminate through new media, rather than in the classical written form.

So all those out there experimenting with this kind of technology in meetings and communication, please continue to share your experiences!

E. Neuroscience and the Behaviour of Meeting Participants

Neuroscience is hot. Book stands at airports have a wide choice of titles on display, all offering essential new insights into the way the human brain works and the impact of this on behaviour. Why is there nothing about the behaviour of meeting participants? In all honesty, we don't know.

In the last three to four decades, behaviour research and neuro-imaging have opened up an exciting treasure chest of data about our brains. Most of the models people used in the past to understand the relationship between the brain, the mind and human behaviour have proved false or too simplistic. Molecules and structures that have emerged over millions of years of evolutionary pressure on the brain have left their indelible mark on possible behaviour choices.

Once again the relevance for meetings and the novel profession of Meeting Designer is enormous. Meeting Design is about making meeting programmes effective and that implies choosing to expose meeting participants to certain stimuli rather than others, in the hope that as a result, they will show behaviours that help to achieve the meeting's objectives. In order to do that successfully, you need to have some grasp of how human behaviour arises in the first place.

Here are two examples of what we mean. We all know that one of the hardest moments during conferences is the first hour or so after lunch. It is the much feared time slot known as 'the post-prandial dip' – a graveyard for speakers confronted with semi-comatose participants. By now it is well-known that avoiding sugar-rich food and alcohol during lunch results in a shallower dip and so leaves participants' attention levels less impaired. But another worrying thing came to light during research on Israeli parole judges who were deciding whether or not to grant applications for bail by crime suspects. It was found that their approval rate gradually declined from one break to the next. When the judges were fresh and rested, they judged parole requests more favourably than when they were ready for a break. Well, common sense tells us, a person's mood naturally swings down when he gets hungry and tired. Doubtless that's true. But are we aware that this affects our ability to make rational judgments? The research showed that the Israeli judges were not aware that their decisions on the cases were systematically different, depending on how close those decisions were to their next break. They were firmly convinced themselves that their decisions were consistent over time. One explanation for this lack of consistency is a decrease in glucose available for brain processes such as critical thinking (the nervous system consumes more glucose than any other part of the human body). As blood tests demonstrated, judges with enough blood sugar to nurture their complex brainwork tend to judge criminals more favourably than judges whose glucose is depleted.[1] So on the one hand, a sugar peak makes us drowsy, while on the other we need sustained blood glucose to keep our pre-frontal cortex going (the brain area responsible for this kind of thinking). What does this mean for the optimum food intake during

---

[1] Reported in D. Kahneman, *Thinking, fast and slow*, London, 2011, pp. 43-44. Original research by S. Danziger, J. Levay and L. Avnaim-Pesso, *"Extraneous factors in Judicial Decisions, PNAS* 108 (2011): 6889-92.

meetings?

We have already referred to some of these issues in Chapters 1.1 and 1.6. but clearly we have not even scratched the surface of the impact of all the brain-related knowledge on meetings, participants' behaviour and how we can guide it. Once again, a lot of incredibly fascinating research is beckoning – research on and with meeting participants with a view to improving meeting programmes in the future.

Finally, when you think about guiding the behaviour of participants you quickly run into a moral issue. It is as if Big Brother starts breathing down your neck. For to what extent is it admissible to guide, influence and prompt participant behaviour? In the US, hiding subliminal messages in television commercials is forbidden. So, is it acceptable to subject meeting participants to specific exercises and experiences that elicit useful, predictable behaviour while participants are not aware of this? Research processes on things like association, jumping to conclusions and anchoring show that people do and decide many things before they become aware of what they choose to do. Knowledge about such processes helps you to understand but also to steer irrational behaviour. The moot point is that if you tell them, the exercise does not work any more... Is it all right to set up an oxygen bar during breaks, rather than a coffee corner, so as to help participants to think more clearly? Or slightly increase the oxygen levels in meeting rooms? Why are coffee and alcohol regarded as acceptable stimulants while amphetamine is not? We already have medicines that improve people's moods and well-being. Would it be a good idea to include one pills in each delegate's pack to make sure that the costly annual corporate sales meeting ends on a high?

Once again, it is probably too early for a book on meetings and cognitive psychology. But one does wonder: How in the world is it possible that no one so far has set up a Meeting Lab? Sigh!

F. Meetings for New Generations in the Network Society

"The times, they are a-changing," there is nothing new about that. In times of change people also change. Thirty or forty years ago, meeting participants would consider it normal to sit and listen to monologues from the mouths of eminent scholars for hours on end. Today that is abnormal: only the abnormally brilliant speaker manages to arouse that level of interest.

What will today's young people expect from meetings? At the risk of being accused of critical crystal ball-gazing, along with many trend watchers we hear and see many paradoxes. In random order and at various levels of societal or individual impact we note: both individualisation and environmental concerns/corporate social responsibility; both the spread of wealth and the need to make sense of it; both materialism and feminisation; both global awareness and local identity; both a need for strong emotions and stimulus saturation/detachment; both multi-tasking and shorter attention spans or impatience; both less factual knowledge and higher information processing capacity; both media convergence and ever shorter life spans of just about anything. All of these societal paradoxes have their impact on meetings, their effectiveness and their programmes. Some of these developments are related to the technology-driven changes touched upon in section C of this epilogue. Others are not, but in general only few of these trends are a recurring concern and topic of debate in meetings about the meeting industry. Perhaps if someone managed a visionary book about them, that might change...

And if that someone does, we would be interested in learning a bit more about long-term changes that seem highly relevant but almost incomprehensible. Such as: how will people deal with time and space? The new generations grow up in a world where the sense of time and space has changed profoundly. The Spanish sociologist Manuel Castells speaks of "timeless time" and "spaceless space."[2] Modern ICT allows people to meet without actually sitting together and to obtain real-time input on just about anything and from just about anyone. As we have seen in the previous sections, this has consequences inside and around meetings. But there is more – changes taking place in the minds of people: the expectations and attention spans of youthful participants; their bonds with networks all over the world; their emotional reactions to things that happen in what we now consider the 'real' world; even their willingness to come to meetings at all.

It is too early to say what the exact consequences of these developments will be for meetings. What we do know is that a different sense of time and space will profoundly alter the experiential value of meetings. Meanwhile many of the characteristics at the heart of meetings as a form of communication will remain unchanged. It cannot be otherwise, because although we change, at the same time we continue to carry inside us the legacy of millions of years of evolution that have made our species into what it is and that we recognise as its essence – an essence that is at the basis of our identities. And so, these long-term developments will show up like the images in the kaleidoscope of ever-shifting receptivity: rational and intuitive, predictable and incomprehensible, useful and wasteful, all at the same time. Whatever the results of these changes will be in practice, they will definitely open up new opportunities for designing better meetings.

[2] Manuel Castells, *The Network Society – A Cross-cultural Perspective*, Edited by Manuel Castells, Edward Alger Publishing Limited, Cheltenham (UK), 2004.